Transformation of Library Services

Transformation of Library Services

Editor

R.C. Ganguly

ISHA

ISHA BOOKS

Delhi-110009

Transformation of Library Services

ISBN: 81-8205-434-6

Published in 2007 in India by
ISHA Books
B-63, 1st Floor, New Gupta Colony,
Near DDA Market,
Delhi-110009
Phone: 9212142040
ishabooks@hotmail.com

Laser Type Setting by: Rudra Computer Graphics, Delhi
Printed at: Salasar Imaging System, Delhi

Preface

Libraries today are no longer repositories of books and other print material. The advent of technology has ensured that traditional libraries that handle large printed materials which are expensive and bulky are being proved redundant and are no longer viable options. Computerised subscriptions, microfilms and the internet have made their presence felt in present age libraries, and the digital age assures us of new infrastructures and capabilities to handle information in ways the 20th century might not have imagined of.

Libraries have, from their very advent itself, changed through time from mere storehouses of knowledge to dynamic service centres, opening new vistas and horizons of information available to a large number of people without delay. The medium of information has evolved from clay tablets to paper and to now electronic and optical media of CD-ROMs. The library is no longer a sacrosanct, formidable looking building with countless books and pamphlets-libraries without walls, which are just a mouse-click away, are now at the beck and call of inquisitive knowledge seekers.

The rapid technological development has opened up additional facilities by providing multiple choice of media, showing through improved performance and assuring greater economy in time, money and effort. The aims behind the construction of an organisation like a library, which includes access to an amazing quantity of information, bridging of the past with the present and as guide for the future, however, should remain unchanged. This means that libraries have to constantly equip themselves with the latest technology, even as technology proves itself redundant after 18 months and cater to the demands of a generation of readers unused to handling bulky and cumbersome material and more used to digital friendly formats.

The present book explores and examines at length the various upheavals and changes in the uses of libraries and they services they offer, as they move gradually from concrete structures towards digital. In an erudite manner, the trends in library management, both past and present are discussed. With its comprehensive discussion of the issues, the book should render to be of great service to students and faculty working in libraries.

Editor

Contents

1 Introduction

In the 500 years since the invention of the printing press, libraries have been at the center of a remarkable flowering of the human intellect, serving as repositories of the human experience while promoting structured inquiry and critical thinking. Libraries are fundamental to the intellectual experience and the natural creativity of the mind; they are core services at every postsecondary institution. Indeed, there are no great universities without great libraries.

In spite of the enormous power to propel human progress, libraries are increasingly asked to justify the resources spent on them, to justify even their very existence. In this climate, libraries must be accountable, responsive, and effective in portraying the value of their services to funding authorities, be they public or private. These imperatives have led to a new emphasis on quantitative assessments to provide hard evidence about the extent of their value to the society or their sponsors.

Online information become more and more available, arguments against funding of libraries are increasing in number and loudness. Therefore, assuring the proper functioning of libraries depends on demonstrating their value in the widest sense and to their widest audiences. Research has produced hard facts that libraries pay fully for their existence, and even produce positive returns on the investments made on them.

Long-term studies of technical libraries using return on investment analysis established that in monetary terms libraries produce 515% annual return on investment, that is five times more than what is invested on them per annum. Cost-benefit analysis also showed that the benefits derived from library services outweigh the cost of providing them. Economic growth has not however, provided solution to rural exodus, marginalisation of the weak, galloping urbanisation, proliferation of shanty-towns, mass unemployment, increased poverty and spread of deadly diseases. Libraries can play direct as well as catalytic roles in contemporary development initiatives.

Libraries increase the value of human intellectual outputs by increasing access to them through professional processing, storage and dissemination. Processing and organisation moves ideas, data and other primary intellectual outputs from raw bytes to information. The world's intellectual outputs would be useless, even constitute a nuisance, if libraries were not there to gather, analyse, classify, catalogue and provide access to them.

The hundreds of bibliographic records of published and unpublished materials ensure their use and reuse to satisfy commercial, educational, cultural and recreational needs. The educational and research role of libraries cannot be over-emphasised. Research has found that libraries make significant contributions to the effectiveness of the education process. Learners from institutions where library use is part of the learning process are more likely to become equipped for the society and occupational effectiveness than those without proper library habits. Libraries are also central for the development of literacy, a critical component of the development of intellectual capital of a community, an attribute which initiates a ripple effect on an individual's ability to become gainfully employed, increase his or her income and make effective contributions to society.

Community members use library services and library programmes for everything from introducing their children to the habit and joy of reading, to tapping into their professional networks. Economic development effort is simply any activity that raises real incomes, thereby offering new hopes of expanded opportunities for people, communities, and enterprises. As both the global and national economies become more and more knowledge-driven, specialised knowledge has become the indispensable asset for further economic development.

Local businesses benefit greatly in specific ways from libraries, including access to new ideas, knowledge and information. In particular, relocating businesses, start-up businesses, and small businesses of all kinds are perceived as enjoying the greatest benefits from library products and services. Indeed, existence of libraries has been cited as a reason for a business' decision to relocate to a particular community. Studies also found that business information resources were significantly more valuable with expert help of library staff.

In other words, not only are information sources themselves viewed as important resources for people seeking mission-oriented information, but professional services provided by librarians are believed by many to be critical factors in finding, accessing and utilising information resources to the fullest extent, especially with regard to electronic resources. The type of information provided in economic development information centres includes: general economic and industry-specific statistics, economic forecasts, trade statistics, market surveys, census data, tax and regulatory requirements, cost-of-living and cost-of-doing-business data, information on general business practices, financial planning, as well as employee benefits and compensation. "How to" materials ranging from starting a business to entering foreign markets are also an important part of a typical core collection.

Training in basic business planning and management could also be provided. A library may offer extension services as part of its service portfolio or develop an economic development information centres unit to focus on local economic development services. Many direct benefits from library services accrue to individuals. These include cost savings from borrowing materials rather than having to buy them; borrowing of such items as audio books and videotapes, which save significant expenditures; and the use of periodicals and newspapers which result in financial benefit. There is a dual nature to this: first, users save the cost of purchasing these items themselves; and second, many users have been better able to manage their lives as a result of information obtained. In fact, some quality of life indexes, for example best places to live, best places to raise children, and best places to retire, include "library books per capita" statistic when profiling communities. Libraries enhance productivity of individuals and organisations.

Access to the right information is a very critical component in the productivity of information workers, and consequently the productivity and good decision-making of the organisations employing them. For the self-employed knowledge worker, use of libraries make them more productive on their jobs, especially as they can obtain job related training in the areas of computer and information literacy skills and good business practices. Libraries perform an important role of social inclusion when they serve the needs of disadvantaged populations such as the poor, the elderly, the physically disabled, the unemployed and those with learning disability, because these are exactly the groups least likely to have the means to acquire such assets as information sources, computers and Internet access.

Libraries also serve as agents of social cohesion. In one study, a participant said: "we are brought closer to other members of our community through the very act of sharing books with them". For this reason, social inclusion and lifelong learning agenda of most developed countries include the founding of new public libraries and increased information and library pr^vision for learners at all levels and of all ages. For many communities and organisations, libraries serve as civic centres, which assist them in meeting their civic duties by offering meeting space for civic organisations, assisting with voter registration, and making government forms available, including tax forms. Libraries also serve as a posting place for proposed changes in local ordinances, and other local government proposals. As a community centre, the library introduces users to new systems of doing things during changeover programmes.

A variety of other programmes are offered, such as story telling, technology.5 education, and recreational activities. Valued in most places is the availability of meeting rooms for voluntary groups, which represent monetary savings to them. Libraries also serve the public by providing assistance in finding answers to many basic questions: from how to find jobs to where to find up-to-date health and legal information. The information the library provides to answer some of these important questions can lead to significant economic benefits and impacts. Research also found that communities value their libraries as physical assets and a source of community pride. Indeed, libraries, especially public and national libraries, are important landmarks in many cities and other communities. Participants in a survey stated many times that the presence of a new library, or the redevelopment of an existing one, favorably impacted on its immediate surroundings.

Effective citizen action is possible only when citizens know how to gain access to information of all kinds and have the skills to become responsible, informed participants in democracies. This is especially so as e-government evolves. Libraries offer real and virtual civic spaces where citizens can speak freely, share similar interests and concerns, and pursue what they believe are in their public's interest. Ultimately, free discourse among informed citizens assures civil society; and civil society provides the social capital necessary to achieve common goals. Through this role libraries prevent the lack of information and idea exchanges which in a closed society stifles creativity, suppresses the imagination and creates a barrier to social, economic and technical progress. E-government is about using the power of information technology to provide better public services.

The main dimensions of an e-government strategy include: building services around citizens' choices, making government and its services more accessible, ensuring social inclusion and ensuring two-way communication between the government and the governed. Governments have always depended on libraries to collect and disseminate government information, but e-government adds very new and valued dimensions: the citizen empowering potential reinforced by virtual access and the possibility to hold governments accountable without physical confrontation. For librarians, a special challenge by e-government is to obtain recognition as the professionals best suited to provide guidance on e-government's need for information analysis, indexing, organising of digital documents, and the design and development of versatile interfaces for information retrieval as well as for data harvesting and communication.

The e-government initiatives that use schools (actually school libraries) and libraries have helped various communities to develop local-global links to information resources and gain markedly improved access to government information. A special feature of the programmes is the two-way communication taking place between the people and government agencies, which helps the various levels of government to improve their efficiency and accountability in addressing the demands and priorities of Canadians. The Canadian Government has largely achieved the goal it set for itself. It is now a leader in e-government when measured by citizens' ability to access a wide variety of government services online. Studies show that, only people and businesses in the higher income brackets are able to afford the hardware, software and connectivity costs required to participate in the information revolution, including e-commerce.

The need for access to the Internet is however not limited to people and businesses with discretionary income, and it is here that libraries are well positioned to help bridge the economic gap along with the digital divide. From individuals who might not be able to afford computer technology at home to many small and home-based businesses, the library can provide the necessary connections to help prevent the division of our society into information "haves and have-nots." The western-style universal access is not a practical reality in African countries where much of the population cannot afford individual access. Instead, focus should be on providing access through community facilities like libraries and schools. In this role, libraries can help in poverty alleviation since information poverty often is the basis of economic poverty. In the information age, access to information has a place alongside adequate food, health care, education, and other basic needs. This phenomenon has broadened the definition of poverty to include information poverty. More so, when it has become clear those people and nations who cannot or will not participate fully in the new information economy will find it all the more difficult to climb out of poverty.

Libraries and Information Society

The information revolution is aiding the library movement by reinforcing the material-virtual duality of knowledge and information and helping in transforming our society into an information society based on a strong foundation of knowledge which is universal, objective, timely and drawing from a variety of sources. In developed countries, libraries are taking the lead in Internetisation, digitalisation and virtualisation of access to knowledge. Special online services are being developed to support lifelong learning, provide health advice and information, and give citizens access to official documents free of copyright restrictions. Thus libraries are becoming not only Internet access points, but also places where people may receive help in using the Internet and other information sources. Governments implementing digital opportunity programmes do them in cooperation with libraries.

Libraries are helping to build viable global communities based on local-global networks that enable individuals and groups to explore their respective and common futures, and create synergy through sharing of knowledge and experience. Local-global networking will become a means of making globalisation to suit local conditions, as knowledge and information sharing will make globalisation desirable through universalism, a new form of understanding that results from shared values engendered by constant exchange of experience. Between 1960 and 1980, libraries in Africa were built and resourced with determination in the hope that they would support the rapid development of their communities. Rightly, then national governments, organisations and donors funded libraries as basic needs. However, since the early 1980's, libraries across Africa have experienced a very deep decline in resources and services. The so-called "great African library decline" can be characterised as follows:

— Funds provided are grossly inadequate. In fact, most libraries do not get up to half of their minimum requirements. In most of the places, available fund just cover staff salaries;

— Libraries lag behind global trends due to inadequate resources, reliance of process inefficient processes, and weak professional networking;

— Lack of current books, journals and other information sources;
— Total lack of, or inadequate application of library information technology;
— Unavailability of, or unreliable access to the Internet;
— Empty reading rooms due to lack of library habit resulting from years of poor customer service;
— Rusty professional skills and·outlook affected by lack of resources for training and development;
— Demoralised management and poor co-ordination within their parent organisations;
— Poor or absence of library support of the learning process across all types and levels of educational institutions across much of Africa, with student to book ratio as low as 30 students to 1 book in certain places;
— Library shelves in public libraries with old and irrelevant books that gather dust;
— Little or no physical development to match current needs;
— Little or no professional library activism and advocacy; and
— Where in existence, library boards that overshadow the libraries they govern.

Some of those organisations are actively funding or implementing projects aimed at alleviating this decline, but the situation may not improve significantly without the attention of all levels of government in Africa nations. This is because of the enormity of the need and the fact that eventually, government whether by design or by chance, determine the course of human progress wherever they operate.

Information Policies

In Africa, national information policies can be viewed as the embracing framework to put into practice the basic notion that social and economic systems will function more efficiently if the right information resources are available to in 'ividuals, households, civil society, businesses and government agencies whenever they are in need of them. Placing libraries and other repositories of knowledge prominently in this framework is the pragmatic starting point, but studies show that in Africa, national information policies usually do not put libraries within the mainstream of issues addressed, instead technology is overemphasized.

National policies and frameworks for information in most countries are fragmented, leading to limited coordination and ineffectual strategies. For example, in most of the countries where library laws have been enacted, national library boards with overly political dispositions were created, resulting in a situation where the boards draw attention to themselves rather than to the libraries they were set up to promote. Library administrators and boards should recognise their economic & human development mission by developing programmes that directly impact on their local economies. In this respect, they should participate in projects that further local and national development, such as export promotions and youth skills development projects.

Specialised outfits such as economic development information centres provide focused means of delivering such services. To be effective e-government programmes must rest on viable libraries and information networks. Therefore, governments at all levels, should strengthen libraries, including university, school and public libraries to enable them to play their central role in strengthening the interactive exchange of information that is the essence of e-government. It is good policy to use libraries as agents for bridging the digital divide because libraries ensure wider access to information technology, the Internet and specialised information networks. In fact modern library services concretise the benefits of the information society to the grassroots of communities. Library governance in much of Africa needs a reappraisal. Library boards in a number of African countries are preventing libraries from developing as strong brands. Successful libraries around the world are recognisable brands. Such libraries attract funds from a variety of sources and have the confidence of information seekers.

National information policies in Africa should have substantial library services component. An information policy without the provision for libraries as the main purveyors of information resources and services is bound to lack substance in the long run. Libraries may not appear glamorous, but any information policy not based on this foundation of knowledge will normally not succeed to serve the aims of development. It is implied that any legislative agenda for the development of a national strategic information framework must include elements for library development in the areas of infrastructure, funding, human resources, technology, information sources, services and governance.

Effective legislative and strategic framework for library-friendly policy environment should include the following elements: A ministerial level organisation with responsibility for policy, resource allocation, introduction and administration of relevant laws, as well as representation of the interests of libraries at the highest level of government. This ministry may cover other related sectors such as science and technology, research and culture. In Africa, a national commission on libraries that provides strategic leadership and cross-ministerial advocacy on libraries, ensures policy and technical focus on how to.maximise resources by coordination and networking across types of libraries as well as governmental departments and the private sector.

The effect that rapid technological and organisational change have had on lifestyles and attitudes to work is such that the traditional division of three stages of life: "education and learning - leading to work - lastly, to retirement" is diminishing, and together with this has been the demise of the "job for life" culture. So 'lifelong learning' is becoming much more than a passing political fad and instead describes a very real change in the lives of individuals and in the activities of societies. New organisations such as the European Lifelong Learning Initiative (ELLI) have been set up to provide input and to be involved in European and international projects on lifelong learning. The World Initiative on Lifelong Learning was formed to develop the sharing of good practice relating to lifelong learning and to set and monitor standards for global lifelong learning.

Many of the Initiative's activities, which include global conferences, books and journals, research projects and lifelong learning projects with Higher Education institutions, were based on recommendations which emerged from the First Global Conference on Lifelong Learning. Initiatives include Community Action for Lifelong Learning (CALL), which outlines recommendations for sectors of the community and the Action Agenda for Lifelong Learning for the 21st Century which includes the following recommendations:

— Creation of Learning Organisations.
— Development of skills profiles.
— Initiation of individual lifetime learning plans.
— Provision of learning opportunities in lifelong learning.
— Creation of a learning passport.
— Improvements in accessibility to learning.
— Increased use of educational technology.
— Accreditation of courses wherever they take place.

— Initiation of portability in qualifications.

— Prioritisation of essential new research.

As a result, there is a growing awareness of the need for individuals to take responsibility for their learning, not just at school, college or university level, but throughout their lives, and to constantly review and update their knowledge and skills. The current unstable job market means people are often forced to re-consider their careers and learn new skills in order to keep up with employers' ever changing needs. The Learning Age will have major implications for all institutions involved in education, which will not find it easy to cope with the massive changes which are implied. Thus, although education needs to operate within some kind of organised structure, it has been noted that "learning is messy". Educators may try to impose order, as may governments and institutions, but individuals will follow their own motivations as they respond to the pressures, challenges and opportunities of learning.

Firstly it is important to recognise that traditional university undergraduate and postgraduate courses, especially when offered in modular formats available through part-time study and perhaps within a well-developed credit accumulation and transfer scheme, will continue to provide many of the opportunities that people seek. However, if lifelong learning does become embedded as the norm for the whole population there will also be challenges to develop new kinds of provision. We can expect increased demand for distance learning, with delivery off-campus to the workplace, home or local learning centre. We can also expect an increase in collaborative provision, involving businesses, community groups, professional associations and universities.

Libraries should also expect to play a central role in the delivery of higher education. As librarians well know, the increase in independent learning which has accompanied increasing student numbers has meant that libraries, learning resource centres and similar facilities are often the place where the bulk of a student's learning takes place. However, 'lifelong learning' is a term that can be and is interpreted in many different ways In the United States it is usually taken to mean pre-school or adult education, i.e. that learning which occurs outside the formal, traditional school - college -university system. Europe often links the term with day release from work. Other terms associated with lifelong learning are "the elimination of inequality in education", and the "democratisation of education", providing a more political and polemical view. It follows that lifelong learning does not necessarily come within the framework of formal education. It takes into account all aspects of learning and provides a framework within which an individual can reflect on the past, undertake informal or formal learning in the present, and prepare for the future in terms of lifetime learning experiences.

Learners are made aware that they are learning by aiming towards specific goals. Achievement of these goals becomes the motivation for what can be called "deliberate learning" . The distinction between one-off or day-to-day learning and lifelong learning is that with the latter, learners should retain what is learnt, and move on through life acquiring new skills to back up existing ones, rather than simply learning for a one-off activity, such as an examination or qualification.

Reference has been made to the fact that both deliberate and one-off learning should occur throughout one's lifetime and that there is a place for both these types of learning within the context of lifelong learning. The need to integrate several types of learning will have implications for higher education institutions, who will have to accept that they make up just one small, but important, part of the system. Higher education institutions will also need to promote the skills needed for lifelong learning and give learners the opportunity to acquire them. This defines an important role for teachers in higher education, who are seen as having a "trickle down" effect on whole generations of potential lifelong learners.

Lifelong learning is a deliberate progression throughout the life of an individual, where the initial acquisition of knowledge and skills is reviewed and upgraded continuously, to meet challenges set by an ever changing society. Academic libraries must be ready to play their part in the support system of this growing and diverse population of learners and would-be learners, and to motivate them to achieving specific goals set throughout a lifetime of learning.

The increasingly technological environment in which we live will change the nature of learning and the role of those who support it fundamentally. Finally, a word of warning! The term "lifelong learning" has been hijacked by every commentator in almost every possible context and is not infrequently used as a substitute for thought about societal change. At the broadest level, learning is of necessity a lifelong experience: every individual action, reaction and encounter involves learning, even if only at the subconscious level. Life is a learning experience. But if life is not to be a process of involuntarily drifting from one experience to another, without direction, and if societies are to function and develop, then learning needs to be planned, directed, evaluated and reviewed. As we shall demonstrate, individuals, organisations and societies all have a stake in ensuring that learning can take place and that, through learning, the well-being of those same individuals, organisations and societies can be secured. Put at its highest, learning is the process through which humankind will achieve its full potential.

At the most basic level, planned and directed learning opportunities are needed to enable individuals to access future learning opportunities: to get a foot on the bottom rung of the ladder of personal development. In the past, literacy campaigns were directed at this goal: the aim was to teach each individual the basic skills so that they could progress. The war which had to be waged for the principle of universal literacy was hard fought, and there are battles still to be won for there are many parts of the world where basic literacy is still a major problem. Even in the UK levels of illiteracy are alarmingly high and stubbornly resistant to action. But even as action to resolve these problems continues, the agenda has moved on. Learning also involves acquiring skills, such as analysis and communication, but these in isolation do not constitute learning. The information explosion, technological change, organisational change and societal change are all factors which will have profound implications for everyone involved in learning. It is not just the individual who needs to be concerned about this.

For all stakeholders, higher education will need to be influential in developing higher levels of literacy such as might be expected of individuals who are equipped both for advanced learning and for positions of responsibility in organisations and society. It is useful, in considering lifelong learning in the context of higher education, to reflect on the experience of adult education over the last few decades. Adult learners and adult learning efforts are varied since prior learning and prior experience mean that it is uncertain how one adult will respond to learning, or to new ideas and skills. Adults also have a tendency toward self-directed learning and adults' self-concepts as learners will have an effect on the success of their learning experiences.

Library staff tend to be very aware of this change because of the increased time they now have to spend assisting students with their coursework and because of the lack of basic independent learning skills which they frequently encounter. At the same time, library staff are ill-equipped to deal effectively with many of these students -

they are unlikely to have been involved in course planning, are not conversant with the learning style being promoted by the course team, and are probably not familiar with the detail of the assessment regime. They may be uncertain as to just where their role lies in facilitating and encouraging learning experiences. As information experts librarians will tend to concentrate on how information is identified, retrieved and used in the learning process, rather than on issues like social interaction as a learning experience. A wide variety of models of education are now in use with an equally wide terminology.

Unlike 'open learning', distance education can be very selective in its student intake, in particular at university and professional levels. Keegan identifies the following elements:

- Separation of teacher and learner, which distinguishes it from face-to-face lecturing
- Influence of an educational organisation, which distinguishes it from private study
- Provision of two-way communication so that the student may benefit from or even initiate dialogue
- Possibility of occasional meetings for both didactic and socialisation purposes
- Participation in an industrialised form of education which, if accepted, contains the genus of radical separation of distance education from other forms

Franchised courses are traditional higher education courses but delivered away from the parent university, usually at a college of further education. The parent institution retains responsibility for validating and reviewing the courses, and students are registered by the franchiser. The franchisee (i.e. the local college) has responsibility for running and managing the courses, including responsibility for providing adequate library resources to students and staff. The course may involve elements of distance learning, including specially prepared materials, but frequently the learning methods are identical to those employed in traditional mainstream higher education. Not infrequently, only the first year of a three or four year degree course is franchised and students join the main in-house cohort for the remainder of their course.

Research on franchised and other partnership courses between higher and further education shows that they are aimed at students who tend to be local, mature, need to study part-time, have been under-achievers, have caring responsibilities and financial difficulties Between 1991-2 and 1992-3 the number of franchised students increased from 10,000 to 35,000. A 1991 EC paper on open and distance learning in Europe defined open learning as "any form of learning which includes elements of flexibility which make it more accessible to students than courses traditionally provided in centres of education and training. This flexibility arises variously from the content of the course and the way in which it is structured, the place of provision, the mode, medium or timing of its delivery, the pace at which the student proceeds, or the forms of special support available and the types of assessment offered.

Sandwich course were developed in the 1960s, and include a lengthy period of work placement mid-way through a (usually full-time) university course. Sandwich courses have strong links with higher education and employment, as the placement is an essential part of the overall qualification. Many vocational degree courses also include a short period of work placement, often at the end of the first or second year depending on the length of the course. This is seen as an important element of the course as it prepares students for entry into the workforce, while still in a learning environment. This type of learning does not necessarily have any obvious links to traditional higher education institutions. Organisations can offer learning in the form of in-house training, external privately run courses and conferences run by relevant professional bodies.

However, the introduction of Credit Accumulation & Transfer (CAT) Schemes and modularised courses which were developed in the 1980s have seen a continued involvement of higher education Institutions and the workforce through partnerships with local organisations such as the Training Enterprise Councils (TECs). Universities and colleges of further education also offer continuing education for the professions, as do many professional bodies and others. Extra-Mural courses are a particular form of adult education traditionally provided by universities in the UK. Their origins are in the use of peripatetic tutors sent to industrial areas from Oxford and Cambridge in the 19th century. This practice was followed by some, but not all, of the redbrick universities. Unlike adult education generally the epitome of university extra-mural work was the "tutorial class", a three year sustained programme at degree level, often in collaboration with the Workers' Educational Association which was founded in 1903.

Extra-mural courses were traditionally viewed as a form of adult education. As a result, extra-mural departments were often viewed as "valuing mainly liberal over occupationally oriented work" which led them to be isolated from the rest of the institution. The current interest in lifelong learning and of "preparing citizens for the learning society" has raised the profile of extra-mural activity which may provide a way forward. Although terminology is changing, what are in effect extra-mural courses are run at many colleges and universities throughout the UK. Independent learning can be understood to have several meanings. At one extreme it has been taken to mean correspondence courses. At the other, as Gagne points out, everyone is an independent learner to some extent, for everyone learns as part of everyday life. In formal classrooms each learner sorts and understands the teachings in his or her own way.

Therefore, "all learners perceive and codify stimuli in an individual, idiosyncratic fashion and to that extent all learning activities are characterised by a degree of independence". Brookfield identifies independent learning, and more specifically adult independent learning, as "learning which occurs independently of the formal education system and which is characterised by learner responsibility for the direction and execution of learning". The motivation to learn can be prompted by work-related reasons or by the desire for personal development, or both. The need or desire to engage in learning can occur at any point during an adult's lifetime. There have been significant changes in the development, structure and delivery of university courses thus allowing adults to undertake a more flexible approach to their studies (by distance learning, part-time and franchised courses) than that required by full-time attendance on traditional courses. Adults are keen to take up the opportunities offered. Between 1991 and 1992, there was a three fold increase in the number of students undertaking locally franchised courses, for example. Work-based learning is incorporated into sandwich courses, employment-based learning programmes, continuing professional development programmes, and other education and industry initiatives involving the higher education sector.

Learning is a process from which the acquisition of and development of skills, abilities, knowledge and understanding are the outcomes. Learning needs to be a structured process involving planning, direction, evaluation and review. Learning is a lifetime experience. Yet we cannot assume that the future will be no more than an extrapolation of the past. Of all the influences on society and on the individual the emergence of the networked information society may prove to be the most profound in the coming decades.

Role of ICTs

Figures for use of the Internet vary wildly, but it is fairly safe to assume that before the end of the millennium in excess of 100 million people will have access to the Internet. Although their access may not be without problems - it may be from an out of date PC or may rely on a slow telecoms line - they will nevertheless be able to access much educational material that was previously not only inaccessible but completely unknown. More than that, the existence of a market of this size will encourage more and more producers of materials, packages and support services to develop suitable software. What may now appear to be rather crude and low level learning packages will become more and more sophisticated and will be much better adapted to the networked environment in the future. Access to the Internet will provide access to such materials and will be a key driving force behind lifelong learning. As technology advances, greater bandwidth will enable products of increasing sophistication to be delivered.

There will be continued development of multimedia products which contain a well-designed mix of video, audio, text and graphics which will incorporate both learning materials and supporting information sources. Such materials may be delivered online, probably using the World Wide Web and with links provided to relevant sites and systems across the world, or may be packaged as CD-ROMs (or equivalent) thus enabling very large amounts of data to be transported very cheaply and used with acceptable response times and without incurring large telecommunications costs. A feature of multimedia packages is that they can be used non-sequentially, so that the learning experience can be tailored to the needs of each individual - providing that the learner has sufficient support and guidance not to become lost in a never-ending maze. For this reason it is to be expected that the role of the "learning designer" will be crucial: multimedia will cease to be a product put together by technical experts but will be the delivery vehicle for well-designed learning experiences which are based on sound pedagogic approaches. Networks will also be used increasingly to enable people to communicate over distances (or merely around the same office) using video conferencing and sophisticated software products.

The Teaching & Learning Technology Programme (TLTP) was launched in 1992 by the then Universities Funding Council with the dual aims to "make teaching and learning more productive and efficient by harnessing modern technology and to help institutions to respond effectively to the current substantial growth in student numbers and to promote and maintain the quality of provision".

The electronic library is becoming increasingly obvious that the support of learning with quality information (i.e. information which is timely, accurate, reliable, accessible and so on) is an essential for learning. In a rapidly changing world in which information can be out-of-date almost as rapidly as it is produced it is important for the learner to be guided to appropriate sources - and to learn the skill of finding such sources for him/herself. Interesting eLib projects in the Access to Networked Resources category may point the way forward, while the new "hybrid library" demonstrator projects which will provide unified resource discovery and resource delivery services emphasise the point. As network-based learning has developed a number of practitioners (both teachers and librarians) have become involved in the complex issue of supporting learners in the networked environment - both on- and off-campus.

A variety of tools will be developed to enable tutors to manage the learning process. It is essential that new technologies are not allowed to swamp individuals with administrative tasks, but are designed to enable the tutor to make maximum use of technology to assist in the effectiveness of the learning of his/her students. A number of JISC Technology Application Programme (JTAP) projects are active in this area. What is apparent from these developments is that ICTs are starting to force a redefinition of support structures and learning environments which goes well beyond the typical 'convergence' of traditional services. These developments illustrate that traditional structures which at first glance appear not to have been unduly influenced by ICTs may in fact be facing profound change.

The social impacts of ICTs within higher education institutions will, almost certainly, be profound. ICTs will, without a doubt, revolutionise learning. To some extent librarians find themselves in the vanguard of these developments since they have felt the impact of ICTs on the services they provide relatively early. However, the lessons which have already been learned from the use of ICTs in learning need to be heeded by librarians as they consider how best to structure their services for the lifelong learner. It is always worth recalling that learning is essentially a social process. Some approaches to technology and learning have seen the future as no more than the delivery of packaged learning to the individual in the home or office. That is an inadequate and deeply inhuman vision. Yet social interaction does not have to mean face-to-face contact between tutor and student all, or even any of, the time. Students can benefit greatly from interacting with fellow students tens, hundreds or thousands of miles away. The key to successful use of technology in lifelong learning lies in designing packages and support from the perspective of learning, not from the viewpoint of technology.

Lifelong Learning

Lifelong learning is the enabler which will help create an inclusive society in which every citizen is valued, in which every citizen can participate fully and in which every citizen can achieve his or her full potential. It will enable the development of communities which support and enrich the lives of each member. It will provide the skills and knowledge base which will secure the economic prosperity of individual societies in an ever more competitive world. Internationally, there is a growing emphasis on education as being much more than a one-off activity, engaged in - or perhaps endured - in early life. As we have seen, the concept of lifelong learning can be traced back decades and even centuries. However, the first Global Conference on Lifelong Learning was held in Rome as recently as 1994. The conference was initiated and managed by the European Lifelong Learning Initiative (ELLI) which was set up to provide input and to be involved in European and international projects on lifelong learning.

The World Initiative on Lifelong Learning was formed to develop the sharing of good practice relating to lifelong learning and to set and monitor standards for global lifelong learning. Many of the Initiative's activities, which include global conferences, books and journals, research projects and lifelong learning projects with Higher Education institutions, were based on recommendations which emerged from the First Global Conference on Lifelong Learning. Higher Education alone cannot achieve this attitude. The learner needs to move on from gaining a higher education qualification towards mastering skills in the workforce. Motivation for learning must be generated from an early age in order to sustain this culture throughout life. Motivation also means developing the capacity to learn, which goes hand in hand with lifelong learning.

Whilst education and training will not necessarily guarantee employment, a lack of it can be seen as "a major factor in unemployment and exclusion". The need for flexible learning pathways is essential in order to address the problem. Some countries have recognised this and offer "second chance" opportunities, with initiatives such as tuition out of normal timetable hours, open learning, and networks for the education of adults who have dropped out of school or university. Organisations need to move towards becoming "learning organisations" in order to survive. Organisational change has been brought about by the rapid movements of modern technology. In order to keep up with changes both within a specific market and as a whole, an "organisational learning approach" is needed. Definitions of the strivers, drifters and strugglers range from "people who know the value of learning, but are not doing enough or applying themselves enough", to people who "neither value learning or intend to practice it".

The Campaign for Learning aims to move as many people as possible towards the "improvers" stage. Other categories could include people who know the value of learning but who find barriers (generally beyond their control), which constantly impede their learning. Such barriers might include age, language, lack of childcare, inflexible courses, lack of access to courses etc. Transferable vocational skills were seen as important since they not only have relevance to specific jobs, but can be used in employment elsewhere. However, the paper also stressed that the motivation to learn throughout one's life must be backed up by relevant legislation and technological provision. The effects of policies and developments need to be monitored, and education and training providers need to continually improve their outputs in order to meet the needs of a learning market which is driven by customers and their choices. Writing almost a year after the new government took office, it is timely to examine in some detail the policy framework that is starting to emerge in this area. The creation of learning organisations was a key item on the Action Agenda in the World Initiative on Lifelong Learning , whilst a key issue in the European Year of Lifelong Learning agenda was to strengthen the foundation for lifelong learning.

The Dearing Report appeared under the title of Higher Education in the Learning Society in July 1997. It proved to be a vast document, the 467 page main report being supported by a further ten bound volumes. As its title implied, a Committee established to "make recommendations on how the purposes, shape, structure, size and funding of higher education ... should develop to meet the needs of the United kingdom over the next twenty years" placed its findings firmly in the context of a vision of learning as fundamental to society itself.

The most important challenge is to recognise that high quality learning is not the exclusive preserve of the educational institution or the training centre. Much.learning has always happened outside these locations, and change, including curricular and technological change, is making it easier for such change to happen. We increasingly need flexibility in the times, locations and forms of learning so that they better suit the needs of individuals and groups.

The further education sector's Quality in Information and Learning Technologies (QUILT) Programme is seen as an encouraging model,.while higher education's use of SuperJANET to deliver collaborative teaching across dispersed sites is also noted. Reference is made to JANET's use "to provide access to remote information sources for both learning and research purposes". The proposals set out a series of ambitious targets for the five-year period to 2002. All serving (school) teachers should be confident to use, and to teach the use of, ICT within the curriculum; the UK should be "a centre of excellence in the development of networked software content for education and lifelong learning"; general administration should "largely cease to be paper-based"; and so on.

The immediate focus should be on the implementation of a public library networking plan, the result of which will be to "ensure that individuals in any area can enter into and interact with resources and learning programmes available outside their immediate area". All public library networks should be interconnected with a minimum bandwidth of 2 Mbps, and all branches should be connected by ISDN or equivalent. This would provide the basic infrastructure on which services could be delivered anywhere in the UK. Links with the University for Industry and the Learning Grid would be fostered. Among the mechanisms which will be required to implement the national information policy are a Public Library Networking Agency to "lead and co-ordinate development and implementation of networking across the UK public library sector" including fostering a development programme for content, services, network infrastructure and staff training. While as a nation we have our strengths, it is also clear that we have our weaknesses. These lie particularly in basic and intermediate skills, where we lag well behind our competitors.

A further challenge is that attitudes towards learning need to be changed so that people want to learn and to continue to do so throughout their lives. At the same time there is recognition that at the individual level people face many obstacles in pursuing learning, including "time, cost, fear, inadequate information, complexity and inconvenience". There can be little doubt that The Learning Age is an attempt to capture a new vision of learning and to make it a reality for the people of the UK. The emphases on ensuring that all young people have basic skills and are fit for employment, the widening of access to further and higher education, the new approach to and emphasis on work-based learning, and the overall emphasis on partnerships as the way forward together set a challenging agenda.

Public and national libraries are thus faced with many challenges if they are to respond to these opportunities. While it is not made explicit, libraries in higher education will also face a series of challenges if they are to play their part in the 'learning revolution'. If higher education is to become more distributed, as people learn at home, at work or in local learning centres, university libraries will no longer be able to deliver their services in a secure, familiar, physical building but will need to be wherever learning is taking place. The role of the library in the lifelong learning process is a topic which has engendered significant debate from a range of philosophical and educational perspectives as well as from strategic and operational perspectives among the library community. Brophy asserted in a recent conference address that libraries are part of a social process "which transforms stored data into knowledge for the benefit of its users, and knowledge into stored data for the benefit of posterity, and that the benefit of having libraries can be seen in the impact they have on individuals and societies.

Wooliscroft predicts that the growth of demand for further & continuing education programmes and the increasing awareness of the benefits of lifelong learning will influence the demand for formal distance programmes. Many institutions, from secondary level up, will be required to become proficient in distance learning modes of delivery within the next few years. This should result in the flourishing of demand for library services from distance learners. Educationalists will seize upon communication possibilities afforded by electronic networks, satellite and cable broadcasting and as Wooliscroft notes, "librarians should and must be the mirror image of the work of educators in this domain". Library services to support adult and lifelong learning in the UK have developed in response to changes in the higher education system, with developments in adult and continuing education and open learning, and in response to demands from independent learners.

These developments are evident in both the public and academic library sectors. In further and higher education, evidence from surveys of non-traditional students indicates the importance of library and information services to such students in supporting formal courses of study, whatever their mode of delivery. In countries with a long history of delivering distance learning courses to remote students, library provision to support distant learners is the norm, rather than the exception as in the UK. In Australia, the USA and Canada some institutions have developed sophisticated levels of service unparalleled elsewhere, largely necessitated by the large geographical spread of the population. These have been partly facilitated by the development of new technologies, including electronic information networks.

The role of the library service is underpinned by philosophies which value research and information skills as fundamental to the educational process. In Australia, Deakin University Library claims a strong user focus and the overarching purpose of the library is summed up in its mission statement as simply "we help people learn". Most Australian universities are funded by the Australian federal government. As a condition of this funding, universities have to comply with government policies, in particular that universities must not charge students for access to resources that are fundamental to their learning (e.g. access to laboratories, test equipment and chemicals and libraries) and that all institutions must aim to provide in their libraries at least 90% of texts and other recommended reading material for a student's course. It is the responsibility of the enrolling university to provide the library and information service.

Recent studies exemplify the marginalisation of library services in the development and delivery of distance learning and other 'non-traditional' courses by some institutions. In 1994, Goodall reported on a survey of 40 higher education institution libraries in the UK in which all respondents indicated that the provision of franchised courses had not significantly altered the way the university library was organised or the range and style of services offered. Non-traditional students generally find libraries daunting places. Perhaps even more significant, however, are the difficulties which such students encounter when attempting to access libraries and utilise library services. A study conducted in 1991 on the library problems of part-time students found a clear demand for longer opening hours, different loan periods, faster procedures for renewing books and more library training.

There was an identified need for improved funding for part time student library services, more co-ordination in establishing services for these students, better liaison between librarians and tutors, wider distribution of reading lists and more instruction. The study concluded that there was a need for the development of specific funding formulae for services to part time students, full borrowing privileges, telephone request services, separate collections of books and arrangements for reciprocal borrowing at other libraries. There are, however, other strategic and operational problems which concern library managers who are attempting to facilitate access to information services for both non-traditional and traditional students. Hall highlights potential difficulties in library collaboration commenting that there is strong resistance between 'unequal partners' such as old and new universities, and between further and higher education institutions. Whilst developments in electronic communications seems to have captured the 'access' label, reality seems to be somewhat different. The value of the slogan 'access not holdings' in relation to library services may need to be reconsidered.

The electronic library could bring as many restrictions in terms of access to information as it brings benefits. Distance learning students are in danger of losing the access which they currently have to browse current periodicals. The arrangements for access to university libraries other than the host institution are illustrated with typical examples of current practice. Formal co-operative agreements are being established between library consortia, although borrowing arrangements are still highly restricted. Sheffield Hallam University offers students a Distance Learning Support Service with a range of services to off-campus students.. The service offers distance learning support to students studying on courses that have been deemed as appropriate to distance learning. Electronic library facilities will play an important role in the University of the Highlands and Islands Project, which aims to develop a new university which will offer students in the remoter areas of Scotland the opportunity to undertake a growing number of higher education courses on a full or part-time basis which can be attended at a specific college or at a remote location. Those students based at remote locations will be able to obtain tutor support through the UHI Network via high bandwidth computer links thus widening the scope for continuous learning in the region. As well as providing electronic library and information management systems, the project aims to provide each campus with networked learning resource centres to support research, learning and information provision, with video conferencing facilities.

Although many university libraries permit members of the public to use their facilities for reference use they do not advertise the fact. Some do invite non-university members to use the library facilities, but are cautious in their invitation. Independent or external users are normally granted access to the library provided they can (a) demonstrate a need to use an academic library and (b) pay a fee or subscription.

The Library's main stated aim, however, is to provide a service to the teaching and research undertaken at the university. Restrictions on access generally seem to depend on the subscriptions that have been paid and to which category the user belongs. So, for example, ex-staff may have different access rights from members of the general public or separate fees may be charged for consultation and for borrowing. In some cases university libraries may restrict the number of external users allowing, for example, up to 30 members of the general public to borrow books from the University Library at any one time. The Robert

Gordon University promotes its library service to potential external members who are studying for a professional qualification or having problems in keeping up to date within a profession, and offers access to anyone undertaking continuing professional development (CPD) activity. Many of the universities which offer services to external members include corporate membership as one of the membership categories. This type of membership may give employees the opportunity to use the facilities of a university library for the purpose of CPD as well as to meet the information needs of their current job or specific task.

Universities may have agreements with other libraries which allow staff and students to have reciprocal access rights. Several consortia have been formalised on a geographical basis. In the United States, library services designed specifically for distance learners have a considerable history. In recent years librarians in this field have been assisted by the development of a series of guidelines and standards, with adoption by regional accrediting agencies providing the 'teeth' to ensure adequate, if not generous, resourcing.

Distance education in Australia also has a long history. The Australian Library and Information Association has a Distance Education Special Interest Group which publishes its own newsletter (DESIGnation). The Task Force on Library and Information Service to remote users issued a report in 1990 which included a number of recommendations for improving access to information for remote users and the Australian Council of Libraries and Information Services adopted a statement of principles on distant provision in 1991. A national library card was discussed but it was never adopted. A number of reciprocal borrowing schemes exist. These include the CLANN network in New South Wales, incorporating university, college and public libraries. The network facilitates reciprocal borrowing for both undergraduates and post graduates. The CAVAL scheme in Victoria comprises academic and special libraries.

The Open Learning Agency of Australia (OLAA) was established in 1992 to broker distance education courses from various universities and FE colleges throughput Australia. Students may register for units from a variety of institutions at any one time. There are no entry requirements. The Open Learning Library and Information Service produces a guide for OLAA students and provides vouchers which the students can use to pay for library services at academic and public libraries. The Open Learning Electronic Support Service (OLESS) currently being developed by the OLAA is described by Van Dyke. A key objective of OLESS is to integrate existing networks to create an 'Australia-wide off-campus student-focused information web'. Collection development is formula driven based on number of off-campus students, location of course delivery and other available titles in the subject area.

Information services are provided via e-mail, telephone, fax and post. Librarians search catalogues and databases on behalf of students and then post on a limited number of books or photocopies. Document delivery is by a courier service or airmail. Distance learning, and similar approaches, are in principle very inclusive, offering opportunities to people in developing countries as much as in the developed world. The role of the public library in lifelong learning in the UK is rooted in the founding principles of public libraries in terms of the Victorian concept that they made available the sources of educational development for those without the financial resources to attend more formal institutions.

The co-operative actions involving public libraries, universities and colleges could prove very fruitful and that public libraries could be used to deliver open and distance learning to employees of small and medium sized enterprises (SMEs), women returning to work, ethnic minority groups, those who have missed out on conventional education and indeed, everyone 'learning through life'. UK public libraries have been proactive in recent years in developing their role as providers of basic skills materials for open learning. One third of public library authorities have staff trained in some elements of educational guidance and over 60% of public library authorities host Training Access points (TAPs) or similar local databases of training opportunities. One example is the Open Learning Club at Croydon Libraries which provides open learning packs for use at home and provides equipment in the library for video, audio and PC-based materials.

Topics in the open learning collection include: writing letters and reports, spelling and punctuation, writing CVs, interview techniques, setting up a business, keyboard skills, word-processing. Much of this kind of material is produced by the Royal Society of Arts (RSA). There have been some recent developments in collaboration between the public and academic library sectors but there is little recent evidence on how such collaboration can improve library services to students engaged on higher level courses of study. An Australian study in 1988 found that public librarians believed that the public library service to distance learning students should be supplementary to what the home institution provides and not replace it. In short, some university librarians may hold the view that in providing excellent library services to support traditional students they are doing all they can to support lifelong learning.

All universities and university libraries hold that their responsibilities are in supporting, first and foremost, the institution's own registered students and staff body Thus, lifelong learners engaged in work-based learning or continuing professional development have access to widely varying levels of library services, dependent on whether they are registered as a student. External library membership schemes do provide such users with access to university library resources, but these usually carry some restrictions relating to, for example, borrowing rights or access to electronic resources. On the whole, quite a depressing picture emerges in the UK regarding library provision for non-traditional students. Furthermore, evidence suggests that some distance learning courses being offered to students are by-passing the institutional library by providing direct to the student all necessary supporting information in a pre-packaged form. Outside the UK, there is evidence of more coherent approaches to the provision of library services to lifelong learners.

Some of this may be described as virtue born out of necessity, given that examples of good practice are drawn from areas which have a wide geographical spread (Australia, New Zealand, US) and a very dispersed user group. There can be no doubt that government and society are serious in their desire and intention to see the development of lifelong learning. Universities may embrace this concept enthusiastically or unwillingly, but they will not be able to ignore it. However, the changes which are required are so fundamental that at this early stage it is difficult to be certain of the shape of the higher education sector in the UK, still less of individual institutions. Librarians have become familiar with the idea that many of their users will in future access these broader services directly, without using their local service as an intermediary or provider. Since many lifelong learners will spend less time on campus than the traditional full-time student or researcher, it is to be expected that they will make even more use of such unmediated services.

The future of any one academic library service, therefore, cannot be regarded as merely dependent on the parent institution. A few academic libraries have made great efforts and can demonstrate good practice - as, for example at Sheffield Hallam - but most treat non-traditional learners either as part of a general category of "external readers" or simply ignore them. In designing services for lifelong learners librarians need to consider the context: the learning objectives, the method of delivery, learning styles and so on. At the same time it is necessary for academic libraries to shift their focus from form to content and to ask themselves how the required content cn be delivered to the lifelong learner - rather than becoming blocked by the difficulties particular forms present.

At present, libraries tend to be organised by form, and frequently budgetary allocations reinforce this approach: it is still not uncommon for library allocations to be split into 'book' and 'journal' funds, with online services treated as an uneasy compromise. Inter-library loans may be seen as an additional service which is severely restricted, not least on cost grounds. Once users gain widespread access to information delivery services, these divisions will be seen to be increasingly irrelevant. Most users will wish to have access to content regardless of form, although they will also wish to be able to state a preference - which increasingly may be for electronic formats which can be manipulated within other documents.

The library role will therefore be to facilitate content access as the primary concern, demonstrating how information sources can be presented within the structures of learning which teaching staff devise and help to repackage content in new ways. Managing this scenario will be a complex task. The rapid development of electronic information sources has changed the nature of academic library provision in a very few years. JISC datasets and eLib services have shown that electronic sources can replace many of the traditional materials which libraries have used, especially in the area of datasets, some journals and new media such as Web pages. However, there is almost universal acceptance that traditional formats (print, audio, video, etc.) will continue to play an important role in the total service.which users require. From this has emerged the concept of the 'hybrid library', which may be seen as a new service model which provides integrated access to the full range of services. The final phase of eLib has provided funding for demonstrator projects in this area.

For lifelong learners, as for others, this concept will have great importance in providing access to the widest range of resources in a manner tailored to the users' own requirements. Librarians have long struggled to try to make the service provided as relevant as possible to the users' requirements. For undergraduate courses this has often been epitomised by the annual struggle to acquire reading lists in time for books to be ordered and put on the shelves.

Librarians will have to gain better understanding of the learning process as a whole and will need to persuade others of the positive contribution they can make. In all the discussions of the future electronic library it is easy to lose sight of one of the key roles of the library - namely, its value as place. Libraries on campuses are often used by groups as places to meet, and with the increase in group work they often provide group study areas. Even for students and researchers working alone, the Library can provide social contact. If there is a continuing reduction in class contact hours, the availability of this 'social-learning centre' may be crucial to the student experience. Where courses are delivered at a distance, there is considerable merit in providing some kind of learning centre to encourage this social interaction as part of the learning experience.

Further education and public libraries would offer obvious centres for this kind of planned activity. The widespread availability of access to Internet resources, including the World Wide Web, has raised considerable concern about the quality of information which is being accessed. While printed publications go through a well-known and tried and tested quality assurance procedure, involving referees, editorial boards and publishers' expert opinions, there is a lack such procedure for electronic resources. In a situation where anyone can publish anything on the Web, it is difficult for users to judge the validity of the information they retrieve. The eLib Access to Networked Resources (ANR) projects are a partial answer to this problem, although at present their long-term future is not assured. Undoubtedly there is a role for systems which provide some kind of authoritative grading for networked resources, but at present it is unclear as to what that mechanism will be. Again, for lifelong learners, the need is likely to be acute as they may well be remote from sources of advice. Librarians will need to consider this issue in the design of their services. Information and communications technologies have much to offer the lifelong learner and may provide the boost which will make lifelong learning a reality. Libraries need to redouble their efforts to assist in the development of networked information resources and in their exploitation.

However, the networked information arena poses questions about how users will be able to identify and retrieve particular information from the vast resources potentially available - the need is to provide the equivalent of a library catalogue which can be used as an access point to world-wide sources. In some cases resource delivery may be a three-stage process, whereby the user, having discovered an item, first requests it, the library then acquires it, and the library then delivers it to the user - this is the classic traditional library process expressed, for example, in a reservations or inter-library loan service.

As part of the management function, decisions will be taken on which resource discovery tools to provide, on how specific resources should be delivered (for example, should they be held locally or accessed from remote servers) and on which tools should be provided to enable users to exploit the information. In addition, management will provide procedures to handle the economic and legal aspects of information provision. Together, these may be described as 'resource management'. Although these functions can be found in the traditional library, in the electronic environment they introduce new levels of complexity, not least because so many of the information resources are not 'owned' by the library in any real sense: issues such as cataloguing of networked resources are therefore far more complex than their traditional library equivalents. The development of information handling skills is now recognised as central to learning. Included within these skills are the ability to identify information requirements, to develop and conduct a search, to retrieve information, to understand it and manipulate it, and to present information in a variety of contexts. Universities have taken different approaches to the development of these skills.

In some, a compulsory module is taken by all first year students to equip them with the study skills, including information skills, that they will need: an example would be the scheme developed by the University of Humberside and Lincolnshire. In others the approach taken is to embed the development of generic skills in the curriculum, so that the relevance of each skill is demonstrated within the learning context of the discipline. There are advantages and disadvantages to both approaches. What is clear, however, is that ways need to be found to ensure that all lifelong learners have the opportunity to acquire these skills, and develop their existing skills, so as to equip them to learn in the future. The provision of adequate helpdesk and other advisory services will be crucial to the success of academic libraries in the future.

Users will expect to be able to access such services in person, by telephone, by email and through web pages and will expect rapid and authoritative responses. Thus the electronic helpdesk service will be designed in as part of the learning environment, not added on as a kind of optional (or perhaps taken-for-granted) extra, and certainly not as the last, desperate port of call for the student who can find nowhere else to turn. The essence of lifelong learning is that each individual will be undertaking learning of some kind throughout life. This provides an opportunity for universities to transform the relationships they develop with their students. Instead of the classic route of a three or four year undergraduate degree course, followed at best by a remote relationship through an alumni society, institutions will have the opportunity to persuade students to return again and again. It is a truism of marketing that it is far easier to sell another product to an existing customer than to recruit a new customer, and universities will need to grasp the opportunities this presents by developing lifelong relationships.

The academic library could have an important role to play in these relationships, perhaps by transforming current 'external reader' membership arrangements into a new type of university membership which includes access to courses as well as to university facilities. Bearing in mind the large numbers of adult learners and scholars who are currently outside institutions, it may be that universities could use access to library services as a means of brining such people into their communities in a much more active fashion than occurs at present. Overlaying all of the changes in academic libraries that a commitment to the support of lifelong learning will bring there will be a need for a high level of management skills.

2

Information Preservation

Everyday information is increasing and so is the userexpectation. So to save the valuable information and fulfill the user's requirement for posterity, digital documents and resources should be managed and preserved at a tremendous rate. Preservation in the digital world is not absolute, but depends instead on the continuing transformative impact of the digital product on the information work of end-users.

The Libraries faces issues of deteriorating books and serial volumes, not to mention maps, manuscripts, and graphic materials such as photographs; reformatting needs pertaining to audiovisual materials that can only be viewed or heard with obsolete technology; and preserving digital materials, including in-house produced as well as commercial or other publications. Guaranteed affordable long-term access to electronic books or journals, for instance, requires collaboration on the part of many stake-holders on the national scene.

In US, the Preservation Office is responsible for activities such as preservation planning and policy, grant writing, disaster planning and response, environmental monitoring, preservation replacement, and preservation education. The Preservation Office also assists with digital projects such as the American Indians of the Pacific

Northwest Library of Congress/Ameritech Digital Library Grant Project. Operational activities such as binding, conservation treatment, and microfilming are decentralised and the responsibility of individual units. In Summer 2002, a pilot mass de-acidification program was implemented. Environmental monitoring with IPI data loggers was implemented in the main off-site storage facility.

The lack of adequate financial resources and organisational dispersal of current preservation resources are major ongoing problems. The Libraries is currently evaluating preservation needs and establishing preservation priorities with the goal of better aligning financial resources with those priorities. Digital Initiatives has moved from a project-focused effort with one librarian to an operational program with a secure funding base and placement within Resources and Collection Management Services. The DI Program has specialised in creating image collections and developing extensive metadata expertise.

The scope of Digital Initiatives has expanded beyond its original focus on images to include more textual, audio/visual, and other forms of information. The main product has been the Digital Collections web page, which received approximately 150,000 discrete visits in the first quarter of 2002. There are more than 40 collections online, with over 20 more in production. Over 44,000 objects have been scanned, primarily images, although gray literature and monographs have been digitised as well.

The digital collections are a mix of Libraries resources, faculty projects, and multi-institutional collaborative projects. Collections are integrated into the Libraries online catalogue and input into OCLC's WorldCat. The DI Program also advises faculty and staff on a variety of projects with digital components. The Metadata Implementation Group, which has been cited as an exemplar, was born out of the DI Program. This group advises others in the creation of metadata and keeps abreast of metadata standards. A Digital Initiative Steering Committee with representation from different areas within the Libraries provides guidance.

Not unlike libraries across the country, the Libraries is challenged by the inflationary costs of maintaining, expanding, and diversifying its collections. In the last six years, the Libraries' purchasing power has eroded significantly despite increases in actual dollars allocated from the University – attributable primarily to price increases for journals that substantially exceed the Consumer Price Index.

In the case of most full-text journals, for instance, electronic access was inseparable from a print subscription. Publisher practices, accompanied by librarian and faculty concern about permanent access to electronic information, dictated that the Libraries pay for the print title along with the electronic version of the same content. Pricing of electronic journals remains volatile and inconsistent, with no one pricing model emerging.

A worrisome trend for a large research institution is the movement by some publishers toward pricing based on the number of students enrolled. In such cases, the cost of electronic access is almost always much higher than the print. The cost for electronic access to bibliographic databases, reference works, and books far outpaces print prices. The combination of these factors –insufficient funding to keep pace with inflation and proliferation of new and costly forms of information – has challenged the ingenuity of selectors and reshaped the nature of the collection. The Libraries has also taken the risk of subscribing only to the electronic version of journals despite the lack of resolution on long term archiving. Yet the percentage of the resources budget going to serials has increased. The Libraries has made significant progress in the area of development and fund raising. The Libraries recognises the desirability of having a work force that can work effectively with a diverse academic community.

The chief academic officer, the Provost, is responsible for the interpretation and implementation of University policies and procedures for academic personnel and has delegated to the Director of Libraries the irresponsibility for administering the Librarian Personnel Code. The Code has been in effect since 1999 and is patterned on the faculty model, which relies upon peer assessment for appointment and promotion. The appointment and promotion policies of the Code are designed to contribute to the academic and scholarly excellence of the University by the maintenance of high standards of librarianship.

Librarians are expected to be active in scholarly pursuits and professional activities that advance librarianship and higher education. The Code also incorporates procedures and policies for performance evaluation; merit salary increases; resignation, retirement, involuntary termination; professional leave; and proceedings for resolution of differences. Librarians are responsible for developing collections, providing access to information resources worldwide, and facilitating use by the Libraries' clientele.

A graduate degree from a program accredited by the American Library Association or an equivalent library science/information studies degree constitutes the primary credential for librarians and is considered the terminal degree. Many hold advanced degrees and specialised training. The noncompetitive nature of librarian salaries continues to be an exceedingly serious problem. Low salaries are not only a source of dissatisfaction among librarians, but they also pose a serious impediment to recruitment.

The Association of Librarians of the University of Washington (ALUW) promotes library service of the highest quality; promotes professional standing for members and encourages professional development; helps to improve librarians' working conditions and benefits; and promotes informal communicatio. ınd fellowship among members.

ALUW is active politically and employs a lobbyist to bring issues of concern to state legislators. ALUW is also responsible for selecting librarians to serve terms on Faculty Senate Councils. Communication across the units in this geographically diverse system is enhanced by the Libraries Staff Web. Other methods of communication include two important online newsletters that are sent to all staff each week. The Libraries has made a significant commitment during the past ten years to providing its staff with training and development opportunities.

The Libraries has official guidelines and application procedures for work-related travel and participation at professional meetings. Travel funds are available not only to librarians, but also to classified and professional staff. The Libraries provides a full range of user services in both physical and virtual settings. Reference assistance, research consultations, check-out and interlibrary borrowing, and bibliographic access to information resources are just some of the services offered.

Preservation of digital information is challenging not only for technological reasons but also for legal reasons. Traditionally, libraries have had a mandate to preserve what they own. Few if any libraries are willing to take responsibility for preserving licensed electronic resources that they do not own, even though they recognise that publishers are not archivers. Increasingly, the preservation of cultural and scholarly resources is becoming the responsibility of all who have a stake in them-creators, publishers, and users-as well as of the traditional custodians in libraries and archives.

Preservation awareness must reach beyond the walls of the library and the grounds of the campus. Therefore, any strategy to preserve these materials must involve many small groups and communities in a coordinated national effort to raise awareness of what is at risk. Among the most widely used techniques for managing long-term access to digital files is migration, i.e., the transfer of digitally encoded information from one hardware-software configuration to another. Migration is intended to keep selected digital information accessible by ensuring that hardware or software obsolescence does not strand files in unreadable formats. It is, in essence, a translation program, and, as is the case with all such programs, some measure of information is lost in the movement from one encoding scheme to another.

In US, the Digital Library Federation (DLF) is the primary manifestation of CLIR's interest in digital libraries. Operating under CLIR's auspices, the DLF is a consortium of 25 leading research libraries that are developing online collections and services. Members work through the DLF to share research and development; identify and promote the application of digital library standards and good practices; and incubate innovative digital library organisations, collections, and services, particularly where these are commonly required but are beyond the ability of any single organisation or consortium to produce. The past year has been one of change and growth for the DLF.

This year, the DLF began to explore a wholly new model for accessing scholarly resources-one that will enable users seamlessly to explore the contents of numerous geographically distributed, and often very different, scholarly information resources. In this model, data providers, such as managers of OPACs and finding aids, e-journals, e-print archives, or online data and image repositories, would agree to provide extracts of their metadata in a common, minimal-level format in response to requests from service providers. Service providers, such as libraries, data repositories, and e-print archives, would use the extracted metadata to build user-oriented services, such as catalogues and portals to materials distributed across multiple sites.

This model would lead to the development of subject portals opening out onto information in all formats, whether print or digital, database or sound, and dealing with a specific topic or theme. Localised or regional services could also arise; for example, to present a wide range of information in a manner appropriate to users in a particular geographically defined community, such as a university campus. In pursuing this work, the DLF and the Coalition for Networked Informations (CNI) have agreed to support the Open Archives initiative, a technical framework that can support harvesting.

The digital library transforms traditional collections through the integration of new formats, licensed content, and third-party information over which the library has little or no direct curatorial control. Collection-development strategies and practices do not yet take account of these changing circumstances, and their legal, organisational, and business implications are not well understood. The DLF is therefore active in identifying, evaluating, and, where necessary, developing collection strategies and practices that are appropriate for the digital library, and in assessing the legal, organisational, and business implications of these strategies. The DLF is also encouraging the development of new kinds of scholarly collections that take full advantage of computer and network technologies. Developing support and other services that enable the digital library to respond to its users' information requirements. In a digital library, how information is made, assembled into collections, and presented online affects whether, to what extent, and how it can be used.

Accordingly, libraries need to engage more effectively with their user communities to build better, more useful, and more usable collections and services. They also need to rethink and restructure user-support services to make them appropriate for library services and collections that are delivered online. An obvious starting point is a thorough review of how scholars and students are using existing online collections and services. However, because there are no standard methods for evaluating such use, no body of data exists to support such a review. The DLF has launched an initiative to identify and seek agreement on appropriate evaluative methods and to deploy them in a comprehensive investigation of how students and scholars are using online collections and services. Gaining experience in preserving digital information.

Identifying standards and practices that enable the digital library to develop and maintain its collections and services cost-effectively. The DLF seeks to identify, document, endorse, and promote the adoption of data-creation standards and best practices for producing digital information that can be managed, exchanged, distributed to end users, and preserved cost-effectively. Effective communications are vital to the DLF. They ensure that its programmes respond to members' needs and interests, and they enable the DLF to inform its members and the broader library community about the strategies, technologies, organisational mechanisms, and legal and business issues that affect the development and cost-effective maintenance of high-quality digital library services and collections. The DLF has taken the following steps to enhance its communications efforts:

— Revised, reorganised, and updated the DLF Web site, its primary vehicle for communicating with the broader community.

— Established several e-mail lists to support communication between the director's office and staff at DLF member institutions.

— Prepared to launch a quarterly newsletter in which the director's office will report to members and members will report about recent developments in their digital libraries.

— Built two online registries to supply information about members' digital library initiatives:

a) *Documenting the digital library*: a database of policies, strategies, working papers, standards and other application guidelines, and technical documentation developed by DLF members to inform or reflect upon their digital library development activities; and

b) *DLF digital collections*: a database of DLF members' Web-accessible, public-domain digital collections.

Drawing professional staff from each of its member institutions, the forums serve as meeting places, marketplaces, and congresses. The changes brought about by digital technology obligate librarians and university administrators alike to consider new economic models for providing information services.

Librarians rely on usage statistics to inform a range of decisions, from acquisitions to storage. In the print environment, librarians developed methods for tracking collection use. With the advent of electronic publishing, however, usage data reside with the publishers, and fewer than half make such statistics available. Given the expense of implementing the statistical-analysis function, many publishers are slow to add this capability.

Libraries face the ongoing challenge of having to account in financial terms for the real value of their chief assets, their collections. The context for collection valuation and the method of accounting vary from library to library, depending on the institution's mission and how its information resources are used to fulfil that mission; however, as information and its products become more important parts of the economy, there is a stronger push to view library holdings from a business perspective. The business risk model treats collections as core institutional assets and defines good stewardship as a dynmic process of identifying risk to the collections and instituting policies and procedures that mitigate the risks. This model is valuable to managers because it is designed not only to identify risk to library assets but also to determine which risks are least acceptable and what measures must be taken to reduce them. It guides management decisions about investments in collections and is grounded in the individual mission of each library.

The library of the future-based on new relationships with many other campus units-calls for a new kind of leadership. CLIR, in collaboration with other organisations, continues to emphasise leadership-development programs that equip librarians to work in partnership with other managers of information resources. Defining the library's role in supporting course-management software and in addressing institution-wide concerns about authorisation and authentication; identifying the kinds of rights management systems that best serve the needs of college and midsize university libraries. Understanding the meaning of "core collections" in the digital environment and the role of off-site storage in collection management; addressing the development of cooperative collections. Communicating library issues to administrators; studying requirements for leadership in the profession; and analysing staffing and recruitment patterns and problems.

An increased awareness of the vulnerability of much of the world's cultural heritage has led to a proliferation of research on preservation science. Researchers and research institutes are making significant efforts to supply conservators and restorers with properly tested means to treat individual artifacts as well as means for mass conservation. CLIR is sponsoring a group of American archivists and librarians, working in collaboration with German counterparts, to explore the adaptation of encoded archival description (EAD) for international exchange. This project, expected to extend over one year, is also receiving funding from the German research consortium, Deutsche Forschungsgemeinschaft.

Library and Information Resources

Library and information resources are the intellectual infrastructure that facilitates the achievement of the University of Washington's primary mission to preserve, advance, and disseminate knowledge. The University of Washington Libraries has been called the "intellectual commons" of the University. The voices of scholars from throughout the ages speak to current students, faculty, and other users. At the same time, individual users pursue solitary intellectual inquiry or work with other students and scholars to explore new ideas. The role of the Libraries as a place for students and other researchers to access information, seek research assistance, do individual work, collaborate with other students and scholars, and engage in lifelong learning activities, will continue to be critical well into the 21st Century.

The mission of the Libraries is to enrich the quality of life and advance intellectual discovery by connecting people with knowledge. The Libraries works to achieve this mission through five key action areas:

— *Any Time, Any Place:* The Libraries works to develop an integrated environment of content, tools, and services in a wide selection of formats and via a variety of delivery mechanisms in order to accommodate its user communities' diverse information needs, far-flung locations and different learning styles. This library—ideally available at any time and from any place—supports and improves the ability of the University to meet its standards of excellence in education and research and to prepare its graduates for a life of learning and global citizenship.

— *Excellence in Collections / Digital Resources* : The Libraries continues to develop and maintain its collections at the highest level possible across all relevant subjects and across an ever broadening spectrum of formats.

Collections include not only the information resources housed by the institution but also remote information resources to which the institution provides access, whether via licensing of electronic resources, free Internet resources, or cooperative collection building and sharing.

— *Capacity Building:* The Libraries proactively creates the means to leverage its priorities by reallocating resources, consolidating, and economising. The Libraries devotes energies to supplementing the funds provided by the State of Washington and secures additional external funding to maintain and preserve collections, facilities, services, and to meet staffing needs.

— *Diversity and Organisational Culture :* Respect for all human diversity is a fundamental value of the Libraries. Staff members who appreciate different backgrounds and perspectives provide a competitive advantage when solving problems and planning for services. This appreciation also allows the Libraries to serve the increasingly diverse communities more effectively and with more sensitivity.

— *Information Literacy:* The Libraries is an active participant in the educational mission of the University. The Libraries seeks, through collaborations with educators on campus and beyond, to ensure that graduates are information literate, able to find, select, and assess information, and therefore prepared to succeed personally and professionally in a global, knowledge-driven society.

Computing & Communications (C&C) is the organisation charged with providing high-quality information technology infrastructure and related services to members of the University community in direct support of the University's teaching, research, health care, and public service missions. Computing & Communications (C&C) is headed by the Vice President for Computing & Communications who reports directly to the President of the University. C&C is divided into eight organisational units: Business & Finance, Communication Technologies, Information Systems, Networks & Distributed Computing, Planning and Facilities Infrastructure, Technology Outreach and Partnership, University Computing Services, and Video and TV Technologies. C&C's mission is to provide convenient, secure, computer-based services and resources that improve the efficiency and effectiveness of the University's ever-broadening constituency, and ultimately add to the region's intellectual and economic capital.

C&C's vision is to create the technology environment necessary to support leading edge teaching, learning, research, and health care, and to advance the University's most important goals — transforming teaching and learning, increasing educational opportunity, advancing human knowledge, and solving regional and global problems. To achieve this vision, C&C has identified the following three critical goals:

— Provide the expertise and infrastructure necessary to enable advanced network computing applications and rich information content.

— Find new and innovative ways to leverage the convergence of voice, video, and data technologies in order to advance leading edge learning, research, and health care.

— Enhance teaching, learning, and discovery by advancing the ability of faculty, students, and staff to do cutting-edge work through high-speed access to information resources, communications tools, and interactive multimedia experiences.

Educational Partnerships and Learning Technologies (EPLT) serves students, faculty, researchers, and clinicians by providing access to tools and resources; promoting fluency with information and information technology; and fostering innovation to meet their needs and goals.

The methods by which information can be collected, assembled, edited, upgraded, archived, displayed, distributed, and accessed interactively are continuously improving. Networked information technology has the potential to support individual and group learning, enhance teaching, and make possible advances in research and clinical practice. EPLT was established in 1998 and is headed by the Vice Provost for Educational Partnerships & Learning Technologies who reports to the Provost. The organisation is divided into two subunits: Educational Partnerships and Learning Technologies.

The Libraries has nationally recognised programs of excellence in library assessment, information literacy, digital library initiatives, international studies support, integrated health information services, and in providing access to networked information. The Libraries is also known for its commitment to collaborative programs to facilitate teaching and learning at the University of Washington. In US, the Association of Research Libraries (ARL) composite index ranks the University of Washington Libraries 12th among its 120 academic research libraries in North America. Yet beyond the strength of local collections and networked resources, excellent service programs, knowledgeable staff, diverse facilities, and size of budget, the Libraries is known for innovation, responsiveness, and an integrated planning and assessment process that makes the user-centered library not just a goal, but a reality.

Students and faculty recognise the value provided by the Libraries and rank the Libraries as the most important source of information for their work. The Libraries also receives the highest satisfaction rating of any academic service on the surveys of graduating seniors conducted by the Office of Educational Assessment.

During the past decade, extensive collaboration with other campus units resulted in the establishment of the largest general computing lab on campus, wired instruction space, and an instructional technology and support centre.

OUGL has evolved into one of the nation's premier student-centered undergraduate libraries. Specialised use space includes 12 group study rooms and four instruction rooms with projection capability. The Health Sciences Library (HSL) supports the teaching, research, and clinical needs of the University's large Health Sciences community.

The HSL has more than 60,000 square feet on two floors with study seating for 490 people and 45 public computers/email stations. The Microlab Learning Commons has an additional 151 work-stations where students gather to work on assignments, research, and other collaborative learning projects. The newest branch library facilities on the Seattle campus are the Physics-Astronomy Library and the Foster Business Library. The Physics-Astronomy Library opened in 1994 with 4,078 assignable square feet in the new Physics-Astronomy building complex. The Foster Business Library opened in 1997 with 16,137 assignable square feet and is a "below garden" facility with an 800 square foot skylight above the reading area. Specialised use space includes 7 group study rooms. The Tacoma campus library is located in a renovated historic building and has 29,081 assignable square feet. It has study seating for 145 students, including one group study room, which accommodates eight students. Special collections include a children's and young adult literature collection, the Foundation Center's Cooperating Collection for nonprofit research, and collections on Russian and English literature.

Teaching, learning, and research at the University is supported by one of the premier library collections in North America, consisting of over 6 million volumes and government documents, 7 million microforms, in addition to manuscripts, technical reports, maps, architectural drawings, photos and slides, audio materials, films, and videos. Beyond the onsite collection, the Libraries provides access to more than 10,000 electronic publications, many of which include additional thousands of journals in electronic form. These electronic resources are available to the academic community anywhere and anytime.

Collections shelved on campus in on-site library facilities are generally heavily used and are in "open stacks," that is, faculty and student researchers are able to browse or retrieve material directly from the stacks without meditation by Libraries staff. Most of the Libraries' collection space is devoted to general stacks, or material that may be checked out from the Libraries. Manuscripts, Special Collections, and University Archives materials are shelved in secure areas, must be retrieved by staff, and are only available for in-library use.

Collection growth has outstripped the Libraries' capacity to provide shelving in traditional campus library facilities. Lesser-used materials have been moved off-site and are retrieved on a regularly scheduled basis when requested by students and researchers. Following a growing trend in academic libraries nationwide, the Libraries developed several remote-shelving facilities to help house and manage its collections. The Libraries houses the largest array of information resources in the Pacific Northwest and several nationally preeminent collections. For example, a number of our area studies collections rank in the top tier nationally, as evidenced by rankings given in the Department of Education National Resource Center competition, among other indicators. Use of the Libraries' special collections is not limited to published scholars or to doctoral candidates.

With the increased emphasis on research on the part of undergraduates, primary source materials such as manuscripts and photographs are becoming even more important to the University's instructional mission. The Libraries resources in scientific, technical and medical journals are especially strong, with serials expenditures generally ranking in the top ten of ARL libraries. These journals are critical to the support of teaching and learning in these areas, as well as to the extensive program of sponsored research. Where possible the Libraries has acquired electronic access to these journals for use by the university community from any of the many locations in which they work.

The Collection Management Services (CMS) unit supports all Libraries units and coordinates collection development and management, the building of on-site collections through purchases, gifts, or deposit arrangements, and provides operational oversight for electronic resources development and access. Subject selectors and library liaisons play a key role in acquiring materials for their discipline, staying in touch with the needs of their constituents, and engaging in instructional and advisory support to their constituency.

The Information Resources Council, which is composed of 26 librarians from across the system, acts in an advisory capacity on issues related to information resources development and management. The head of CMS chairs the Washington State Cooperative Library Project's Databases Committee and oversees its competitive bid processes, which have resulted in favourable group purchase terms for databases from the Institute for Scientific Information and ProQuest, among others.

The Libraries is also represented on the Administrative Committee of the Washington State Library's Statewide Database Licensing Project, and is a member of the Greater Western Library Alliance (GWLA), a group of 30 research libraries in the western U.S. GWLA is currently pursuing group purchasing opportunities and strategies to help reform the system of scholarly communication. The Libraries was a founding member of the Pacific Rim Digital Library Alliance (PRDLA) and the Digital Library Federation (DLF).

In other library units a consolidated service desk staffed by librarians, staff, and students handles reference and information queries. Reference and service points also handle telephone inquiries. Electronic reference service is offered in several modes. Asynchronous service is provided through electronic mail to a designated library unit address, library staff person, or through LibQuest.

The Libraries have licensed access to a wide array of bibliographic databases that provide coverage of most subjects as well as more generalised ones that contain full-text. Most material in the Libraries can be checked-out by University faculty, students, and staff as well as by non-affiliated users who have borrowing privileges. In general, reference materials and items in Manuscripts, Special Collections, and University Archives do not circulate.

Some library units restrict the circulation of periodicals. While there is some variation in loan periods, books usually circulate for 28 days (undergraduates) or an academic quarter (graduate students and faculty), while the check-out period for periodicals is 3 days. During the past several years, a number of libraries have moved from closed (mediated) reserves to open (non-mediated) reserves. This change supports the collaborative learning model favoured by most University classes by eliminating individual responsibility for checking out reserve materials, allowing longer in-library use of materials, and effectively avoiding most reserve fines. Circulation services are offered in every library location that circulates material.

Initial check-outs must be done within the library. However, subsequent renewals can be done remotely without staff mediation. The Health Sciences Library currently provides a "self check-out station" that enables borrowers to borrow without staff mediation. Through the Libraries web site, users can see what items they have checked out, have on hold, or have borrowed through interlibrary loan; they can renew the books they have checked out; and place holds on books that are checked out. Users can also request through the Catalogue that circulating books at any site (including Bothell and Tacoma) be sent to another library unit for pickup. The University community can already perform a number of library-related activities without coming physically to the library.

There has been a significant decline in the in-library use of material from more than two million items in the 1995-96 year to just over one million in 2001-02. The decline has been most pronounced in those libraries where a significant proportion of information resources are now available electronically such as business, newspapers, scientific, and medical journals. The quality of the Libraries' information resources is not only acknowledged nationally, but is strongly valued by the Libraries' primary clientele, the campus faculty and students.

The Libraries has used networked computing technology to expand the resources available for education and research for almost two decades. The infrastructure needed to provide access to this array of global resources is jointly supported by the Libraries and Computing & Communications (C&C). The computing infrastructure supporting library services at the University is robust and extensive. C&C has a long history of working with the Libraries and their network services are critical to the delivery of digital information resources. Public access to networked information resources is provided through both remote servers around the world and locally mounted databases. Library systems host over 200 databases on clustered Dell servers running Windows 2000. Data is kept on a Storage Area Network (SAN) and all systems are UPS protected. This combination provides outstanding performance and reliability, as there is no single point of failure in the entire server system. This fully redundant server environment is capable of storing several terabytes of data.

The catalogue database is part of the Integrated Library System (ILS) that uses Innovative Interfaces Inc. software running on an IBM AIX server. This is maintained by C&C and is also protected with redundant disk storage, off-site backups, and emergency power. C&C also maintains a second computer using software from the same vendor (INN-Reach) to provide a union catalogue and statewide lending service for the 6 public baccalaureate institutions. The public can access these resources in any library unit from over 300 public access workstations running Windows 2000.

Some applications requiring older operating systems are provided on stand alone units. Staff computing is supported with over 500 desktop PC's that are being migrated to Windows XP during the 2002-2003 timeframe. The Libraries uses the same robust server environment throughout the libraries network to facilitate collaborative work through stored and shared documents. Access is coordinated via a staff web intranet.

As a heavily wired, and now wireless-ready, networked environment, Odegaard Undergraduate Library (OUGL) has made great progress toward adopting the best of technology to enhance teaching and learning at the University of Washington. In 1994, the Libraries and OUGL were open to innovative uses of space and staff to support student learning in the most effective ways. OUGL was to serve as the gateway, the entry point for the undergraduate student, the novice researcher, and the inexperienced user of information technology.

The importance of the library as place for academic coursework and research is evident in these high entry numbers. The OUGL partnered with the Computer Science and Engineering (CSE) Department to create a cultural laboratory supporting digital animation. The library provides the space and information specialists to research aspects for the animation subject. The partnership is mutually reinforcing. For the future, the Libraries and CSE imagine integrating even more—physically and intellectually. The Libraries has offered instruction to University students, faculty, staff, and to a lesser extent to the non-affiliated community in a variety of modes for decades.

Over the past ten years, however, significant changes in the educational and societal environment have prompted re-examination and experimentation in the mode and objectives of these educational programs. Through a series of collaborations the Libraries is seeking innovative means to shift the vision for its educational mission from one focused internally upon the tools and resources provided by the Libraries to a vision that embraces the larger, and rapidly changing, learning and information environment.

The Libraries' goals for its instructional efforts in the 21st Century are to ensure the information literacy of University graduates, to enhance their ability to function as scholars and citizens in a rapidly changing, knowledge-based economy. Information literacy is defined as a set of abilities requiring individuals to "recognise when information is needed and have the ability to locate, evaluate, and use effectively the needed information" and is further elucidated in the ACRL. Information literacy is not a static skill set, but is developmental over the course of a degree program and indeed, the lifespan.

A curricular basis for information literacy learning requires collaboration with individual faculty as well as with departments, schools, and colleges in order to identify the appropriate information literacy learning outcomes for the individual discipline/program, and to situate information literacy learning opportunities throughout the curriculum. Current modes of instruction provided by the Libraries include tours, orientation sessions, individual and small group consultations, drop-in workshops, course-related instruction, credit courses taught by librarians either as part of Informatics 220, General Studies or courses offered through academic departments, web-based tutorials such as UWILL (UW Information Literacy Learning), online help, and interactive "chat" which addresses point of need assistance. Course-related instruction remains the primary means of providing library instruction within the academic curriculum. Faculty members frequently direct requests for instruction for their classes directly to the appropriate subject selector or library liaison.

Instructional strategies must change in order to address the changing educational needs of students. There are many challenges that the Libraries face in achieving a curriculum-based approach for information literary learning at the University. The curriculum structure at the University is highly decentralised, as are the curriculum development and approval processes.

The challenge for the Libraries is to make connections with multiple departments, programs, and instructors in order to identify and negotiate the curricular location for library research instruction. The lack of standardised and ongoing linkages with the curriculum and curricular development has contributed to the inconsistent integration of the use of library and information resources into the learning process.

3

Information Retrieval

Information retrieval (IR) is the science of searching for information in documents, searching for documents themselves, searching for metadata which describe documents, or searching within databases, whether relational stand-alone databases or hypertextually-networked databases such as the World Wide Web. There is a common confusion, however, between data retrieval, document retrieval, information retrieval, and text retrieval, and each of these has its own bodies of literature, theory, praxis and technologies. IR is, like most nascent fields, interdisciplinary, based on computer science, mathematics, library science, information science, cognitive psychology, linguistics, statistics, physics.

Automated IR systems are used to reduce information overload. Many universities and public libraries use IR systems to provide access to books, journals, and other documents. IR systems are often related to object and query. Queries are formal statements of information needs that are put to an IR system by the user. An object is an entity which keeps or stores information in a database. User queries are matched to objects stored in the database. A document is, therefore, a data object. Often the documents themselves are not kept or stored directly in the IR system, but are instead represented in the system by document surrogates.

Today, school decision-makers for school library programs-school boards, superintendents, principals, teachers, even school librarians themselves-are unaware, or insufficiently aware, of the impact that good library information programs are having in many schools, and could be having in others. In October 1998, Commonwealth Libraries made a Library Services and Technology Act (LSTA) grant to PCBL for this purpose.

The learning and teaching role supports the instructional goals of the school in both content (standards and subject curriculum) anu process (information literacy skills). The information access and delivery role encompasses the more traditional responsibilities of the school librarian, those of developing the school library's collection and services and providing access to them.

Program administration, includes both management of the program and larger training and advocacy functions within the school community. The mission of the library program is to ensure that students and staff are effective users of ideas and information. Guidelines for School Library Media Programs dealt with the value of the mere presence of a library with a professional librarian, reflecting the lack of centralised library service, particularly at the elementary level. Willson showed that students demonstrated superior gains on the Iowa Test of Basic Skills (ITBS) in elementary schools with a centralised library and a professional librarian. Likewise, Becker compared ITBS scores between students in elementary schools with and without libraries and found that the presence of a library and the guidance and function of a librarian appeared to exert significant influence on pupil achievement in some information-gathering skills areas.

Student access to the school library was also significantly greater in schools with professional library personnel than in schools without them. Yarling found that the addition of a well-equipped and managed centralised library had a significant impact on the performance of elementary school students in library-related skills, particularly outlining and note taking. Students who used a new fully staffed and equipped elementary school library also showed significant improvement in library skills test scores in the study by Ainsworth.

Guidelines for School Library Media Programs in 1988 referred to various aspects of the school librarian's teaching role. Aaron studied a group of eighth grade students who participated in a program in which a full-time school librarian was added to the teaching team. In addition to showing significant improvement in language arts, spelling and math computation, the students in the experimental group experienced improvement in their self-concept. Gengler looked at differences in the ability to apply selected problem solving skills between sixth grade students who were instructed by a classroom teacher and those who received additional instruction from an elementary school librarian.

Findings showed that the mean score on a problem solving skills examination for the librarian-teacher instructed group was significantly higher than for the teacher instructed group. Hastings and Tanner looked at whether improved English language skills could be developed at the tenth grade level through systematic library experiences rather than the traditional emphasis on formal English grammar. In a study by Hutchinson, English teachers gave tenth grade students special library skills instruction and practice over a two-week period.

Library usage among the students increased regardless of their academic grade point averages. Hale found that an experimental group of twelfth grade students who were given a variety of library services and resources and the opportunity to work independently under the supervision of the librarian showed "remarkable enthusiasm" for learning. Barrilleaux focused on a comparison of the achievement of junior high school students in general science classes in which textbooks were used with students who used reference materials in the school library rather than a textbook.

Results showed that for all investigated educational outcomes, the use of library materials without a basic textbook was the superior method of instruction. Much of the research taking place after the introduction of Information Power: Guidelines for School Library Media Programs in 1988 focuses on the instructional role of the school librarian. Lance, Welborn and Hamilton-Pennell found that students whose school librarians played an instructional role, either by identifying materials to be used with teacher-planned instructional units or by collaborating with teachers in planning instructional units, tended to achieve higher test scores. A study by the Library Research Service in Colorado also found that students earned higher reading scores in schools where the librarian played a vital instructional role, including planning instruction with teachers, providing information literacy instruction, providing in-service training for teachers, and evaluating students' work.

Nevertheless, several researchers have identified a gap between theory and practice. Person found a discrepancy between the real and ideal role perceptions of school librarians. While they were aware of the roles identified in the Guidelines, they didn't perform them as often as they would have liked.

Pickard also studied the gap between theory and practice of school librarians performing the instructional role and found that less than 10 percent of her sample appeared to be practicing the role to a great extent. Angelo verified this finding in a study which showed that the majority of school librarians were performing duties of the traditional librarian, such as student orientation and assisting students and teachers in finding materials, while a low percentage were performing planning and consultation roles. Kuhne concluded that school libraries need to be more integrated into the curriculum and that the school librarian could play a much more distinctive teacher role than he or she does today. Van Deusen and Tallman found that more than half of her sample of school librarians did not assess student work at all during the study period.

Today, school librarians successfully involved in resource-based learning were energetic, healthy and enthusiastic; showed leadership abilities; had theoretical understanding of resource-based learning; had the ability to translate theory into effective instructional plans; and were knowledgeable about specific learning resources. These librarians saw teaching as their primary function. Farwell found that school librarians could play a pivotal role in the successful implementation of collaborative planning if they were knowledgeable about the curriculum, the library collection, information literacy instruction, and instructional design and delivery.

Another aspect of the school librarian's learning and teaching role identified in Information Power: Building Partnerships for Learning found that teachers and school librarians both strongly agreed that the librarian should work with teachers in helping students to develop the habit of reading. In the school library field, a few research studies to date have looked at the connection between integrating information literacy skills into the curriculum and improved student learning.

In Australia, Todd, Lamb and McNicholas studied Year-Seven and Year-Eleven students and found that integrating information skills into subject content, with collaboration by classroom teachers and school librarians, had a positive impact on student learning, including better understanding of subject content and improved test scores. Todd analysed the impact of integrated information skills instruction in a Year-Seven science class. The two treatment classes recorded significantly higher annual science scores than the control classes.

Information Access

The information access and delivery role includes providing quality resources and technology that support the curriculum, offering convenient and flexible access to the school library's resources and services, and providing a welcoming environment which is conducive to learning. Early studies focused on service level and collection size as predictors of academic achievement. Greve discovered that the most valuable predictor of student test scores was the number of volumes in the school library.

Thorne examined the reading comprehension and library skills of students using the augmented services of a Knapp Project library versus the nominal services of a second junior high school library in a two-year study. Findings revealed a significant difference in the mean gains of the experimental group over the control group in reading comprehension and library skills.More recent studies have focused on the connection between students' achievement in reading and access to print resources, particularly in libraries. The Colorado study by Lance, Welborn and Hamilton-Pennell concluded that the size of a school library's staff and collection is the best school predictor of academic achievement. Elley compared the scores of students from 32 countries on the 1992 International Association for the Evaluation of Educational Achievements (IEA) Reading Literacy Study with data on the home environment and school and public libraries.

A Library Research Service study reported that students are likely to earn higher reading scores if there is a relationship between the school library program and local public libraries. Such a relationship might include public library staff presenting booktalks at the school library, and the local public library providing a summer reading program.Several researchers point to the potential importance of the school library as a factor in equalising access to print resources for disadvantaged children. McQuillan found a strong negative correlation between poverty and print resources at home. He concluded that school and public libraries could help increase access to print for low-income communities and schools, thus improving their students' reading achievement.

Halle, Kurtz-Costes and Mahoney reported that the number of books in the homes of low-income, African American children was related to children's reading scores at the end of the following year. They concluded that providing access to children's books through libraries may be one of the most important things disadvantaged communities and schools can do. McQuillan studied the public library use of language minority students and found that Spanish-speaking households are much less likely to have access to books, and therefore fewer opportunities to further literacy development.

Unfortunately, school libraries often appear to reflect the economic conditions of their communities. Krashen and O'Brian reported that socio-economic status was the most powerful predictor of student reading achievement in the Los Angeles Unified School District. Both Krashen and McQuillan made the point that the low student reading scores in California could be traced to the deplorable state of its school and public libraries.

Size of the school library collection has been shown to be a positive predictor of student academic achievement. Similarly, McQuillan reported that SAT scores were positively correlated with the number of books per student in the school library. Koga and Harada investigated the attitudes of students in Australia, Japan, Korea and Thailand towards school libraries and found that students with a keen attitude toward learning tended to use the library more often and demonstrated better academic achievement.

A Library Research Service report showed that states with above average reading scores on the 1994 NAEP reading test have schools where students visit the school library more frequently and borrow more books and other materials. The role of the school librarian in developing and providing access to the library program has received a fair amount of attention in the research. Pembroke found that, when school librarians provide reading guidance or a bibliography, reluctant fifth grade readers can be motivated.

Martin found that as library services increased (including reference, information skills, curriculum integration, interlibrary loan, reading guidance, and technical assistance), third grade test scores also increased. She found a statistically-significant relationship between all the school library variables (collection size, expenditures for the collection, staffing, and services) and overall achievement in grades 3, 5, and 11, indicating that the whole is greater than the sum of its parts. A Library Research Service study reported that students are likely to earn higher reading scores if there is a collection development policy for the school library. K. G. Alexander's study of four exemplary school librarians found that they all provided continuous access to their libraries; assisted individual users; designed flexible circulation policies; used innovative methods to promote their libraries; and developed collections which supported all areas of the curriculum.

Gehlken reported that in all three blue ribbon high schools studied, the school librarian flexibly scheduled classes; organised and cataloged the collection; provided an inviting climate conducive to learning; assisted students in traditional and electronic methods of information access; and involved faculty in the selection of materials. The libraries in all three schools were organised, automated, easily accessible, and provided materials in a variety of formats across all levels and subject areas. The library facilities were inviting, aesthetically pleasing, safe, and user-friendly.

The role of technology in promoting student achievement has been the focus of some recent studies. In their review of educational technology research, Sivin-Kachala, Bialo, and Langford concluded that using technology has a positive effect on student achievement, attitudes toward learning, and student self-concept. Paul, VanderZee, Rue and Swanson reported that using the Accelerated Reader technology-based literacy program had a positive affect on student academic performance and attendance rates, especially for socio-economically disadvantaged children in urban areas. Wenglinsky found a positive correlation between computer use and academic achievement in mathematics, but only if computers were used to convey higher-order skills or engage in learning games. Use of computers for drill and practice, the lower-order skills, was negatively related to academic achievement for both fourth and eighth grade students.

Significantly, disadvantaged groups had less access to those aspects of technology that positively affected educational outcomes. There is perhaps no place where the school librarian's role has changed more in the last ten years than in the integration of technology. McCarthy found that less than 50 percent of the New England school libraries in her sample had automated circulation and cataloging systems, and these were mostly in middle and high school libraries.

High-achieving schools tend to have more technological resources. Baule found that schools with exemplary technology were also more likely to have high-quality school library programs. Yetter observed that the school libraries in successful resource-based learning schools had modern, spacious facilities designed for flexible use and access to technology.

Gehlken noted that all three blue ribbon schools studied had libraries which were committed to increasing student access to technology, and which had the flexibility and electronic capabilities to accommodate the changing needs created by new technologies. Students identified the electronic catalog, computer printer workstations and copying machines as some of the most important services provided by the school library program.

As Wenglinksy demonstrated, it is not the amount of technology or computer use that counts in promoting student achievement, but how it is used. Many researchers have found no correlation between reading achievement and amount of computer software available. Technology must be integrated into the school library program.

A Library Research Service report concluded that students earn higher reading scores if their school library programs incorporate the latest information technology. Such technology includes a district-wide catalog, access to online databases, resources available through a local-area network, and access to the World Wide Web and the statewide library network. The program administration role involves effective management of the human, financial and physical resources of the school library program.

This role also provides leadership within the larger learning community. Adequate staffing, budget, and administrative support are key to the success of this role. Yetter found that schools that had successfully implemented resource-based learning had a common understanding and support from the principal, teaching faculty and school librarian about the centrality of the library program in the school's instructional process. These schools provided planning time for teachers and school librarians to work collaboratively, clerical support for the school librarian, flexible scheduling in the school library, and principal support of the library program. Likewise, Farwell determined that in schools with successful collaborative planning, the principal served as an advocate for collaborative planning and information literacy instruction, and provided financial support for the library program, adequate clerical staff, and time during the school day for school librarians and classroom teachers to plan together.

There appears to be a two-way relationship between administrative support and school librarians performing the instructional role. In schools where there was fiscal and organisational support for the library program, including automated systems and paid support staff, van Deusen found that school librarians performed the instructional consultation role to a greater extent. Lumley concluded that instituting a curricularly integrated and flexibly scheduled library program required leadership on the part of the school librarian as well as principal support, resulting in strong leadership roles for the librarian in curriculum, instruction and staff development. Martin also found a significant positive relationship between school library staffing and student achievement, especially in high school reading. Schools employing more library staff had higher achievement test scores.

A Library Research Service study showed that student reading scores were higher in schools where there is a state-endorsed school librarian and where the school librarian is supported by an aide. School librarians in effective schools tend to have good planning, communication and management skills. The basic library procedures and processes in their school library programs functioned smoothly. A Library Research Service report indicated that students are likely to earn higher reading scores if there is a plan for the development of their school library program. The involvement of a school librarian in technology-based staff training can support student achievement. Wenglinsky found that teacher's professional development in technology and the use of computers to teach higher-order skills were both positively related to academic achievement in mathematics and the social environment of the school. A very important administrative role for the school librarian is to obtain an adequate budget for the library program.

Angelo's study of Massachusetts school library programs revealed that more than 90 percent were operating at the minimum level according to state standards in the areas of personnel, collection, and budget. Lance, Welborn and Hamilton-Pennell found that students at schools with better funded libraries tend to achieve higher average test scores, whether their schools and communities are rich or poor and whether adults in the community are well or poorly educated. Bruning also reported a positive relationship between student achievement measures and the proportion of a school district's budget spent on library materials, for both high- and low-income districts.

These findings are particularly significant since studies seeking a relationship between school spending as a whole and student performance have shown mixed results. Traditionally, conventional wisdom dictated that the larger the collection, the better. As electronic sources of information proliferate and the value of up-to-the-minute information increases, this assumption becomes more questionable. Another wildcard related to this issue is the age of library collections.

A larger collection is not necessarily a better one, if it consists increasingly of deteriorating volumes of obsolete information. Although few school libraries have budgets that include personnel costs, many have budgets for print and non-print materials, electronic access to information, and miscellaneous operating expenses. Additional items called for expenditures on computer equipment and other capital purchases. Partial correlation was used to weigh the effects of school library staffing on academic achievement while controlling for each of several school and community conditions.

This technique is especially useful in assessing complex relationships among several potential predictors, because it weighs the importance of each predictor variable while ruling out the effects of another. It is intuitively obvious that the status of library information programs may depend on more general school circumstances, just as those circumstances, in turn, may be driven by community conditions.

The community and school variables included represent major antecedent conditions that might explain away that impact. For instance, the possibility that a correlation between the level of school library staffing and test scores might be a spurious result of generally high levels of staffing in a school was addressed by including the teacher-pupil ratio. For all statistical techniques, separate analyses were conducted for elementary, middle, and high school levels. After the direct effects of all school library conditions on test scores were determined via bivariate and partial correlation, their indirect effects from one to another were calculated.

Several characteristics of school library programs beyond staffing help to explain the relationship between library staffing and academic achievement. These characteristics include: school library expenditures, information resources, information technology, and staff activities that help to integrate information literacy into the school's approaches to standards and curricula. The success of any school library information program in promoting high academic achievement depends fundamentally on the presence of adequate staffing-specifically each library should have at least one, full-time, certified school librarian with at least one full-time aide or other support staff member. When the relationship between school library staffing and test scores is controlled for socio-economic differences, the relationship reveals itself to be a dynamic one in several ways. When the relationship between school library staffing and achievement is controlled for differences in adult educational attainment, the relationship is weakened for all three tested grades.

The relationship is weaker still, however, at the high school level compared to the elementary and middle school levels. This finding suggests that school library programs can compensate better for a lack of parental education before rather than after students reach the mid to late teens. When the relationship between school library staffing and achievement is controlled for the race/ethnicity of students, it is weakened slightly at elementary level and remains little changed at middle school level, but increases dramatically at high school level.

This finding suggests that, while school library programs are challenged to compensate for the cultural disadvantages of many minority children in the early years of public education, those programs are more successful at compensating for such disadvantages as students mature. Predictably, economic differences (e.g., median family income, percent of families living in poverty) have the most consistently undermining effect on the relationship between school library staffing and reading scores. It is difficult for the best school library program to foster students' learning when their home life is defined by the privations of poverty. Children from poorer families are less likely to live in homes where books and other information sources are readily at hand, and where a home computer providing access to the World Wide Web can be taken for granted. Nonetheless, even when economic differences are ruled out, the relationship between school library staffing and test scores remains both positive and statistically significant.

While controlling for some school and community conditions (e.g., average teacher's salary, community socio-economic conditions) weakens the relationship between school library staffing and achievement, more often there is little change, and, in one case (e.g., race/ethnicity), the relationship is even strengthened over time. Because none of these other factors explains away the relationship between school library staffing and achievement, that relationship is likely to be one of cause-and-effect. At both elementary and secondary levels, increases in library staffing are also linked to increased access to computer resources.

Notably, computers counted in this study are those either in or under the jurisdiction of the school library program as well as any computer elsewhere in the school-in classrooms, computer labs, studios, or offices-that have networked access to library resources. An interesting distinction in these findings between elementary and secondary levels is that, for both levels, as library staffing increases, computers with access to licensed databases increase, while, for secondary level alone, staffing increases are linked with increases in computers with Internet/World Wide Web access. These findings probably reflect the increasing time and money commitments of most librarians to licensing and promoting use of well-organised, up-to-date, high-quality databases as well as the active concern of some public officials and interest groups about very young children having completely open access to the Web.

The mere presence of a large collection of books, magazines, and newspapers in the school library is not enough to generate high levels of academic achievement by students. Such collections only make a positive difference when they are part of school-wide initiatives to integrate information literacy into the school's approach to standards and curricula. Rich collections of information resources can only help to improve the learning environment if the school librarian is in a position to mobilise them to that end. The relationship between having access to such resources and having school librarians who are actively engaged in enriching the learning environment is important at all grade levels, but is especially important at the elementary level.

The successful integration of information literacy into a school's approaches to standards and curricula depends on more than traditional library resources alone.

In today's global information-based economy, information technology plays as important a role in promoting students' academic achievement as it does their later financial success. At both elementary and secondary levels, activities involved in integrating information literacy happen more often where school library programs have carefully developed, well organised, widely deployed computer networks.

The successful integration of information literacy in a school depends, in part, on the school library program managing a computer network that provides access to the library's catalog, and the Internet/World Wide Web. Such networks are not limited to computers in or under the jurisdiction of the school library program, but can-and should-include networked computers throughout the school, so that students and teachers can access needed information in classrooms, labs, studios, and offices.

Students at the highest scoring schools averaged reading scores in the upper 80's, while their counterparts at the lowest scoring schools averaged scores in the mid-70's. Higher achieving schools often spend twice as much-or more-on their school library programs as lower achieving schools. At the elementary level, annual school library spending average over $14,000 and just over $7,000, respectively, for higher and lower achieving schools. At the high school level, higher scoring schools spend about $22,000, while lower scoring schools spend less than $10,000. Such differences in buying power have been demonstrated to have a direct effect on the size of the school library program's collection of information resources.

While school librarians are common among the schools participating in this study, the level of such staffing varies.

The level of certified school librarian staffing varies as much as six hours per week in middle schools. Differences in the level of support staffing are even more dramatic. At elementary and middle schools, higher achieving schools have 25 to 35 hours per week, respectively, of support staff, while lower achieving schools average half as much help, if any at all.

When support staff is limited or non-existent, school librarians are not free to manage library expenditures, resources, and technology or to engage in key activities that ensure the integration of information literacy into a school's approaches to standards and curricula.

School Library Programmes

The numbers of print volumes, periodical subscriptions, and CD-ROM reference titles available via school library programs at higher and lower achieving schools also vary substantially. While the collection at a typical lower achieving elementary school is only about 9,000 items, its counterpart at a higher achieving school exceeds 12,000-a difference of almost one-third. This gap closes somewhat for middle and high schools, but higher achieving schools still tend to have six or seven items in their collections for every five items found in lower achieving schools. The most dramatic statistical difference between lower and higher achieving schools is in the area of information technology.

The typical higher achieving elementary school has 40 to 50 computers either in or networked to the school library, while lower achieving schools average only 6 to 10. At the high school level, higher achieving schools average 75 to 100 computers compared with 20-25 for lower achieving schools. Finally, higher and lower scoring elementary schools are distinguished by the amount of time school library staff spend in teaching students and teachers how to access and use print and electronic information resources.

At higher achieving schools library staff spend three days on such activities for every two by lower achieving schools. Small investments of time in key activities pay off. Pennsylvania System of School Assessment (PSSA) reading scores increase with increases in the following characteristics of school library information programs: staffing, information technology, and integration of information literacy into the curriculum.

In addition, as staffing, information resources, and information technology rise, school library staff spend more time teaching students and teachers how to access and use information resources. In the twenty-first century, digital libraries became a prominent research area. Main goals of projects involving digital libraries are the application of the several information retrieval techniques developed in the 80's and the realisation of new distributed technology to manage information resources.

The typical problem of document retrieval in a digital library can be overcome if users have the possibility to manage their own personal library. The Private Digital Library (PDL) project that represents a service of the Corporate Digital Library (CDL) prototype, developed at the LACAM Laboratory.

The aim of this project is to enable users of CDL to generate locally a personal library where to store their preferred documents once they are retrieved from the CDL. Moreover, the PDL system incorporates an assistant agent to help users in formulating their queries, in case they are inexperienced or have not made clear their information need. When the user receives satisfactory results of a query (performed through the CDL) he may choose to store all or part of the results in his/her private library. On the other hand, if the user is not satisfied by the results of the query, he can select, from the documents found, only some portions of text units, and use them to populate a repository of text units. The documents in the private library are organised by the Cataloguer module in proper folders, according to user preferences.

The user can decide to find documents contained in his private library, by activating a local Search Engine. By means of a certified applet, the whole system can be hosted on a server and the user can access the system through a client. The user is central in the architecture. When the user starts the interaction by proposing an initial query, he receives the results of the query (documents found in the CDL) he may choose to store all or part of the results in his/her PDL.

On the other hand, if the user is not satisfied by the results of the query he can select, from the documents found, only some portions of text units, and use these portions to populate a repository of text units. This repository represents the input to the Query Suggester, one of the services offered by the PDL. This agent, on the basis of the text units stored in the repository, helps to formulate queries in a more convenient way, so to retrieve more documents of interest from the CDL to be subsequently inserted in the PDL.

The query suggester module performs the extraction of keywords to be proposed for new queries, exploiting the reduced amount of text units stored in his personal repository that, in a way, represents the user interest.

As we move into the electronic era of digital objects it is important to know that there are new barbarians at the gate and that we are moving into an era where much of what we know today, much of what is coded and written electronically, will be lost forever. Enormous amounts of digital information are already lost forever. Digital history cannot be recreated by individuals, and organisations cannot recreate a digital history because it was not archived or managed properly or it resides in formats that cannot be accessed because the information is on out-dated word-processor files, old database formats, or saved on unreadable media.

Many large data-sets in governments and universities world-wide have been made obsolete by changing technologies and will either be lost or subject to expensive 'rescue' operations to save the information. There will be a demographic bulge of electronic materials coming into libraries and archives as the Baby Boom generation of authors and academics begin to wind down their careers and begin off-loading their materials to various libraries and archives. These materials will come to libraries on a wide variety of storage devices, perhaps even in entire computer systems, and will probably have equally significant paper collections associated with them. Information technologies are essentially obsolete every 18 months.

This dynamic creates an unstable and unpredictable environment for the continuance of hardware and software over a long period of time and represents a greater challenge than the deterioration of the physical medium. Many technologies and devices disappear as the companies that provide them move on to new product lines, often without backwards compatibility and ability to handle older technologies, or the companies themselves disappear. There is a proliferation of document and media formats, each one potentially carrying their own hardware and software dependencies. Copying these formats from one storage device to another is simple. However, merely copying bits is not suffi-cient for preservation purposes: if the soft-ware for making sense of the bits is not available, then the information will be, for all practical purposes, lost. Libraries will have to contend with this wide variety of digital formats. Many digital library collections will not have originated in digital form but come from materials that were digitised for particular purposes. Those digital resources which come to libraries from creators or other content providers will be wildly heterogeneous in their storage media, retrieval technologies and data formats.

Libraries which seek out materials on the Internet will quickly discover the complexity of maintaining the integrity of links and dealing with dynamic documents that have multimedia contents, back-end script support, and embedded objects and programming. Financial resources available for libraries and archives continue to decrease and will likely do so for the near future. The argument for preserving digital information has not effectively made it into public policy.

There is little enthusiasm for spending resources on preservation at the best of times and without a concerted effort to bring the issues into the public eye, the preservation of digital information will remain a cloistered issue. The importance of libraries has been diminished in the popular press as the pressures from industry encourage consumers to see libraries as anachronistic while the Internet and electronic products such as Microsoft Encarta are promoted as inevitable replacements. Until this situation changes, libraries and archives will continue to be asked to do more with lessÑboth in terms of providing traditional library services, as well as new digital library services: preservation will have to encompass both kinds of collections.

Increasingly restrictive intellectual property and licensing regimes will ensure that many materials never make it into library collections for preservation. These will be corporate assets and will not be deposited into public collections without substantive financial and licensing arrangements that few libraries will be able to afford. From a positive perspective, this fact will allow libraries to essentially ignore the preservation question for many kinds of key information resources as these may be preserved by their corporate owners.

The flip-side of this argument is whether corporate owners will develop a public-spirited interest in providing this archival role for future generations and whether the resources will be accessible to the public. The archiving and preservation functions within a digital environment will become increasingly privatised as information continues to be commodified.

Companies will be the place where the most valuable information is retained and preserved, and this will be done only insofar as there is a corporate recognition of the information as an asset. But companies have no binding commitment to making information available over a long term. Those librarians who suggest that legal deposit is the means for addressing this issue are not likely to be successful. The first line of defense against the loss of valuable digital information rests with the creators, providers and owners of digital information. This fact is a critical one for preservation purposes as it strongly suggests that the role that librarians and archivists must play will be an increasingly public one. Preservation is a desktop issue, not merely an institutional one.

The role of preservationists must be to interact with users and to address preservation and information management issues on their desktops, not the archivists' desktop. Standards will not emerge to solve fundamental issues with respect to digital information. The challenge in preserving electronic information is not primarily a technological one, it is a sociological one.

The dynamism of the market for information technologies and products ensures the fundamental instability of hardware and software primarily because product obsolescence is often key to corporate survival in a competitive capitalist demo-cracy. Product differentiation manifests itself at the very level of the document standard.

Proprietary systems provide commercial enterprises with profitable products whereas static formats do not create a continuing need for upgrading which software and hardware companies depend upon. This situation conspires against standards that create a stable nexus of hardware, software, and administration. Libraries and archives will be required to continue their existing archival and preservation practices as the current paper publishing boom continues. Clearly, digital collections are not going to be a substitute for existing and future library collections and plans must be made to accommodate both. A significant concern of libraries and archives is that the financial resources necessary to address expensive IT upgrades, embark on data rescue operations, and undertake digital preservation will have detrimental impacts on other aspects of library and archival operations such as building collections and providing services for the public.

Preservation Nexus

Sustainable solutions to digital preservation problems are not available. The research programme for digital preservation is still being established. For example, the Preservation of Electronic Materials: a Programme of Studies funded by the U. K. Joint Information Systems Committee of the Higher Education Funding Councils has recently put forward a research agenda which illustrates the situation. This programme includes:

— Developing a topology of major data types and formats and identifying issues affecting preservation of each category of material.

— Investigating the attitudes of originators and rights owners to the responsibilities of digital preservation.

— Examining costing models for long-term preservation of digital materials.

— Examining the three main methods of digital preservation: technology preservation; technology emulation; information migration.

— Investigating the digital preservation needs of universities and research funders.
— Investigating progress towards permissive guidelines for digital preservation.
— Reporting on sampling methods and techniques for collecting materials, on the nature and extent of institutional electronic archives, and or the relevance of current archival practice to digital preservation .
— Investigating post hoc rescue, or data archaeology, of high value digital material which cannot be accessed because the required IT environment is no longer available.

Digital Preservation

The preservation of digital materials is not complex. As long as the relationship between hardware, software and humanware is maintained, a kind of'preservation nexus' exists and a digital object can be preserved forever. The problem is the centrifugal forces such as time and money that pull each of these elements away from each other software and hardware become outdated, migrating information may require expensive recoding, and organisations lack resources to address the problems. This creates an environment where the object is basically left in a digital limbo-trapped in an obsolete format or captured on an unreadable medium, or lacking the administrative capacity, resources, or willingness to refresh the data. The archiving of digital information is not a conservation problem. To quote a conclusion of the Technology Assessment Advisory Committee to the Commission on Preservation and Access, 'Preservation means copying.' It is the 'contents' that must be preserved not conserved. Unlike conservation practices where an item can often be treated, stored and essentially forgotten for some period of time, digital objects will require frequent refreshing and recopying to new storage media. Keeping the 'original' digital artifact is not important.

Further, refreshing or 'copying' of digital information will not be confined to merely moving from one storage medium to another but will also entail translation into new formats or structures. It is also likely that this translation will be an imperfect copy, as well as a costly and ongoing expense that must be budgeted for accordingly.

Some types of digital objects will not be transferable to either new media or to new formats, for example: software executable files; self-extracting archives coded for particular operating systems; and formats unique to a software implementation. Even maintaining materials on a particular storage media like CD-ROM will not be easy. Multimedia materials that require particular hardware and software platforms to access the contents will disappear and will not be easily migrated to any new system. It is quite possible that a significant portion of multimedia CD-ROM titles presently in-print today will not be accessible to the next generation operating systems.

The handling of the physical storage of the digital object is the least of our worries. However, as a profession, librarians and archivists know how to do this wellÑhow to have climate controlled environments, how to conserve and store materials of various types, how to ensure that disaster recovery practices are in place, and so on. What is lacking in our knowledge base, and in that of technologists, is how to preserve over time, and on a cost-effective basis, the relationship between the storage, retrieval and display hardware and software. Preserving digital objects over time and in a cost-effective manner, requires technologies and formats to be stabilised to a greater degree than we have presently. But market forces drive the introduction of newer, faster, bigger, 'better' technologies for the production, distribution and storage of electronic information. No standards process can keep up with the dynamic changes which have occurred in the past 20 years.

Documents are becoming complex, dynamic creations made of multiple objects, embedded programming and hypertext links. This is a significant departure from the solitary book or artifact with which preservationists traditionally work. Organisations are being asked to make fiscal commitments to creating complex technical infrastructures that change every 3-5 years and which require increasingly expensive technical expertise to keep functioning.

Future Challenges

There are a number of key areas in which concerned institutions and professionals can contribute:

Knowledge Creation

There is an urgent need to augment research in the area of digital preservation. Projects which further our knowledge in the challenges of preserving various types of materialsÑmaps, archival materials, color documents, bound volumes, data-sets, music, and electronic formats like SGML, PDF, ASCII, HTML must be undertaken. The research needs to include a careful accounting of the actual costs of preserving these materials. If projects do not provide cost-effective preservation solutions or have only marginal benefits, we need to be informed of this. If some techniques or strategies work better than others, we need this information clearly stated.

Digital Triage

There should be informed skepticism about the claims of organisations that say they will archive the Internet. The library and archival communities already know that not everything can and should be saved. What is key is selecting which digital resources to preserve and which ones not to preserve. Librarians and archivists must develop digital collection development and evaluation guidelines to assist in deciding what can be saved and what should be saved, and what can't be, on a case-by-case basis. The Research Libraries Group's Preservation Working Group on Digital Archiving, as well as that of the JISC in the UK, have identified the development of guidelines for appraisal, selection, and priority setting for preserving digital information as being a key task for future work.

Rescue Operations

Digitally produced images of documents are not a substitute for microfilm preservation. Digital copying will not necessarily ensure the preservation of a digital document. The fact is that digital information may be outputted to microfilm for preservation purposes and it may even be appropriate to print an electronic document on acid-free paper and handle it according to established archival practices. These hybrid methods may be an effective transition step until stable guidelines and technologies evolve for long-term digital preservation. Librarians and archivists need to work with industry to develop simple and cost-effective print-to-microfilm systems; this will enable archives to preserve documentary collections that are provided in proprietary formats such as word-processors in a cost-effective fashion to be effectively preserved.

By transferring electronic information into non-electronic form there will be a loss of functionality for some kinds of information. Paper or microfilm documents may no longer have active hypertext links or be searchable by keyword and there will be some cases where it is not reasonable to migrate the information to non-electronic forms as it would render the information useless, e.g.

software or large data-sets. Recoding information of this type will be sharply constrained by the resources and in many cases will not be feasible.

Document Formats

Mixed media and multiple document formats will continue to remain the fly-in-the-ointment of digital collections. Multiple formats may require maintaining multiple hardware/software platforms and will confound simple migration to new storage media. Whether possible or even preferred, requiring that data be stored in a common format is unlikely for the foreseeable future. Similarly, existing translation software available for the migration and translation of document formats illustrates that the problems are significant and the results are often less than satisfactory.

The simple case of conversion between the most popular document formats, MS-Word and WordPerfect, provide ample illustration of the challenges that are faced and argue for skepticism about claims for future systems which will make this task easier. There will probably be no effective solution to this problem. If a library will be receiving electronic objects from content providers such as authors or publishers, they may want to specify a limited range of acceptable document formats. Working with creators to bring these problems to their attention and providing guidance on how to organise files and which formats to use for purposes of archiving will help. Once again, more research and effective communications with content and technology providers are required to address the issue of multiple formats.

Being Legal

The management of rights and access controls for electronic objects is an increasingly complex area of concern for libraries and archives. A library may have the rights to access and use electronic materials, but the right to preserve the materials may not be the same thing. Restrictions on access placed by rights-holders or by licensing arrangements for particular resources need to be addressed when questioning whether the information can be preserved. A simple example is the case of whether a library can retain old versions of a CD-ROM database to which it may subscribe or whether the CD-ROM must be discarded after the subscription is finished or destroyed when a new version is issued.

More complex legal issues arise with the automated collection of Internet information for preservation purposes in efforts such as the Internet Archive, where it seems that intellectual property rights are being ignored. Similar intellectual property concerns about the legality of unauthorised and automated indexing of Internet WWW sites are also being raised. Licensing will be one of the most important things that a library will be required to do in the electronic realm. The management of diverse licensing arrangements promises to be a significant administrative and technical challenge for preservation purposes. For example, the University of California Digital Library framework is quite explicit about the need to ensure that where digital materials are printable, the licenses and contracts associated with them allow you to print a copy on acid-free paper for preservation purposes.

Librarians need to work on contractual issues. There must be a concerted effort on the part of all libraries to work together to get the best contractual arrangements possible and to be more aware of the contractual issues associated with the licensing of electronic resources.

Importance of Preservation

Librarians and archivists must engage in a concerted effort to raise the profile of preservation. The Commission on

Preservation and Access and Research Libraries Group (RLG) in the United States, the Joint Information Systems Committee (JISC) in the UK and PADI Working Group and National Library in Australia, among others, have all been active in framing the problems of digital preservation within their constituencies. As a profession, librarians and archivists need to encourage critical thinking and be highly pragmatic about the nature of the new medium and the challenges of digital preservation.

Although there are positive benefits to digitisation, particularly in providing remote and enhanced access to information, as Klaus-Dieter Lehmann, Director General of Die Deutsche Bibliothek warns, there is a danger here as well. The problem is that 'digitisation may come to be regarded as a panacea for all of the real and imagined problems libraries now face in connection with the preservation of physical collections: the growing need for storage space, the deterioration of books due to acid paper, and the rising costs of library operation.' Only by increasing public support and understanding of the issues of preservation, both digital and analog can we hope to address the shortfall in fiscal and human resources that continue to hinder preservation efforts and impact upon library services.

Archiving decisions for materials which are common to many libraries will be made in consultation with other libraries to deter-mine the appropriate forms and sharing-mechanisms. Few libraries will be positioned to effectively archive large quantities of electronic information.

Any given library will necessarily be required to select re-sources that they can archive and preserve according to their particular mandates and user requirements. In many cases, it will not make sense to duplicate efforts. Digital pre-servation efforts will need to be coordinated. In other situations, it may make perfect sense to duplicate archival efforts, particularly if the information is too valuable for historic purposes to be entrusted to only one institution. Efforts such as the U. S. National Digital Library Federation and the Canadian Initiative on Digital Libraries are examples of important first steps.

Digital Preservation as a Public Good

Librarians and archivists protect the public interest by making information available to the community and by asserting the importance of maintaining a record of our collective intellectual heritage. This task will be a continuing challenge because libraries and archives are too often considered to be competitors to publishers, document delivery services, and other private sector content providers. It is unlikely, unless a substantive ground-swell of public support is generated, that libraries will win in the battle against commodification of infor-mation resources or be able to generate the public support necessary to meet the challenges. Despite the present lack of public interest in digital preservation, it is necessary to believe, perhaps as an article of faith, that the efforts of librarians and archivists will be appreciated in the future. The traces of information that we are able to save from our digital vellum will be valuable sources of information to the future. Even if the task of digital preservation remains thankless, it is a vital one and must still be undertaken. The objective is a noble and necessary one even as the many problems appear insurmountable. Digital collections facilitate access, but do not facilitate preservation. Being digital means being ephemeral. Digital places greater emphasis on the here-and-now rather than the long term, just-in-time information rather than just-in-case.

The research programme for digital preservation has only recently been initiated to develop strategies, guidelines, and standards. Although tremendous work has been undertaken in defining the problems and challenges, much more remains to be done, and the tough task of actually doing digital preservation remains ahead. A critical appraisal of where we are vis-a-vis our digital culture, and what we want for the future something which may not be defined in technical terms at allÑis required both inside and outside of the library and archival professions. If history and cultural heritage are to be important, then it will likely fall to librarians and archivists, the monastic orders of the future, to ensure that something of the heady days of our 'digital revolution' remains for future generations.

The challenges to digital preservation are considerable and will require a concerted effort on the part of librarians and archivists to rise up to these challenges and assert in public forums the importance of protecting a fragile digital heritage.

Technological advances come equipped with both affordances and unintended consequences. Preservation has its own well-known examples of technological advances leading to problems for librarians to solve:

— "Brittle books," the product of nineteenth-century technological innovations that had produced inexpensive paper;
— Bulk microfilming techniques employing scanning equipment that required the spines of books to be cut off;
— Reformatting of analog tapes to digital, only to discover that the digital media are more fragile than we realise.

Preservation of new media is even more problematic than preservation of earlier ones. By one estimate, as much as half of the global motion picture library may become inaccessible in 10 to 15 years because the storage media have degraded.

Today, preservation suffers more from inadequate funding than from negligent librarians, and today's libraries have much more material than in old time, both in quantity and in kind, that needs preservation. Part of the problem reflects our uncertainty about who is responsible for preservation of library resources. In some developed countries, a national library typically has responsibility for acquiring and preserving a country's published output. In USA Library of Congress serves as a national library in some respects but has no universal preservation charge for the nation — although it has recently been assigned the responsibility for forging an infrastructure to support long-term preservation of digital content through the National Digital Information Infrastructure and Preservation Program (NDIIPP).

Historically, the Library of Congress has been first and foremost the Congress's library. The personal library of Thomas Jefferson — the core from which the Library of Congress grew — was a broad collection but certainly not an assemblage of all books published in the United States. While the Library of Congress attempts to collect widely, and even comprehensively in many subjects, following a collection policy like every other American research library, it does not collect in such fields as medicine and agriculture. What the Library of Congress particularly preserves tends to be its special collections — those unique maps, manuscripts, photographs, films, radio broadcasts, and materials in other formats held only by the Library of Congress.

Books and the News-paper

Through the twentieth century, preservation methods focused initially on achieving permanence and durability for two core kinds of materials in library collections: the book and the newspaper.

Technological innovations in the mid-nineteenth century had produced a less expensive kind of paper made from wood pulp, which made possible an explosion in printed materials that contributed to public literacy and to the organisation of public libraries with print collections.

The unintended consequence of the new paper technology was the later "brittle book." The chemistry of paper and of paper processing was not fully understood at the time.

Indeed the chemistry of paper was the subject of fairly substantial research in the early twentieth century. The new, cheaper books, which were a boon to literacy and libraries, turned out to deteriorate fairly quickly. Spofford and his contemporaries already had seen books begin to decay. In 1897, his successor as the Librarian of Congress, John Russell Young, took note of the "grave questions arising out of the modern conditions in the manufacture of paper". Young presented a plan to Congress calling for materials presented for copyright protection to be printed on good-quality paper.

Late-nineteenth century librarians like Mr. Spofford could see that parts of their collections were crumbling but did not fully understand the scientific reasons. But by 1910, federal scientists had begun to explore the chemistry of paper and paper products, and these efforts continued. Some in the professional library community tried to stay abreast of the research. Nonetheless, for most librarians in Spofford's professional lifetime, binding and repair were conservators' primary preservation activities, along with managing library buildings protectively, training staff in the proper handling of materials, and trying to persuade patrons not to mark, abuse, or steal the books. Little systematic effort occurred in professional librarianship programs or in libraries themselves to address the source of the problem until the late 1950s and the 1960s. In that period, the Council on Library Resources (CLR) made a number of grants to support preservation efforts. CLR sponsored research by W. J. Barrow into the causes of paper deterioration and the possibilities for development of a "permanent/durable" text paper.

Barrow horrified the library world when he reported research indications that only three percent of the books published between 1900 and 1949 would last more than fifty years. In 1960, the Association of Research Libraries (ARL) appointed a Standing Committee on the Preservation of Research Library Materials, which recommended establishing a central federal agency to preserve a physical copy of every "significant written record" and to provide copies to other libraries as needed. Microfilming, in use in a few libraries as early as the 1930s, was endorsed as a method to preserve rare and endangered texts and to reduce use of fragile originals. Televised images of the great floods in Florence of 1966 further increased awareness of preservation among research libraries and collections in the U.S., provoking research into preservation, conservation, and disaster recovery methods for books and other artifacts.

Many preservation specialists went to Florence to help save materials and learned much about preservation techniques in the process.The 1960s also saw the inauguration by Chicago's Newberry Library of the first local conservation program, the organisation of professional associations for conservation, the introduction of formal training programs for conservators and museum professionals, and more publications dealing with preservation and conservation in libraries and museums. In 1972, the Library of Congress established a research laboratory, headed by John C. Williams, which spearheaded work on diethyl zinc de-acidification, work that continues to be important at the library. More recently, the Library of Congress awarded contracts to Pittsburgh-based Preservation Technologies, L.P. (PTLP) for de-acidification. Other preservation methods have been explored at the Barrow Laboratory and the Public Archives of Canada.

Institutions of higher education such as Carnegie-Mellon University and the Rochester Institute of Technology set up centers for studying the chemistry and technology of paper, binding, paints, inks, and varnishes. Realising that the cycle of deterioration would not end unless alkaline paper was adopted in book manufacture, the library community worked with other concerned communities and standards-setting organisations to promote guidelines for and use of durable paper.

The Council on Library Resources initiated work on production guidelines for book longevity in 1979. A committee, headed by Herbert Bailey of the Princeton University Press, made important studies of "permanent" paper and binding. And in 1981, the Z39 Committee of the American National Standards Institute drafted a standard for permanent paper for printed library materials.In the 1970s, major university libraries began to undertake large, cooperative preservation projects. An important by-product was that preservation departments became commonplace in research libraries. Unfortunately, institutional preservation programs were not generally funded as a regular part of the research universities' budgets. Instead, many preservation efforts were made possible by external funding from the National Endowment for the Humanities (NEH) and private foundations, especially The commission estimated that at least 3.3 million and possibly more than ten million books remained at risk in the U.S., and that de-acidification would cost between $250 million and $1 billion.

NEH expanded grant-making for preservation, setting a goal of helping research libraries microfilm at least three million of the most at-risk volumes. NEH also promoted standards and guidelines for microfilming so that individual library preservation activities would produce a decentralised but nationally accessible collection of works on durable microfilm. Book deterioration may be slower than was projected, but microfilming seemed essential at the time to ensure preservation of the content of millions of valuable texts that librarians feared would crumble on research library shelves. Librarians also recognised the need to conserve unique paper artifacts in special collections.

The biggest debate during the brittle books era focused on centralisation. Patricia Battin, president of the Commission on Preservation and Access, believed that centralisation would finally link preservation and access. She argued for the creation of a central repository for microfilm masters that would serve as an archives as well as a distribution system. Any library microfilming a book would add a permanent master copy and a service master to the central repository.

Any library wishing to add a preservation copy to its own collections would be able to acquire, at cost, a copy of the service master. Though NEH funding encouraged collaboration among libraries, centralisation lost out because libraries aspiring to research status established their own individual preservation offices, and preservation became a recognised career track within individual institutions.Federal and philanthropic funding continues to support preservation within individual libraries and archives rather than to promote centralisation of preservation in a single institution or handful of institutions. Thus, NEH has supported microfilming nineteenth century newspapers state by state and the National Agricultural Library has supported microfilming projects in state libraries to protect endangered materials documenting agricultural history.

Not surprisingly, this decentralised and local approach coincided with the local history movement in the 1980s and increased attention to conservation and preservation of local heritage resources of all sorts. NEH supports brittle-book microfilming at a number of university libraries that avoid redundant effort by sharing information about materials scheduled for filming. Today preservation has become part of the management of a modern library, embracing not only the reformatting of texts but also the improvement of library buildings and their internal environments, the conservation and repair of items in library collections, the adoption of commercial standards for books and paper, the education of readers and staff about handling and caring for fragile materials, the training of librarians in preservation, and the adoption of disaster planning and recovery strategies.

We have learned a lot from scientific study about library materials and how to manage them, and awareness of such research must become part of professional librarians' training and library management. Effective preservation programs require organisational coordination to ensure an appropriate and consistent standard, to reduce unnecessary redundancy, and to enable future users to find the materials. Preservation increasingly requires value judgments about whether to retain an original book, journal, or other artifact or just its intellectual content. That question is growing as libraries confront a huge additional set of preservation concerns and challenges associated with digital content.

Significance of Digital Technology

Digital technology causes us to look at content in new ways. The degradation of books and newsprint, which was an unanticipated adverse consequence of technological innovation, provoked the modern, scientific study of preservation requirements. One solution has been re-formatting, first to microfilm and subsequently to digital media. High-quality film is a relatively stable medium. Microfilm readers are simple, if not always pleasant, to use, and conscientiously microfilmed images of printed artifacts — including the binding, the pages, the illustrations, and even surviving handwritten marginalia — convey information that these artifacts frequently embody beyond their texts. More recently, the rise of electronic publishing, first in creating scholarly e-journals and then in digitising rare texts, decoupled content from the artifact, so that information became separated from its original vehicle and expressed in a new form — as text on a screen that might look different depending on which computer program presented it. For at least some forms of communication, such as scholarly journals, electronic delivery of information in digital form has been a godsend. Researchers quickly recognised the convenience of having electronic information delivered to their desktops and being able to search it.

Librarians grew concerned, however, over questions about the stability of electronic materials. Concern that long-term preservation represented an early barrier to the acceptance of electronic journals as a form of publication equivalent to print has led many publishers to treat electronic versions as add-ons they provide in parallel with print formats. JSTOR, Project Muse, and related programs arose to provide electronic journals consisting of digitised page images with so-called "dirty OCR" behind them to support searching.

Other programs provide straight text delivered from aggregated databases or make material available in one of the mark-up languages. Thus the same journal article may be delivered in multiple formats, which raises preservation questions. Is any one electronic version more authentic than the others, and which, if not all, should be preserved?The research literature is fundamental to the research endeavor, which is deeply embedded in higher education and in industry. But journal publication has become increasingly expensive since the 1970s as prices of printed journals have risen. Options for electronic publishing have engaged the attention of both the library and the publishing communities. We are already seeing all kinds of information created in digital form only — scientific databases, visualisation tools, geographic information systems, e-journals, and a wealth of cultural history contained in images, sound, television, radio broadcasts, and cinema. Librarians are concerned about preserving these resources, too.Electronic storage media degrade, just as paper does, only perhaps more quickly.

Signals stored on electronic media also degrade, and not at a consistent rate, and hardware and software become obsolete. Data must therefore be transferred to new media or migrated to newer platforms, operating systems, and program applications. An alternate strategy is to emulate the original; that is, to provide a way through software to mimic the hardware on which a given system ran. Either way, each item in a digital archive requires active management. Discs, tapes, and other electronic media, like print, must be maintained in controlled environments, but may take more labor than print to preserve. Finally, metadata is vital for information management but is labor-intensive and hence expensive to create.Assuming, however, that we solve the problems of preserving electronic data, we then must deal with questions about who owns it and what can legally be done with it.

Libraries hope to provide future scholars with the production elements and the performance. However, we do not yet know how to do that in the digital world. Today's information technologies have been justly celebrated as democratising information production and access.

There is also evidence that the entertainment, publishing, and other content industries are coming to realise the potential commercial importance of future use of their content, which means attention to preservation now. Librarians inherit a tradition of local and global coordinated practice and procedures — namely, interlibrary loan, shared cataloging, and the development of directories of microform and manuscript collections, practices that are perpetuated through library school, professional training and continuing education. Just as preservation of analog required libraries to expand their organisational functions and librarians to alter the professional curriculum, we can expect that learning to manage digital resources will require similar adjustments.

4

Digital Collection

The mission of the Library is: to collect, preserve and give access to recorded knowledge, in all documentary forms, for the benefit of all engaged in research and learning, or with other information needs. In Australia, Wales, the fundamental nature of the Library's work was determined by the Royal Charter that established the Library's existence in 1907.

The current wording of the Charter gives as the Library's functions: the collection, preservation and maintenance of manuscripts, printed matter, maps, photographs, visual and audiovisual material relating to Wales and the Celtic peoples and similar material which furthers the aims of higher education and literary and scientific research.

The Charter is the basis for several key features of the Library:

— its emphasis on material of Welsh (and Celtic) interest
— its wider collecting responsibilities (these are based on legal deposit and purchase)
— the fact that it collects material in such a wide variety of media
— its mission to support researchers and those in higher education

Valuable pointers to the future of the Library were provided in 1999 by the many responses to Choosing the future, the first large-scale public consultation exercise ever conducted by the Library. Individuals and organisations expressed clearly and at length their strong views on how they think the Library should evolve.

The existence and work of the Library depend on certain principles and values, shared by those who govern it, work in it and use it. They are seen as complimentary to the values and principles of the National Assembly in guiding the Library's work. The Library has a vital role as a collector and guardian of the intellectual record of the life of Wales and the Welsh people. This is important in itself, and is also an important element in defining the cultural identities of the country.

The new political status of Wales is a product of, and will itself contribute to, a renewed concern with cultural identities. The Library is likely to have an important part to play in reflecting, recording and even forming those identities. This intellectual record is not confined to any particular medium, format, period or language. From its beginning the Library has been more than what is conventionally recognised as a 'library', that is, a collection of printed works. It stores a wide - and still widening - range of formats capable of carrying intellectual content. Among these are: books and periodicals, manuscripts and archives, pictures, photographs and maps, sound and moving images, and electronic material. This record of the 'matter of Wales' is, however, part of a wider, indeed world-wide, domain of recorded knowledge, produced in many languages and over many centuries, which the Library attempts to represent in its collections for the benefit of its users.

The Library's wider collections, mainly acquired in print form through legal deposit, are essential to its ability to support study and learning, not only in Welsh or Celtic domains, but also in a very wide range of other subjects. The Library's collections and services exist to meet the needs of all those who can benefit from them.

The Library is proud of the fact that it is a public library, in the sense that any adult is able and welcome to use its collections for reference with little formality and without charge. Among the groups that make use of the Library at present for consultation and reference are academic and personal researchers, students and other learners, businesses, the media, and visitors from Britain and overseas. This right of unrestricted access is part of the democratic rights of citizens in pursuit of information, knowledge and enlightenment, and contributes to the promotion of 'social inclusion'. The Library has a duty not merely to 'hold its doors open', but to encourage awareness and use of its collections and services, by all the means at its disposal.

The Library has an important function, as by far the largest and most significant institution of its kind in Wales, in leading, co-ordinating and supporting the development of library and archive services in Wales. This is not an optional part of its mission, but an essential role in a country where library and archive services tend to be small and scattered. In its turn the National Library is part of a wider, interlocking structure of library, information and archive institutions in the United Kingdom and throughout the world. It co-operates with them to make the best use of the resources that are available to all.

The National Library seeks to do everything it does - whether providing answers to enquiries, publishing books, mounting exhibitions, or any other relevant activity - to the highest possible standard, with excellence as a constant ideal in mind. In short, as a thriving, relevant and well-regarded cultural and information resource for the people of Wales and the world. These will be among the defining characteristics of the Library:

— all of the Library's central functions will remain relevant, although how they are performed will change over time. In particular, more information and services will be delivered through the internet and will therefore be capable of reaching a much larger number of people. Among these will be: detailed information about items in the collections; digitised copies of many items; and transactional services, such as the sale of goods from the shop and reprographic services.

— many more people, and a wider range of people, will make use of the Library's services than in the past.

— as well as continuing to serve researchers and learners wishing to study the collections, the Library will welcome many more visitors interested in exploring the history and culture of Wales through the collections.

— a range of information services will be developed to satisfy the needs of specific groups of users, including those interested in family and community history.

— the systematic collection of electronic material, published and archival, will become a major element of the Library's activity, especially as web archiving becomes established, and if the law of legal deposit is extended to embrace electronic publications. The Library may gain the status of a 'Trusted Digital Repository' for the whole of Wales.

— the Library's services to readers and visitors will be backed up by a strong and well-organised series of collection, technical and administrative services.

— the Library's already well-developed partnerships with other organisations will be further strengthened.

The degree to which the Library will be able to realise this vision will depend on a number of factors:

— the availability of sufficient resources to maintain existing functions and fund new developments

— the speed and ease with which new technical systems and tools can be harnessed to the achievement of our objectives othe success with which the Library can nurture innovation and adaptive thinking among its own staff.

The essence of what the Library does is contained in its five 'core functions'. These set the minimum boundaries of its policies and practice. The core functions are defined below, with in each case an indication of the chief means by which they are performed.

To collect materials by legal deposit, purchase, donation, bequest, exchange and deposit, in accordance with agreed collection development policies. This function is carried out through:

— assembling as complete a collection as possible, in all media, of published material relating to Wales, including printed publications and sound and moving image material

— maintaining (mainly through legal deposit and purchase) the most comprehensive collection in Wales of printed material published in the United Kingdom and Ireland, and of research material from other countries

— developing collections of unpublished materials relating to or deriving from Wales, including archives and artistic works

— accessioning, processing, cataloguing and storing material acquired

To preserve and conserve materials in the collections. This function is carried out through:

— ensuring environmental, storage and handling conditions favourable to the continued preservation of materials

— intervening to conserve materials and hence arrest deterioration or repair damage

— transferring, in some cases, information to more suitable preservation formats

To provide satisfactory access for users of the Library to its building, collections and services, and adequate information about them. This function is carried out through:

— providing access to public spaces, collections and facilities within the Library's building
— providing document delivery, enquiry and information services to those wishing to use the Library, in person or remotely
— providing easy access to catalogues and lists of the Library's collections, and surrogates of selections from them

To raise awareness and disseminate knowledge of the Library's collections. This function is carried out through:

— issuing guides, leaflets and other publicity material
— publishing printed monographs and serials
— mounting material on the Library's website
— staging exhibitions derived from the collections
— arranging lectures and seminars

To collaborate with, and where appropriate give leadership to, related professional and other bodies in the fields of library and information services, archives, museums and galleries. This function is carried out through:

— acting as a focal point for library and archive bodies in Wales
— working with bodies in Wales, in Britain and beyond to pursue co-operative initiatives and partnerships, and advance professional practice

The Library underpins the performance of these five core functions through the following 'supporting functions':

— management and development of its human resources

— budgeting, control and accountability of its financial resources, and income generation
— maintenance and development of the Library's information and communication technology infrastructure
— maintenance and development of the Library's building and its facilities
— continuing investigation, monitoring and analysis of user needs

Many of the Key Objectives below belong to the two major development initiatives of the Library: the Digital Library Initiative and the Open Library Initiative. These are priorities for increased funding

Digital Library Initiative

The *Digital Library Initiative*, begun in 2001-02, seeks to make a substantial contribution to this objective. In particular, it will extend significantly the ability of the Library to cater for teaching and learning in Wales.

The interlocking elements of the Digital Library Initiative that require additional funding over the next three years are:

— Collecting and archiving Welsh websites
— Acquiring a Digital Store and a Content and Digital Asset Management System
— Improving online access to collections and items within them
— An accelerated digitisation programme

Open Library Initiative

The fundamental challenge facing the development of the Library is to open its collections and services to more people, for a wider range of purposes - in particular to contribute to education and lifelong learning. The elements of the Open Library Initiative that require additional funding over the next three years are:

— Developing services and facilities in the visitor centre, including exhibition and public programmes
— Improving reader facilities and opening hours
— Establishing services for local authorities
— Founding a Family and Community History Centre
— Extending promotion and marketing of the Library
— Implement improvements to the Library's grounds
— Improving facilities for disabled users

The following will be necessary:

— Drastic reductions in collecting and cataloguing of collections
— Reduction in opening hours, including the closure of the reading rooms for one day a week
— Fewer online services
— Cutbacks in preservation activity
— Fewer exhibitions
— Reduction in staff training and development
— Failure to contribute to co-operative initiatives including the Shared

In Wales, the Library's activities are dependent for the most part upon the Grant-in-Aid (GIA) received from the National Assembly. The GIA covers the main operating activities as follows:

— revenue expenditure
— capital expenditure
— purchase of collections and individual items

In order to maintain the ability of the Library to fulfil its core functions and to aid new developments and projects the GIA provided is supplemented by the use of private funds. The Capital Grant is intended to cover the costs of capital items including computer hardware, software, equipment and the repair and enhancement of the Library building.

The demands on the capital budget far exceed the grant provided. This has resulted in a significant backlog of works on the building and has restricted the Library's ability to invest in equipment to support existing activities or develop new important areas. Providing navigational tools to support effective access to the resources in the growing digital archive will be a challenge.

Some users will have limited time and a very specific task at hand; they will benefit from the ability to search with precision. Others will have plenty of time and want to gain an overview of what is available in the entire archive or on a general topic before searching for anything in particular. They may prefer to read introductory presentations, take guided tours, browse lists of topical headings, or perform a general search and look at large numbers of individual items. The American Memory archive of historical materials is being assembled collection by collection; these collections have different characteristics.

Collections currently available over the World Wide Web consist of a single general type of material (text, image, audio, or movie), but collections in process incorporate several types. Later, two thematic anthologies comprising textual documents and images will be released, one on the American variety stage and one on the history and development of the environmental conservation movement. Another collection in process, covering the presidency of Calvin Coolidge and the transition to a consumer economy in the 1920s, includes all four types of material.

Some digital collections will have individual bibliographic information (catalog records) for each item, with individually assigned subject headings. Others will be described primarily in a finding aid, a structured document with links to the items listed. The intellectual context and depth or breadth of focus for collections also varies. Some comprise a large proportion of the output of an individual creator.

Some are personal selections of collectors or scholars. Others are collections of materials in a particular physical format with no single topical theme. Initially, the only way to access American Memory was to start by browsing a list of the collections. Each collection was described by a sentence and a list of broad subject topics. By early 1996, there was a full list, of about eight collections, and a subsidiary list for the four general types of material.

For a cross-collection search, the list of hits identifies the parent collection and the item type, as well as the item's title. Each collection currently consists of digital reproductions, a group of linked HTML pages providing archival and intellectual context, and one or more access tools for exploring the collection.

Limitations

The computer offers rapid access to an array of resources, but its screen is less convenient than a large table for studying images and than a book for skimming through indexes and pages of text to determine its relevance. The images the Library has disseminated to date have been sized for display on today's computer screens, usually between 500 and 1200 pixels wide. For photographs and page images, these "reference" images are satisfactory for many uses, although many researchers and publishers will still want to see the original or take advantage of a high-resolution version at the cost of time to download (not currently supported). However, if maps and large posters are scaled to fit on a screen, too much detail may be lost for all but the most cursory scanning.

The Library hopes that other organisations will develop approaches allowing users to zoom in on selected areas with progressively higher resolution. A promising line of research is the application of wavelet transformations to a browsing model for large images at the Alexandria Project at the University of California, Santa Barbara. Visitors to the Prints and Photographs reading room can explore image collections by skimming quickly through a folder full of similar images. They can pick out those that catch their eye and lay them out on the table. This is particularly valuable for comparing similar images.

One approach to providing equivalent functionality is to display many thumbnail images in a grid. Although an increasing volume of primary textual materials is available online, there is no consensus on how best to present long documents in a way that supports convenient use.

Today, users of MS Windows who are comfortable with the technology can download a free SGML viewer. This free viewer can present a structured table of contents derived from chapter and section headings. Headings act as direct links to corresponding sections of a document. However, the internal search feature of Panorama Free does not take advantage of the structural information encoded in the SGML format.

The book-length works are somewhat clumsy in their HTML form, but this format does allow any user to download or print the text of the entire work reasonably conveniently — absolutely necessary for use in schools where equipment for access to the Internet is, at best, a scarce resource. The problem of networked access to book-length works is not unique to the Library of Congress. As an increasing array of documents are available in SGML format, the Library hopes that a more powerful SGML viewer will become widely available or that WWW browsers will be extended to handle SGML.

Meanwhile, the Library will be experimenting with other options, such as Adobe's PDF format, the use of frames within HTML, and the development of viewer modules using the Java programming language. Meanwhile, a variant approach using HTML will be taken for the Country Studies/Area Handbook Program.

These studies have been prepared by the Library's Federal Research Division for over 60 countries around the world. Currently, contractors deliver files to the Library on CD-ROM. As for many other imaging projects, the highest-resolution images have been stored offline to save disk space. Compressed files for on-line delivery of images are loaded onto disk drives attached to the WWW servers.

The CD-ROMs serve as an archival copy for the uncompressed versions. As the size of the archive grows, these CD-ROMS require formal inventory control. Ensuring the continuing usability of the archival files is also important since the accumulated effort involved in their creation will be valued in millions of dollars.

The need to manage vast archives of computer files is not unique to libraries; solutions are appearing from the commercial sector. To address the estimated need for 50 terabytes of managed storage by the year 2000, the Library will be installing a commercial hierarchical storage management system over the coming months.

Storage management software will transfer files automatically between high- performance disk drives and less expensive storage media from which retrieval will take longer. Typically, the location is based on time since last access, but more complex rules can be enforced. Since the highest resolution images will be accessed only occasionally, they will usually be resident on the slower medium.

The allocation is transparent to applications accessing the files; "stub" files left in the logical file hierarchy point to the physical location of files that have been relegated to another "layer" of storage. For its second layer of storage, the Library has chosen high capacity magnetic tape cartridges under robotic control. The tape unit has been installed and is already in use for regular backup and restore operations.

Generation of archival copies of collections on tape cartridges is also possible for preservation of the digital materials. The hierarchical storage management software will be installed on individual computers over the next few months, in conjunction with system upgrades. Direct access to the archival digital reproductions will also support other functions.

Online access to high-resolution images could facilitate digital reproduction as an alternative to the Library's current service that provides users with photographic copies of graphical materials for a fee. The expectations of users in the Prints and Photographs reading room have already been raised. After identifying the images they need in a few minutes, some users express dismay that photoduplication requests may take several weeks.

In US, the National Digital Library Program also plans to disseminate materials in other forms, perhaps supplying source files to companies or organisations that will assemble subsets and tailor them to particular markets. Providing source files will be easier and more reliable with on-line access than by manual sorting through CD-ROMs and copying large numbers of files.

The hierarchical storage management system will address issues related to physical storage of files, but there is also a need for more formal management of the collections and objects themselves than can be provided by the Unix file system. The organisation of collections is currently through the relationships between naming schemes and Unix directories.

There is no automatic enforcement of naming conventions. If a digital item has several component files, there is no way to treat that item reliably as a unit. One of the custodial divisions keeps track of directories on charts posted on an office wall. While the number of collections is small, this approach is feasible, but the Library recognises that it will need enforcement of unique names, more automatic adjustment of all pointers when files are relocated, and a structure that recognises key relationships between items and their component files, and between collections and the items they comprise.

Since no adequate system has emerged from the commercial marketplace to support effective access to multimedia resources of this complexity, the Library has begun work with collaborators to design and build two prototype "repositories" as experiments in this area. A preliminary set of attributes or fields has been developed for use in both repositories, a set that is limited to metadata relating to the "physical" digital object, and its creation, modification, retrieval, and display.

This "physical" metadata includes the logical name, access privileges, the digital format, key structural relationships, and administrative data such as the unit or person responsible for the item, date created, and number of times accessed. In US, one prototype repository is under development with the Corporation for National Research Initiatives (CNRI). This repository will also be used for the CORDS project in the Copyright Office.

The repository provides a secure environment from which the items in the collections and their metadata can be accessed together or separately. This permits negotiation over access terms and conditions for a digital object to be an integral part of every access, access which must be possible through many protocols, such as HTTP and Z39.50. The repository will allow for an essentially limitless range of formats and for objects from the repository to be transformed before dissemination into a format which may be very different from the stored form. The implementation of the repository uses modern concepts of distributed objects. For interaction with other systems, it uses CORBA (the Common Object Request Broker Architecture) implemented through Xerox's Inter- Language Unification (ILU) system. IBM is currently developing a program that will load the images already scanned into the VisualInfo repository.

This program will integrate data from three sources: database records, created at scan time, that contain logical names and values for certain physical metadata fields; information recorded automatically in the TIFF header of image files; and the image data files. The development of these prototype repositories is at an early stage, and design details will probably change in the light of practical experience, and as the strengths of each approach become clear. The prototype stage is important in testing the Library's model which separates the storage of primary descriptive information from the digital representation of the items described.

The Library's model allows for multiple repositories, but all repositories must coordinate with independent external indexes and support standard external access protocols. One important aspect of tests is to explore how well the different approaches scale, as the number of objects grows and additional formats must be supported.

The repositories will also support experiments in the handling of access restrictions. Restrictions may be necessary for some items not only to comply with copyright law, but also because of conditions set by donors and the general legal concerns of privacy and publicity. Information has been gathered on the status of many items. Some items have not been digitised or have been withheld from distribution because of the need to restrict access or re-use. Some digitised items may be accessible in the Library's reading rooms but not over the Internet.

Within this changing environment, research libraries understand more keenly than ever the new ways in which clients are seeking and using information. Libraries see an expanding base of users and, in many instances, changing service demands. There is ample evidence that when libraries make quality content available through the Web, its use increases and it reaches more people within the institution. In addition, the user base for any individual library has expanded to include users beyond the institution. This has been achieved through more efficient resource-sharing arrangements (often statewide) as well as by targeting new user groups for digitised content and e-services. In many cases, openly accessible digitised collections on the Web are also being used heavily by people from beyond the educational world.

Despite press accounts to the contrary, research libraries report that use of the library's physical facility remains heavy, especially for collaborative learning and research activities and for access to computers and information technologies. As a result, many libraries have moved to provide 24/5 access to the library buildings. At the same time, there is growing evidence in the data collected from ARL member libraries that the service demands of users may be changing. Many libraries see declining use of some traditional services, such as use of some print materials, circulation transactions, and reference transactions.

However, the data confirm that the demands for interlibrary borrowing and for user education are steadily increasing. These trends signal a shift in the behavior of information users that is being closely monitored. Research on the information-seeking behavior of people is growing almost as fast as the Web itself. The Pew Internet & American Life Project5 creates and funds original, academic-quality research that explores the impact of the Internet on children, families, communities, the workplace, schools, health care, and civic/political life.

The project aims to be an authoritative source for timely information on the Internet's growth and societal impact, through research that is scrupulously impartial. An overwhelming number of college students reported that the Internet, rather than the library, is the primary site of their information searches. "Many students are likely to use information found on search engines and various Web sites as research materials....A great challenge for today's colleges is how to teach students search techniques that will get them to the information they want and how to evaluate it....While few universities require college students to take courses on information seeking, many include a session on it during freshman orientation meetings. To better understand how usage patterns are changing, the Digital Library Federation (DLF) and Council on Library and Information Resources (CLIR) commissioned Outsell, Inc., to conduct a large-scale study of over 3,000 undergraduates, graduate students, and faculty members from a wide range of academic institutions.

The results revealed that the highest percentage of resources used were print materials, which students ranked higher than library and non-library electronic sources in four out of five factors. The Internet-based sources scored high only on the factor of convenience, while print materials scored high on the factors that make a difference in the quality of research and learning: generating the information for which the student is looking, the usefulness of the material, its reliability, and the availability of assistance.

There are differences across disciplines in terms of how information is used and to what extent new technologies are being embraced; libraries are recognising these differences as they offer new services.

There are also differences in the pace of change in different institutions; institutional cultures that allow, for example, some flexibility in personnel policies and practices as well as in budgetary reallocations, are more accommodating of experimentation and change. In this rapidly changing environment, libraries must continue monitoring trends, assessing their performance by seeking feedback from current users, and anticipating the needs of future users. To meet and anticipate these needs of the academic and research communities, libraries are collaborating as never before, forming partnerships both within and outside their own institutions, often sharing control in order to effect critical change.

While circumstances will vary from library to library, the results of the task force survey demonstrate many ways that libraries are responding to user expectations. Libraries are expanding the amount and variety of high-quality information resources that are directly available to academic and research users via the Web. They are also expanding the definition of collections to include "born-digital" content that is neither owned nor licensed by the library. T

he varied efforts toward this goal may be characterised as follows: changing collection development policies to emphasize the acquisition of electronic resources, engaging in digitising and electronic publishing projects, and assuming responsibility for managing and servicing born-digital content that resides outside the domain of the library. Even in the electronic and networked environment, the economic model continues to feature the library as the central agency on campus that buys and/or manages information resources on behalf of the institution. Libraries have shifted the focus of their collection development policies to the acquisition of more electronic content, much of it via consortia. While aggregate data documenting the quantity of e-resources currently being made available by libraries has proven elusive, there is data on the spending trends.

Over the last decade the average percentage of a research library's materials budget that is spent on electronic resources has grown from 4% to 16%. One hundred six ARL university libraries report spending more than $132 million on electronic resources in 2000-01. The vast majority of that was spent on electronic serials and subscription services, expenditures which have increased sharply, from just $11 million in 1994-95 to more than $117 million today. To support this increased spending on electronic content, libraries have reallocated resources from the purchase of print. The extent of such reallocations will vary depending on institutional user expectations and financial circumstances.

Many libraries have adopted a policy of adding the e-version of journals when available and are showcasing titles of e-journals available to users via the Web by making this a staff priority and by applying software management tools for titles included in aggregated electronic databases. The processes for selecting, budgeting, and acquiring electronic materials are continually changing and greatly differ from those for the selection and management of print. The print process is orderly: discrete amounts of money are allocated by discipline, the marketplace is fairly predictable, and materials are selected and ordered using established procedures. By contrast, the processes for selection and management of electronic resources are chaotic. The migration from print to electronic varies in speed and extent by discipline; electronic products are interdisciplinary and expensive, giving rise to selection by committee; projections for future funding are guesswork; and archiving and content control are problematic.

Legal and negotiation skills are now mandatory. To complicate matters, decisions are often made through a consortium. The process for acquiring electronic resources turns the traditional acquisitions and user service model topsy-turvy. In building electronic collections, libraries must also constantly respond to changing publisher behavior. The most profound influence on a library's collection management and access strategies has been the extraordinary price increases for scholarly journals, combined with publishers' use of licensing to define the terms under which a library may make the content available and to whom. It is reasonable to speculate that these phenomena, driven by some of the larger publishers but now employed widely, make up one of the forces that prompted libraries to blend the previously distinct operations of collection management and access.

Some libraries have fully embraced initiatives stimulated or endorsed by SPARC (the Scholarly Publishing and Academic Resources Coalition) and other affordable publishing venues and are using acquisitions funds as investments in the future of scholarly communication. These libraries focus acquisitions on publications from scholarly societies and less expensive publishers, nonprofit and for-profit, that provide high-quality titles at affordable prices. These less expensive titles tend to be the most highly ranked by faculty but labor intensive to obtain, since each publisher has only a few titles and often lacks sales and technical staff.

These libraries try to consistently view collection expenditures as investments, and to seek out publishers likely to contribute to a sustainable future for scholarly information. Libraries are also supporting open access projects that experiment with alternatives to the current subscription-based funding model or the current journals-based publishing model for scholarly communication. These approaches are seen as those of a good citizen, especially in an institution whose needs for funding include many urgent priorities in addition to library needs. These libraries are investing in initiatives that may help solve the long-term problem of high prices for journals.

It is clear that the role of the online catalog has changed. That catalog has become one of many databases available to users; libraries are linking to and from the catalog to integrate all of these resources. In recognition of this broader role for the library catalog, some libraries are considering modifying cataloging to favor timely access to a wider variety of formats. One proposal called for reallocating funds that are devoted to describing books and journals to materials that are proportionately underrepresented in today's catalogs, such as films, music, photographs, and digital objects. Libraries are also reconsidering their current efforts to collect and catalog free Web resources, concluding that these labor-intensive activities can be avoided by perfecting nascent machine harvesting and cataloging techniques.

A small number of libraries and library organisations are participating in experiments funded by The Mellon Foundation to test the application of harvesting and search engine technologies. Using the recently developed OAI metadata harvesting protocol, these libraries are delivering information from the "hidden Web" not normally found by Internet search engines and from databases with retrieval formats that present special processing or presentation problems. Several libraries are working with vendors to adapt existing portal software into multifunctional products with features and services desired by users in research communities. Other examples of library involvement in development of software applications are ILL management systems, instructional tutorials, management of content and services for digital libraries, and institutional repositories.

Although where information resides matters less to the user, the library as place—the physical entity—remains more important than ever and performs a host of functions vital to learning and research. Much research library space is busier than ever before. Library facilities are being reconfigured to provide space for collaborative learning and research. There are classrooms and media labs where faculty and librarians may interact in providing student learning experiences, group study spaces, and community spaces where students can meet to discuss ideas.

The transformation of library space has also become an opportunity to attract new academic collaborations such as writing studios and academic skills tutoring. Library space is now seen as learning space on an equal footing with classrooms and laboratories. Libraries are being renovated to expand e-access and foster community by providing electronic classrooms, wireless data networks, offering laptops, and expanding library hours.

Libraries are establishing spaces called "information commons" where library reference services are offered jointly with information technology support. At the same time, libraries are responding to decreasing use of in-person reference service by combining service points and shifting resources to online reference service and online tutorials. To make the best use of prime real estate, libraries are adopting new approaches to managing large print collections by using storage centers with delivery services for less frequently used materials and engaging in cooperative approaches to long-term preservation copy retention.

The branch or departmental library remains valuable but its role too is changing. While access to information and library services is far less geographically based, branch and departmental libraries still play a role in development of community and serve as sites for collaboration. Yet, in the Internet world there are opportunities to rethink the role of multiple libraries and their configuration within an institution. One library reported establishing a program to replicate the opportunities for personalised services and contacts that characterise branch library service without the cost of creating additional branches.

Some of the same opportunities for reorganisation may present themselves when libraries work in collaboration with other libraries outside their institutional boundaries. Libraries are active participants in building awareness among researchers, faculty, and students of uses of high-quality content and information technology in teaching and research. Curriculum review and changing expectations for teaching faculty present opportunities for libraries to contribute expertise and resources.

Libraries provide classrooms; training and consulting in finding and evaluating information; and assistance with creating electronic theses and dissertations, displaying and visualising data, publishing journals on the Web, and using geographic information systems (GIS) and remote sensing. Recognising that disciplines are adopting new technology at different rates, librarians are:

— Working with faculty to integrate information literacy skills and digital content into the course curricula

— Expanding the number of people reached by offering basic information literacy and fluency training through online tutorials

— Assisting researchers in acquiring, accessing, displaying, and visualising spatial and numeric data by providing training in use of software and partnering with faculty to provide classroom instruction in its use

— Developing systems and instructional tools for pedagogical use of digital resources, including images

— Managing campus instructional technology initiatives

— Making Organisational Changes within the Library to Innovate and Improve Services

Libraries are embracing change—being willing to change what libraries do and how it is done—and, as a result, are reorganising their operations and re-deploying staff to respond to the new environment.

Libraries are assuming leadership within their institutions to advocate for enduring institution-wide knowledge management policies and programs that contribute to a robust system of scholarly communication. Some libraries are accomplishing this goal by:

— Sponsoring scholarly communication seminars to broaden faculty and graduate student awareness of trends that threaten the long-term sustainability of the current system of scholarly communication

— Advocating for institution-wide intellectual property policies that balance the rights of copyright owners and those of users and libraries in educational settings, including the development of principles that guide the licensing of electronic resources for the institution

— Promoting individual behavior and building institutional support that contributes to the long-term health and viability of scholarly communication channels, including developing infrastructure for such alternative publishing practices as publishing open access journals or creating institutional repositories

All research libraries are innovating and adapting to the changing needs of their patrons, as well as to the changing requirements of their institutions. There is no clear evidence to suggest definitive trends in change based on the size of the library collection. There are specific types of innovation, however, that seem to be related to library or institution size. There is anecdotal evidence that library size has been influential in the development of digital library programs; libraries with more mature digital library programs tend to be libraries with larger collections and more staff members.

On the other hand, smaller institutional settings may encourage innovative collaborative activities, either because of the financial necessity to join forces to make something happen or because of the potential in smaller communities for more interaction across campus units. There is also anecdotal evidence that the institutional climate for change and the active support of groups and key individuals within the institution play a central role in the library's orientation and opportunities to innovate; to the extent that the size of the institution impacts this climate, size may be a contributing—if not driving—factor. Research libraries' ability and desire to collaborate with other research libraries, with non-university libraries, or with other organisations and industries will determine the success of many library programs. Motivations for collaborations vary greatly and include leadership, political support, the lure of available funding, and the desire to transform the library, to move it into the digital age.

An increasingly important collaboration is consortial buying of print and electronic content and services. Consortial buying and licensing for access to electronic resources have become central in every research library's arsenal of strategies for acquiring information more economically than could be accomplished by acting alone. Many libraries find user-initiated consortial borrowing combined with rapid delivery a successful avenue for making their users' access to books as easy as access to electronic resources.

There is evidence that fast delivery of books within a consortium has increased book use, especially by undergraduates. Consortia also offer accompanying services that greatly expedite the discovery and delivery of non-book content for users affiliated with libraries participating in the consortium; some consortia are centrally managing image data banks, electronic theses and dissertations, and other digital materials. Consortial structures vary and reflect the political framework of the state or region in which they operate and the institutions they represent. In some cases, a state legislature appropriates funds centrally to support consortial activities on behalf of libraries; in others, individual libraries pay to a common fund.

External funding facilitates the process of individual institutions' making the adjustments and compromises that consortia require and tends to support consortial relationships among libraries of varying sizes and characteristics. Consortia funded solely by the participating libraries tend to be formed of libraries of similar size and characteristics. Consortia are on the front line of controversies between libraries and publishers about pricing, the terms of use defined by licenses, and publisher practices that make it difficult for a library to cost-effectively tailor its purchases from the publishers' lists or to reduce the total amount of money spent with that publisher. The tendency of consortia to acquire or license electronic resources from the larger, commercial publishers raises concerns that content from scholarly societies or other smaller publishers will be overlooked.

Research library staff are actively working with their partners in consortia to assess the benefits and challenges of consortial licensing and to influence publisher behavior in favor of scholarly communication needs. A closely related factor to collaboration is the degree to which the organisations involved in a joint effort are willing to share control, at both the intra- and the inter-institutional levels. This sharing of control has implications for many activities such as archiving; consortial buying; expanding online resources; collaborative efforts with faculty, information technology groups, instructional technology centers; and cooperative publishing projects. Libraries are promoting team operations to advance collaborative projects and to encourage a convergence of different organisational cultures where control is truly shared.

Many research libraries are willing to establish new partnerships and share control in order to innovate. Research libraries' ability to recognise their strengths and their willingness to leverage those strengths influences the success of library integration into the research institution. Libraries have a special kind of space on campus, space that is seen as politically neutral and representative of the intellectual commons--public-good space.

This nature of space gives libraries leverage to attract and nurture collaboration with other parts of the institution. Libraries also have human talent they may deploy for the institution. Research library staffs have a wide range of expertise that can support new approaches to meeting user and institutional needs. Many libraries are leveraging their space and human resources to the advantage of the institution, for example, in creating an information commons, establishing an institutional repository, or providing campus management of copyright clearances.

A major factor in innovation is the degree to which research libraries and their institutions are willing and able to embrace change. The willingness of the library leadership (at all levels) to change its vision of what a library is and does, and to transform library operations to reflect that vision, obviously influences innovation. However, the culture of the institution itself also influences how the library engages and supports change. Many research libraries find themselves in the impossible position of being expected by some disciplines to implement systemic change while continuing to be responsive to the needs of other disciplines that have slower rates of adoption of new technology.

During this period of transition, this is a major factor influencing how libraries implement change and how that change is received within the institution. The degree to which people in the institution exhibit "interdisciplinarity" or demonstrate effectiveness in working with the various cultures of the institution—library, faculty, and information technology cultures—is another important factor in innovation. Success in collaboration depends on some degree of convergence of these cultures.

Convergence or integration of cultures is being approached in several different ways. Examples include convergence of cultures in shared space; convergence of technical and bibliographic expertise; and convergence of human capital to consolidate efforts, encourage cooperation, and provide institution-wide access to the latest equipment, software, and support as well as a wide and deep collection of high-quality content. Experience reported in the task force survey suggests there is a need to support greater cultural integration.

Some libraries pursue this goal by establishing cross-cultural task forces, developing cross-training and mentoring programs for effective performance across and outside traditional roles, adopting position classification schemes that reflect the changes required of staff, providing opportunities for staff to cross boundaries, and by giving people time to work through the process of cultural convergence. Converting existing collections and new acquisitions from paper to electronic-only is currently inhibited by the nascent state of strategies for preserving digital content.

Internationally, publishers are working with national libraries (or their proxies) for them to assume the role of the publishers' archives for digitised texts; the reliability and terms of use of these archives are still being determined. When library, publisher, and technology communities reach consensus on how best to manage the preservation of digital resources, the transformation of library collections to largely electronic will accelerate. In this rapidly changing environment, there are many opportunities for entrepreneurial activities, which often require the financial risk of investing resources in new activities even as budget pressures tighten.

Entrepreneurship may also create new activities that bypass or challenge the standards, rules, and policies that are part of library operations. Success depends on the library's ability to reach informed judgments, usually with less than complete information, on the strategic importance of an opportunity and whether it warrants the financial and other risks that accompany change.

Preservation of Digital Content

Responding to user expectations for easy searching and convenient access to an expanding array of information sources, libraries are spending increasing amounts of their materials budgets on electronic resources. While up to now many libraries have actually also maintained the print, where dual versions exist, recent budget and space constraints have led many to make a choice of the format they collect.

The nascent state of strategies for preserving digital content makes some libraries reluctant to relinquish print editions. However, seeing that these preservation issues are now being addressed, and given the significant advantages of the electronic editions, many libraries have decided to collect electronic-only. Libraries are also offering printing services to meet users' expressed need for print.

As professional print-on-demand technologies become more cost effective, this option may offer, for users who require it, a way to generate high-quality bound printed editions from electronic information resources. At the same time, libraries have not abandoned print. They continue to acquire print in disciplines that are not moving as quickly into the digital world as others and in formats, such as monographs, that are still published primarily in printed form. Thus, integrating print and electronic resources and making print resources almost as easy to access as electronic content are challenges facing libraries in this hybrid environment.

Portal software is being designed to enable users to search library catalogs simultaneously with both open and licensed databases to find content regardless of format, thereby building a bridge between the library's print and digital collections. Timely, self-service resource sharing and other user-initiated services such as book renewals and book- and article-delivery are also making access to print resources much easier. In the future more information will be created, stored, delivered, and preserved digitally, but print—because of its physicality, flexibility, perceived reliability, ease of reading and sharing—will be used for reading and editing for some time to come. Even as print retains importance, the library's physical space has increasing value for other activities, especially collaborative learning and research. Thus, to free up prime real estate, libraries are moving lesser-used print collections to storage centers (with rapid delivery service) and are exploring cooperative approaches to long-term preservation copy retention. For now, research libraries' print collections continue to play a critical role for users even as that role and how users gain access to the material are changing.

Given the rapidly changing environment, however, libraries are carefully monitoring the information-seeking and reading habits of their users to see how their use of print and digital resources changes or does not change over time. Institutional repositories—digital collections capturing and preserving the intellectual output of a single or multi-university community—provide a compelling response to two strategic issues facing academic institutions. Such repositories:

— Provide a critical component in reforming the system of scholarly communication--a component that expands access to research, reasserts control over scholarship by the academy, increases competition and reduces the monopoly power of journals, and brings economic relief and heightened relevance to the institutions and libraries that support them; and

— Have the potential to serve as tangible indicators of a university's quality and to demonstrate the scientific, societal, and economic relevance of its research activities, thus increasing the institution's visibility, status, and public value.

Institutional repositories represent the logical convergence of faculty-driven self-archiving initiatives, library dissatisfaction with the monopolistic effects of the traditional and still-pervasive journal publishing system, and the availability of digital networks and publishing technologies. This convergence manifests itself in several ways:

— *Attitudinally*: Institutional repositories build on a growing grassroots faculty practice of posting research online, most often on personal web sites, but also on departmental sites or in disciplinary repositories.

— *Economically*: While the variety of institutional contexts and potential implementations make it difficult to project institutional repository development and operational costs with any precision, the evidence so far suggests that the resources required would represent but a fraction of the journal costs that libraries now incur and over which they have little control.

— *Technically*: Digital publishing technologies, ever-expanding global networking, and enabling interoperability protocols and metadata standards are coalescing to provide practical technical solutions that can be implemented now.

The rationale for universities and colleges implementing institutional repositories rests on two interrelated propositions: one that supports a broad, pan-institutional effort and another that offers direct and immediate benefits to each institution that implements a repository.

While institutional repositories centralise, preserve, and make accessible an institution's intellectual capital, at the same time they will form part of a global system of distributed, interoperable repositories that provides the foundation for a new disaggregated model of scholarly publishing. This model unbundles the principal functions of scholarly communication, thus presenting the potential to realise market efficiencies previously hidden by the vertically integrated publishing model that now characterises academic journal publishing. Altering the structure of the scholarly publishing model will be neither simple nor immediate.

The stakes are high for all the well-entrenched participants in the system--faculty, librarians, and publishers--and the inertia of the traditional publishing paradigm is immense. In the near-term, large journal publishers have both the power and the incentive to maintain the status quo: the prestigious journals they control appear integral to the very structure of academic professional advancement. However, digital publishing and networking technologies, harnessed by an increasingly dissatisfied library market—as well as by authors themselves--are now driving fundamental changes to this publishing model at an accelerating pace. And new communications paradigms, especially when constructed by the scholars themselves, can eliminate seemingly insurmountable publisher advantages in relatively short order. Institutional repositories, by capturing, preserving, and disseminating a university's collective intellectual capital, serve as meaningful indicators of an institution's academic quality.

Under the current system of scholarly communication, much of the intellectual output and value of an institution's intellectual property is diffused through thousands of scholarly journals. While faculty publication in these journals reflects positively on the host university, an institutional repository concentrates the intellectual product created by a university's researchers, making it easier to demonstrate its scientific, social and financial value. Thus, institutional repositories complement existing metrics for gauging institutional productivity and prestige. The current system of scholarly communication limits, rather than expands, the readership and availability of most scholarly research.

Rounds of journal price increases and subsequent subscription cancellations act to reduce the audience further. The role of alternative scholarly publishing models, such as institutional repositories, in breaking the monopolies of publishers and increasing the awareness of university intellectual output grows increasingly clear. Further, institutional repositories can serve this function whether they are implemented on individual campuses or in collaborative consortial projects.

Institutional Repository

Stated broadly, a digital institutional repository can be any collection of digital material hosted, owned or controlled, or disseminated by a college or university, irrespective of purpose or provenance. A particular type of institutional repository—a digital archive of the intellectual product created by the faculty, research staff, and students of an institution and accessible to end users both within and outside of the institution, with few if any barriers to access.

In other words, the content of an institutional repository is:

- Institutionally defined;
- Scholarly;
- Cumulative and perpetual; and
- Open and interoperable.

Institutional repositories can assume many forms and serve a variety of purposes. Indeed, the technical and administrative infrastructures developed by academic institutions for existing digital library initiatives might often be modified or repurposed to serve the requirements of an institutional repository. The institutional repository might form a component of a more comprehensive institutional initiative, one encompassing virtually all of an institution's digital assets. In contrast to discipline-specific repositories and subject-oriented or thematic digital libraries, institutional repositories capture the original research and other intellectual property generated by an institution's constituent population active in many fields.

Defined in this way, institutional repositories represent an historical and tangible embodiment of the intellectual life and output of an institution. And, to the extent that institutional affiliation itself serves as the primary qualitative filter, this repository becomes a significant indicator of the institution's academic quality. Depending on the university, an institutional repository may complement or compete with the role served by the university archives. University archives often serve two purposes: 1) to manage administrative records to satisfy legally mandated retention requirements, and 2) to preserve materials pertaining to the institution's history and to the activities and achievements of its officers, faculty, staff, students, and alumni. Compared to institutional repositories, which aim to preserve the entire intellectual output of the institution, university archivists exercise broad discretion in determining which papers and other digital objects to collect and store.

Developing institutional repositories does not require that each institution act entirely on its own. For many colleges and universities, existing state or regional institutional or library consortia will provide a logical infrastructure for implementing institutional repositories via collective development. Such cooperation could deliver economies of scale and help institutions avoid the needless replication of technical systems. Indeed, consortia might well prove the fastest path to proliferating institutional repositories and attaining a critical mass of open access content.

Depending on the goals established by each institution, an institutional repository could contain any work product generated by the institution's students, faculty, non-faculty researchers, and staff. This material might include student electronic portfolios, classroom teaching materials, the institution's annual reports, video recordings, computer programs, data sets, photographs, and art works—virtually any digital material that the institution wishes to preserve.

This content may include pre-prints and other works-in-progress, peer-reviewed articles, monographs, enduring teaching materials, data sets and other ancillary research material, conference papers, electronic theses and dissertations, and gray literature. To control and manage the accession of this content requires appropriate policies and mechanisms, including content management and document version control systems. The repository policy framework and technical infrastructure must provide institutional managers the flexibility to control who can contribute, approve, access, and update the digital content coming from a variety of institutional communities and interest groups.

Several of the institutional repository infrastructure systems currently being developed have the technical capacity to embargo or sequester access to submissions until the content has been approved by a designated reviewer. The nature and extent of this review will reflect the policies and needs of each individual institution, possibly of each participating institutional community.

Essential to the institutional repository's role both within the university and within the larger structure of scholarly communication is that the content collected is both cumulative and maintained in perpetuity. This has two implications.

First, whatever the content submission criteria for a repository, items once submitted cannot be withdrawn--except in presumably rare cases involving allegations of libel, plagiarism, copyright infringement, or "bad science." This removal would be the functional equivalent of revoking the registration initially granted to the contribution on accession into the repository. This does not necessarily mean that all content will be universally accessible in perpetuity. Institutions must develop criteria and policies--and implement rights management systems--for allowing access to a repository's content, both inside the institution and from outside, that balance the goal of the broadest available access with the reality of encouraging faculty participation.

The cumulative nature of institutional repositories also implies that the repository's infrastructure is scaleable. While initial processing and storage requirements might prove modest, institutional repository systems must be able to accommodate thousands of submissions per year, and eventually must be able to preserve millions of digital objects and many terabytes of data. Second, institutional repositories aim to preserve and make accessible digital content on a long-term basis.

Digital preservation and long-term access are inextricably linked: each being largely meaningless without the other. Providing long-term access to digital objects in the repository requires considerable planning and resource commitments. The institution needs to balance the desire to accept the farrago of file formats popular with various disciplines, in order to simplify content submission and encourage faculty participation, with the complications that migrating some of those formats or media might present as new standards evolve. While it is possible for an institution to dictate digital formatting standards for students—in the submission of electronic theses and dissertations, for example—prescribing such formats for faculty, for both attitudinal and practical reasons, proves far more problematic.

The goals motivating an institution to create and maintain a digital repository—whether pan-institutional, as a component in the changing structure of scholarly communication, or institution-centric--require that users beyond the institution's community gain access to the content. For the repository to provide access to the broader research community, users outside the university must be able to find and retrieve information from the repository. Therefore, institutional repository systems must be able to support interoperability in order to provide access via multiple search engines and other discovery tools.

An institution does not necessarily need to implement searching and indexing functionality to satisfy this demand: it could simply maintain and expose metadata, allowing other services to harvest and search the content. This simplicity lowers the barrier to repository operation for many institutions, as it only requires a file system to hold the content and the ability to create and share metadata with external systems. Given the disparate publishing practices amongst academic disciplines, an institution's content accession and access policies need to accommodate legitimate researcher concerns about access to pre-publication material deposited in the repository.

Institutional repositories typically do not permit content to be removed once submitted. However, a variety of legitimate circumstances might require an institution to limit access to particular content to a specific set of users. These circumstances might include copyright restrictions, policies established by a particular research community, embargoes that an institution's Sponsored Programs Office might require to keep the institution in compliance with the terms of sponsor contracts, and even monetary access fees for certain data.

The goal of the OAi is to contribute in a concrete manner to the transformation of scholarly communication. The proposed vehicle for this transformation is the definition of technical and supporting organisational aspects of an open scholarly publication framework on which both free and commercial layers can be established. The origins of the Open Archives initiative lie in the growing number of electronic preprint (eprint) archives. While several of these began as informal vehicles for the dissemination of preliminary results and non-peer reviewed "gray literature", a number of them have evolved into an essential medium for sharing research results among the colleagues in a field.

These archives demonstrate a shift in the traditional scholarly communication model, which has relied on formally published scholarly journals. There is a growing consensus that the scholarly journal system is facing significant challenges:

— The explosive growth of the Internet has given scholars almost universal access to a communication medium that facilitates immediate sharing of results.

— The rapidity of advances in most scholarly fields has made the slow turn-around of the traditional publishing model an impediment to collegial sharing.

— The full transfer of rights from author to publisher often acts as an impediment to the scholarly author whose main concern is the widest dissemination of results.

— The current implementation of peer-review-an essential feature of scholarly communication-is too rigid and sometimes acts to suppress new ideas, favor articles from prestigious institutions, and cause undue publication delays.

— The imbalance between skyrocketing subscription prices and shrinking or, at best, stable library budgets is creating an economic crisis for research libraries.

The e-print archives exemplify a more equitable and efficient model for disseminating research results. An important challenge is to increase the impact of the e-print archives by layering on top of them services-such as peer review-deemed essential to scholarly communication. This is the focus of the Open Archives initiative. The aim of the archive initiatives described above is to try to create a more effective scholarly communication mechanism that addresses problems that exist in the established system. The approaches that are taken by individual archives differ in a number of ways.

Some initiatives build on a centralised model, others on a distributed departmental, or by extension, institutional model. Some deal with gray literature only, others incorporate metadata of peer-reviewed papers or try to establish some form of peer-review outside of the established system. Some deal with metadata only, others with both metadata and full content. Yet all share the attribute of offering scholars a vehicle to conveniently and immediately disseminate research results to peers.

The reason for launching the Open Archives initiative is the belief that interoperability among archives is key to increasing their impact and establishing them as viable alternatives to the existing scholarly communication model. The Open Archives initiative has been set up to create a forum to discuss and solve matters of interoperability between author self-archiving solutions (also commonly referred to as e-print systems), as a way to promote their global acceptance. Interoperability is a broad term, touching many diverse aspects of archive initiatives, including their metadata formats, their underlying architecture, their openness to the creation of third-party digital library services, their integration with the established mechanism of scholarly communication, their usability in a cross-disciplinary context, their ability to contribute to a collective metrics system for usage and citation, etc. Interoperability among archives offers substantial benefits to the scholars that use them.

An important attribute of the traditional research library as an information provider is its role as a common entry point for a variety of information resources, not necessarily divided along disciplinary or institutional boundaries. The move from physical to digital sources should not be accompanied by the breakup of this entry point into a collection of fragmented archives. An increasing number of scholars move fluidly in their research across domain boundaries; the technology for delivering digital information should facilitate rather than hinder such fluidity.

Mechanisms for interoperability offer the potential for discovery tools and virtual collections that extend across the contents of multiple archives. Interoperability is also beneficial to the archive and service provider. Rather than having to provide an entire suite of services for its users, individual archives can instead establish a welldefined interface on which external providers can build enhanced services. A variety of such services can be envisioned, including those that facilitate discovery, linking, and reviewing. An intriguing and essential set of services would be those that provide metrics to assist in the evaluation of the impact of certain scholarship and aid in tenure review and promotion decisions. Although interoperability has been a watchword for a variety of efforts in digital libraries and networked information, the actual meaning of it and the implementation thereof has often proven elusive.

In addition, the convention introduces an organisational framework for making information available about archives that adhere to the technical recommendations of the convention-the data providers-and about trusted parties that build end-user services for data originating from such archives-the service providers. As such it provides a communication mechanism between providers of data and providers of services and creates a community of open archives. The Santa Fe Convention builds on on a number of definitions and concepts that are essential for its understanding. The Convention considers the following to be crucial components of an e-print archive:

— A submission mechanism;

— A long-term storage system;

— A management policy with regard to submission of documents and their preservation;

— An open machine interface, that enables third parties to collect data from the archive.

The last item is crucial for enabling third parties to create services that support the discovery, presentation and analysis of data in the archive. Most e-print archives will also provide native end-user services. However, facilitating the broad dissemination of archive data through third party services is a crucial feature of an e-print archive. Therefore, the open interface is a key part of the Santa Fe Convention.

The convention uses the notion of a record in an archive. Some archives may store metadata that describes full content without storing the full content itself. In this case, the metadata is a record. Other archives may also store full content. However, the convention assumes that if full content is stored, there will always be associated metadata stored in the archive as well as a mechanism to tie metadata and content together. In this case the combination of metadata and full content is a record.

Open Archives Metadata Set (OAMS)

The Open Archives Metadata Set (OAMS) is a collection of nine metadata elements intended to facilitate coarse granularity resource discovery among the records in distributed and dissimilar archives. The semantics of this set have purposely been kept simple in the interest of easy creation and widest applicability. There is no provision for qualification or extension of the nine elements. The expectation is that individual archives will maintain metadata with more expressive semantics and the Open Archives Dienst Subset provides the mechanism for retrieval of this richer metadata.

Open Archives Dienst Subset

The Open Archives Dienst Subset is a set of protocol requests that are delivered via HTTP. This protocol is a subset of the full Dienst protocol. The protocol requests in the subset provide the following functionality:

— List the full identifiers for records stored in an archive. An optional argument permits the client to specify that the list should only include records added after a specific date. Another optional argument allows the client to specify that the records should be accompanied by the metadata associated with the identifier.

— Return the metadata for a specific record in a requested format.

— Return the list of metadata formats supported by an archive.

— Return the list of metadata formats available for a specific record.

— Return the structure of the partitions by which an archive is organised.

Metadata

The requirement to have a shared, basic metadata set to facilitate interoperability across communities was reconfirmed. Also the notion of parallel metadata sets that serve specific needs of communities and archives was reconfirmed.

The shared metadata set developed during the original Santa Fe meeting-the OAMS-was deemed inappropriate for cross-community use due to some e-print specific aspects.

Instead, the Dublin Core Element Set was selected as the common metadata set. This selection leverages years of work in the Dublin Core Metadata Initiative in developing cross-community consensus. Initial steps were taken to encourage the development of community-specific harvestable metadata sets. Representatives of the e-print community at the meeting decided to propose a metadata set targeted at the e-print community under the name EPMS by the beginning of 2001.

Representatives of the research library community proposed a similar effort and calls for proposals from other communities (e.g., the museum community, Open Language Archives) will be issued. To distinguish between metadata specific to harvesting functionality and other metadata (both shared and community specific), a carrier syntax in XML was developed. This syntax transports packages of specific sets (e.g., Dublin Core, EPMS) within a contextual wrapper that contains metadata specific to the harvesting interactions between data and service providers. The concept of unique identifiers within an OAI namespace has been maintained. Its implementation has been revised for compliance with general URI principles and to allow for the building of resolution mechanisms and services across OAI-compliant archives.

OAI Harvesting Protocol

At the heart of the technical agreements of the OAI is the metadata harvesting protocol, which provides a simple interface to transfer metadata from a data provider to a service provider. The original specifications for this interface in the Santa Fe Convention were a subset of the more expressive Dienst protocol. This protocol contains the following service requests:

— *Identify* - returns a self-description of the archive, containing information submitted at time of registration and other administrative information;

— *ListMetadataFormats* - returns a list of identifiers of metadata formats that are offered by the archive in general or for a particular record;

— *ListSets* - returns a structured list of sets within which records may be located;

— *ListRecords* - returns a list of record identifiers, and optionally metadata, within a specified range of dates and/or a specified Set. Flow control is achieved by the use of server-generated continuation tokens;

— *GetRecord* - returns the metadata associated with an identifier.

These service requests and their parameters are encoded into standard HTTP URIs. Responses to the requests are XML documents. This allows for simple implementation using CGI scripts or similar technology for data providers while service providers can exploit the proliferation of XML parsers to ease the harvesting of data.

Dienst System

The word "Dienst" refers to a number of things:

— A conceptual architecture for distributed digital libraries.

— A protocol for service communication in that architecture.

— A software system that implements that protocol.

Conceptually, Dienst is a system for configuring a set of individual services running on distributed servers to cooperate in providing the services of a digital library. The open architecture of the Dienst system - exposure of the functionality through an defined protocol - makes it possible to combine Dienst services in flexible ways and augment the existing services with other mediator services, which build on the functionality of the existing services.

The Dienst system originated with the Computer Science Technical Reports Project, a DARPA-funded collaboration to establish a digital library of computer science technical reports. Broadly speaking, there are three ways that Dienst is used:

1. Organisations that wish to join an existing digital library built using Dienst.
2. Organisations that wish to create a new distributed digital library with Dienst.
3. Organisations that wish to undertake research in digital libraries using an existing Dienst digital library or by experimenting with the software.

The modular nature of the software encourages researchers who wish explore mechanisms for enhancing existing services or using the interfaces to existing services to built other services. Notice: While the software has been built and tested according to conventional software engineering standards, we stress that it is research software. Organisations wishing to use it for mission critical applications should consider a thorough review of the architecture, protocol, and software for robustness and security.

The distributed Dienst software is configured to handle textual resources (documents) in a variety of formats. However, the Dienst architecture includes a sophisticated document model that accommodates a wide variety of digital resources. Using the Dienst software for these other resources will require some programming. The Dienst protocol and software is copyrighted but is available for free and can be used and redistributed for non-commercial uses. The Dienst protocol and software is used in a variety of existing digital libraries and projects. In short, the Open Archives Initiative is providing a framework for the extensive interoperability of archives of scholarly research literature.

For this initiative to become a widespread reality, the participation of large numbers of individuals and institutions is required. In order to be able to participate, what institutions need is working, interoperable, configurable software that is freely available and easy to set up. It is this need that the EPrints software was developed to fulfill. EPrints is a feature-rich open archive software system that is as simple to install as any normal application. It runs right "out of the box" with a comprehensive default setup that should serve most people's needs.

However, it has also been designed to make it extensively and flexibly re-configurable for customised needs; almost any aspect of the archive's operation can be adapted to suit a particular requirement. This means that the archive can be used by institutions, individuals, journals or any other organisation wishing to interoperate with Open Archive services. This adaptability is achieved by using a modular design methodology. The system is divided into two main components: The core archive component, which provides the functionality required for all open archives, and the site-specific component, providing details about exactly what is stored in the archive, how it is presented and how it may be searched. The system is supplied with a richly featured site-specific component that requires minimal changing to set up a fully working, interoperable open archive.

5

Digital Automation

The term automated digital library can be used to describe a digital library where all tasks are carried out automatically. Computer programs substitute for the intellectually demanding tasks that are traditionally carried out by skilled professionals. These tasks include selection, cataloguing and indexing, seeking for information, reference services, and so on.

The common theme is that these activities require considerable mental activity, the type of activity that people are skilled at and computers find difficult. Automated digital libraries should not be confused with library automation, which uses computing to reduce routine tasks in conventional libraries. The underlying question is not whether automated digital libraries can rival conventional digital libraries today. They clearly cannot. The question is whether we can conceive of a time when they will provide an acceptable substitute.

Quality of service in automated digital libraries will not come from replicating the procedures of classical librarianship. More likely, automated libraries will provide users with equivalent services that are fundamentally different in the way that they are delivered. Within the foreseeable future, computer programs are unlikely to be much good at applying the Anglo American Cataloguing

Rules to monographs. But cataloguing rules are a means to an end, not the end itself. They exist to provide services to users, notably information discovery. Automatic methods for information discovery may not need traditional cataloguing rules.

The criterion for evaluating the new methods is whether the users find what the information that they require. Consider the contrast between web search engines and conventional abstracting and indexing services or library catalogs. Almost everything that is best about a library catalog is done badly by a web search service. The selection of which materials to index by a web search engine relies on arbitrary considerations, the indexing records are crude at best, authority control is non-existent, and the elimination of duplicates leaves much to be desired. On the other hand, web search services are strong in ways that catalogs are weak. While cataloguing is expensive, indexing the web is cheap.

The leading web search engines index several hundred million web pages every month, more than the total number of MARC records that have ever been created. It is wrong to claim that conventional catalogs or indexes are superior because of their quality control, and it is equally wrong to claim that the web search services are superior because of their coverage and currency. The value to users depends on what the user wants to achieve. In US, for medical research, no web search engine can approach the National Library of Medicine's Medline service. Medline has over 11 million references and abstracts. It is built by a team of indexers who have knowledge of bio-medical research, using indexing rules and MeSH subject headings that have been developed laboriously over decades. In contrast, web search services such as GoogleSM are entirely automated.

The indexes are built by a team of computers with no knowledge of what they are indexing. Google has the advantage over Medline of indexing hundreds of millions of web pages, and doing so repeatedly every month. It is quite useful for finding general information on medical topics, but it does not index the major scientific journals, its indexing records are crude, it has no understanding of medical terminology, and makes no attempt to separate sound medicine from quackery. It is a long way from being a substitute for Medline. On the other hand, consider the trade-off between Google and Inspec, which is the leading abstracting and indexing service for computing. In many areas of computing, Google's restriction to open access web materials is relatively unimportant, since almost every significant result first appears on a web site and only later reaches the printed journals, if ever. In computing, substantially the same information is often available from several sources.

Google provides a direct link to an open access version. Inspec references a formally published version, which is usually printed or online with restricted access. For my purposes, Google's broad coverage and convenient links more than compensate for its weaknesses. A scientist judges a library catalog simply as a tool for information discovery, while, for a humanist, the catalog may be a bibliographic source in its own right. Any predictions of the future value of web search engines compared with conventional abstracting and indexing services depend heavily on the publication and reading habits of people in different disciplines. The rate of progress in computing power is described by Moore's Law, that the number of transistors on a semiconductor doubles every eighteen months. This is roughly equivalent to saying that computing power increases 100-fold in 10 years or 10,000-fold in 20 years. Few people can appreciate the implications of such dramatic change, but the future of automated digital libraries is likely to depend more on brute force computing than on sophisticated algorithms.

Many of the most successful methods of artificial intelligence apply simple methods to huge volumes of data. An interesting example comes from the computer programs that play chess. The IBM system that is now equal to the world's greatest grandmasters is descended from Deep Thought, a student project at Carnegie Mellon University. The members of the Deep Thought team were not chess experts. Their breakthrough came from expertise in developing exceptionally fast hardware, which could analyse immense numbers of chess variations. The potential for automated digital libraries lies in the simple observation that:

- — Simple algorithms plus immense computing power often outperform human intelligence.
- — Moore's Law tells us that the computing power will be available.
- — The state-of-the-art in automated digital libraries
- — The introduction of automated digital libraries is a continual process, much of it happening outside conventional libraries. Here are some current examples.

Information discovery illustrates the complementary skills of computers and people. Humans are skilled at reading a few thousand words and extracting complex concepts. Faced with a billion pages (roughly the size of the web), they are helpless. Computers can index every word in a billion pages and search the indexes for simple patterns almost instantaneously. The web search services represent the state-of-the-art in automated information discovery. Within each service lie a number of separate processes, each of which is carried out automatically, and each of which is constrained by the current state of computing.

To build the indexes, a web crawler must decide which pages to index, eliminate duplicates, create a short index record for each page and add the terms found on the page to its inverted files. To search the index, the search engine must convert the user's query to a search command, match it against the inverted files, rank the results and return them to the user. To anticipate the potential of automatic systems to rival the functionality of Medline in all disciplines, we need to examine the components of a system like Google and see how they could be improved. Moore's law predicts that computers will be 10,000 times more powerful in twenty years. With such computer power available, we know that the automatic search systems will be extremely good, even if no new algorithms are invented. To decide how closely a document matches a query would seem to require human judgment, yet standard methods of information retrieval do remarkably well. They use the power of computers to match simple patterns as a surrogate for the human ability to relate concepts. As humans, we use our understanding of language to observe that two texts are on similar topics, or to rank how closely documents match a query.

Computers can estimate closeness of match by comparing word frequencies. One basic concept, developed by Gerald Salton at Cornell University about 1970, represents each document as a multi-dimensional vector and uses the angle between their vectors as a measure of the similarity of two documents. Evaluating the importance of documents would appear to be another task that requires human understanding, but Google's ranking algorithm does remarkably well entirely automatically. The idea behind this algorithm is simple. Google ranks web pages by how many other pages link to them. It gives greater weight to links from higher-ranking pages. Calculating the ranks requires the algorithm to iterate through a matrix that has as many rows and columns as there are pages on the web, yet with modern computing and considerable ingenuity, Google performs this calculation routinely.

As a result, Google is remarkably successful in presenting a user with the most important page on a topic or a well-respected overview. This algorithm was developed as part of the NSF-funded Digital Library Initiative. The Internet is an extremely important part of modern culture and contains many materials that should be preserved for future generations. Each month, a web crawler gathers every open access web page with associated images. The Internet Archive preserves these files for the future and mounts them on computers available for scholarly research today. The Internet Archive is not perfect.

Only HTML pages and images are collected, no Java applets or style sheets; the materials are dumped into a computer system with no organisation or indexing; broken links are left broken; and access for scholars is rudimentary. Yet the simple fact is that without the automated approach of the Internet Archive, these materials would already have been lost. Attempts to catalog and collect web materials using skilled librarians and archivists have floundered on the scale of effort needed to do even a rudimentary job.

Citation analysis is a long-standing success story of applying computers to library information. Inspired by the efforts of Eugene Garfield, the founder of Science Citation Index, there is a long tradition of using citations as bibliographic measures. Hyperlinks are the web's equivalent to citations. Since they are already in machine-readable form, they are amenable to algorithmic analysis. Google's ranking algorithm can be seen as applying the concepts of citation analysis to the web. Hyperlinks refer to items or copies of a work, but citations normally refer to the work itself or a specific manifestation.

Automatic systems are becoming capable of extracting a reference from a document and linking it to the digital object that it references. Currently, the most fully automated system for reference linking is the SFX system, created by Hebert Van de Sompel and colleagues at the University of Ghent. Reference linking is one of the building blocks that are being used to build large-scale automated digital libraries. ResearchIndex is a digital library of computer science materials, created entirely automatically by Steve Lawrence and colleagues at NEC. It makes extensive use of citation analysis and reference linking. It downloads papers from the web. If they are in PostScript or PDF, it converts them to text. It parses the papers to extract citations and the context for the citation. It provides users with services such as searching the entire text or the citations, listing the references within a paper, following the citation links, or displaying the context in which references appear. An interesting aspect of ResearchIndex is that it provides a way for users to submit corrections, automatically of course.

Metadata is one of the foundations of librarianship. There are a number of projects that extract metadata from digital objects automatically. Perhaps the most remarkable is the Informedia project, led by Howard Wactlar at Carnegie Mellon University. Informedia has the extremely ambitious goal of providing access to segments of video, such as television news, entirely automatically. Thus it includes algorithms for dividing raw video into discrete items, for generating short summaries, for indexing the sound track using speech recognition, for recognising faces and for searching using methods of natural language processing. Each of these methods is a tough research topic and, not surprisingly, Informedia provides only a rough-and-ready service, but overall it is surprisingly effective. Moreover, many of the weaknesses of Informedia could be overcome by applying huge amounts of computing power.

The job of a reference librarian ranges from helping users with the mechanics of using a library to tasks that require deep intellectual understanding. The ugly term "disintermediation" is used when users perform for themselves tasks that used to be carried out with the help of a librarian. Information retrieval provides a good test case. The mechanics of searching have been almost completely assumed by computing. The current generation of scholars never experienced the tedium of reading through long lists of abstracts, searching huge card catalogs and following citations laboriously from journal to journal. Searching a card catalog required skill. Because of the labor in creating and filing cards, only a small number of entries were provided for each work. Since few users ever mastered the complex rules for the main and supplementary headings, or the intricate filing conventions, serious users turned to reference librarians for help. Automated digital libraries can clearly help with the mechanics of searching, but information seeking is more complex.

In disciplines with complex organisation of information, searching for information remains a skilled task. Often, knowledge of the subject matter is paramount and the experts develop their own skills. For example, carrying out legal research online is a basic skill that every law student learns. Historically, most doctors needed the help of a medical librarian to carry out an in-depth search. Now, even in medicine, the tools available to the user are sufficiently good that most searches can now be carried out directly by the user. It seems that automatic tools are steadily reducing the need for reference librarians in these fields. For many years, we have had computer systems that can search enormous collections of text for the phrase "space station", or simple variations. For this purpose, computers clearly out-perform human searching for both speed and accuracy.

Computing power is much cheaper than human expertise, more so every year. When money and time are available in abundance, skilled professionals have no equal. But they are always in short supply. In the United States, the National Library of Medicine is funded by the government and provides open access to Medline, but only rich lawyers can afford to use the legal services provided by Westlaw and Lexis. Because of the cost, traditional library systems are selective. Indexing and abstracting services restrict their coverage to a carefully selected set of publications. Catalogs do not include potentially useful information from monographs, such as individual items in anthologies, subheading, captions, and so on. There are essentially no attempts to catalog the content of web sites, below the level of the whole site. Even so, these services are very expensive. Automatic systems have no trouble with being inclusive; they have problems when they attempt to be selective. Their weakness is lack of precision.

They exhibit what, in a human, would be called very poor judgment. Both ISI's Web of Science and ResearchIndex provide users with interlinked scientific documents. Web of Science is a splendid service, but its production is not fully automatic, since ISI relies on skilled personnel for election and for key parts of the input process. Because the ResearchIndex methods are automatic and are applied to raw data, ResearchIndex inevitably has errors, while the skilled staff at ISI eliminate almost all errors, but at a cost. A library subscription to the Web of Science costs $100,000 per year. Automated digital libraries combined with open access information on the Internet offer to provide the Model T Ford of information. Nobody would claim that the Model T Ford was a peer to the handcrafted cars of its generation, and automated digital libraries cannot approach the personal service available to the faculty of a well-endowed university. But few people could afford a hand-built car, and few people have easy access to a major research library. The low cost of automated digital libraries is already bringing scientific, scholarly, medical and legal information to new audiences.

The library and information services were recognised as a key service within the newly established knowledge management group that also consisted of e-business strategy, data warehousing, management and analysis services and web services. In Australia, an integrated structure for the Department of Human Services (DHS) libraries was endorsed in July 2000 paving the way for new library innovations supporting a departmental knowledge management approach. The Department of Human Services has adopted a knowledge management approach that supports key organisational outcomes. There are five major strategic directions that scope out the future for the DHS. They are:

— Improving services for better outcomes;
— Increasing the state's capacity to promote quality of life;
— Redistributing resources in a changing environment;
— Strengthening a culture of working together;
— Providing sound management.

These strategic directions are underpinned by the strong focus on leadership, service excellence, accountability, valuing staff, innovation and enthusiasm, respect for customers and staff and acting with integrity. During 1999 the knowledge management group of functions aligned under the management of the Director for Knowledge Management (KM), Iolanda Principe. Functions currently contained in this group include:

— e-business and e-records management strategy;
— knowledge strategy;
— library and information services;
— organisational information services (data warehousing, management and analysis);
— web services.

Since this time, a Framework and Guide for Knowledge Management in the Department of Human Services was written in June 2001 and recently endorsed by the department's executive management group. This framework outlines key definitions, principles, objectives and responsibilities for KM within the department. It is designed as a practical guide for staff in the department in implementing a KM approach within their business unit while mapping out an organisation-wide approach. The principles articulate a range of elements from valuing employee knowledge as a key asset, to sharing knowledge and working collaboratively through to employees having the right to access the information / knowledge they need through appropriate systems.

The key KM objectives are:

— Leveraging the use of existing departmental knowledge;

— Fostering the creation of new knowledge;

— Enhancing the retention of knowledge (especially when people leave); and

— Improving knowledge transfer to clients.

Within this framework, the development of a knowledge centre has been identified as a key initiative for the KM program. This knowledge centre is a focal point for knowledge skills and the facilitation of knowledge flow within the organisation and requires the transformation of the current library and information services to fulfil this function. The KM framework is focussed on:

— The evolution of knowledge workers;

— The links between organisational strategic directions and KM;

— The links between knowledge / information / new economy initiatives (state, national and international) and KM within the DHS strategic plan;

— Effective measurement or evaluation of KM strategies and initiatives;

— Demonstration of KM best practice;

— Capturing organisational intellectual capital and effectively measuring how this occurs particularly within an organisational cultural context.

The DHS in South Australia is leading the way in the successful implementation of knowledge management within the public sector. The current challenges for the library are:

— Support the development and meet the needs of knowledge workers.

— Provide access to knowledge for improved decision making and innovation.

— Enhance the department's capacity to capture its knowledge and its ability to use this knowledge to further strategic objectives.

Individual training for library staff focussed on specific skill set acquisition Library culture that supports learning and innovation for strategic benefits. The current challenge for the library within this emerging knowledge enabled department is how to further this shift and overcome the barriers identified above. With clear evidence that customers want more tailored services delivered in an appropriate and timely way, it has become clear that the library must shift from a passive knowledge facilitating role to a pro-active knowledge broker role.

There are numerous creative and innovative ways in which the library can achieve these value added services and become a re-intermediary knowledge agent. For example, in working with departmental projects, the library can provide its expertise with the support of additional resources from the project allocations.

This also requires that library staff work with its customers beyond the library walls. This type of work already happens informally on an individual and ad hoc basis and, consequently, is not currently captured by existing library measurement tools. What is a knowledge centre? It:

— identifies sources of important knowledge, both inside and outside the company

— catalogues and indexes material so that retrieval is efficient and effective

— maintains and sustains the knowledge repository (the knowledge bank)

— provides a one stop shop for multiple information needs

— knows who can help - pointers to people as well as information

— runs a client advisory service - offering expertise on sources, their availability, relevance, quality and overall usefulness to the business.

While it can be argued that the library already does this to some extent now, within the KM framework, the shift for the library to a knowledge centre relies on extending what it already does well and formalising some of the informal or intangible knowledge processes that occur. The library team has an extensive knowledge base about the work being carried out in the department.

In addition, there have been several initiatives that assisted the library team to position itself for these and other changes in the future. They are:

— Enhancing partnerships with customers through knowledge need assessment processes;

— The development of a Balanced Score Card for the library and information services;

— Evolving library culture for innovation and learning;

— The realignment of Communications and Public Relations, Health Promotion South Australia and Knowledge Management groups.

A key activity in the integration of library services for the DHS was the implementation of a qualitative focus group process to identify customer needs. The strategic benefit of these initiatives is that knowledge workers now have improved access to quality, evidence based knowledge.

Specifically, this knowledge is available easily and quickly, potentially seven days a week, 24 hours a day. The next challenge is to ensure that future customer participation processes enable clearer identification of knowledge worker and organisational needs and that innovative service delivery strategies are implemented to meet these needs. The balanced scorecard is one tool that will assist in this process. The DHS in South Australia has adopted the balanced scorecard as a key reporting tool for the measurement of strategic and intangible outcomes. The scorecard methodology enables the measurement of objectives that target organisational change, and, specifically, innovation and creation.

Critical to the successful integration of the library service, so that is truly reflective of knowledge management principles, is the evolution of a learning culture, that is, modelling the KM approach within the library team. As a first step, the team has undertaken customer service and team building activities. Through the provision of a tailored training program, the library staff have been able to:

— Identify the issues that prevent us from embracing change;
— Identify the existing gaps in skill set and knowledge that are required to become a knowledge enabling service for the department;
— Improve the way we communicate with one another and, consequently, with our customers;
— Extend our collective understanding of the department's strategic directions and need to integrate and extend our business to support innovation;
— Create a culture of learning within the library team so that we are better positioned in the future to adopt new technologies and innovative service delivery solutions.

Learning to share the knowledge within the team and creating an environment where it is safe experiment with new ideas will enable us to more effectively contribute to the organisational knowledge base. For the library it means a new opportunity for closer partnerships with key departmental knowledge workers who have skills and expertise in:

— Communication systems and strategy;

— Publicity, promotion and marketing and customer relationships;

— Capacity building for organisational change and knowledge creation, capture and retrieval; and

— Organisational publishing (ie creating knowledge assets).

The benefit for the library, in the first instance, is a more cohesive departmental approach to capturing organisational knowledge through improved publishing policies and protocols. Currently, the library strongly advocates for its involvement in these processes to ensure legal deposit requirements are met and copies are available, not only within the department, but also nationally and internationally. The potential within this expanded group for further service delivery innovations and the enhancement of relationships with customers is great and an opportunity the library will take up eagerly. Specifically, the library will also be looking to expand its expertise in processes for engaging with customers through partnerships with the staff in these functional areas. The challenges and barriers have been clearly defined previously. The library has commenced its journey, beyond its traditional library role, to support the organisation's knowledge management approach. The initiatives that have contributed to this reorientation have also been described. Future directions for the library that will build on these initiatives, at least in the short term, are:

— Establishment of a service delivery strategy that articulates the knowledge centre approach and shift to knowledge broker and enabling service including the building stakeholder and customer partnerships

- Development of improved processes for the mapping of future customer and organisational knowledge needs;
- Adopting reporting tools that measure the strategic and intangible benefits of library service delivery innovations, eg the Balanced Scorecard;
- Continuing reorientation of library culture to foster learning and knowledge for innovation within the library team;
- Participating as key partners in the KM program and initiatives to build the organisational knowledge base that captures both explicit and intangible knowledge.

Delivering and Preserving Information

Libraries have experienced a strong shift in focus over the past decade towards digital formats for information resources. In a growing number of libraries, there is now an attitude that user demands will be met through digital media and electronic dissemination as much as through paper-based media. Universities are investing to provide improved teaching and learning resources via digital media. Other institutions, including the British Library and the US Library of Congress, are developing large technical infrastructures. The implementation of technical infrastructure and the improvement of access to the digital world is seen as hugely important for regions such as Africa, which lacks overall investment in social economic growth, and Latin America, where development has been limited by the relatively lower economic status of the library. These shifts at the library or institutional level are a reflection of the macro economics of the global economy, which contains a much larger informational and digital element than ever before.

Today, many institutions have realised they must put in place information policies, services and technologies with a firmer long-term economic strategy than might previously have been considered. The business plan driving MIT's development of DSpace is one such example. DSpace is MIT Libraries' innovative institutional digital repository designed to manage, host, preserve and enable distribution of the scholarly output of MIT's faculty. There is a clear intent to roll out the DSpace model to many other institutions. Another major economic institutional issue is the long-term preservation of large documentary collections. Almost all libraries have to think about preservation in both analogue and digital worlds. Even if they do not themselves preserve materials, they need to be sure that some institutions are doing so if they are to direct their users to them.

The purchase of digital resources remains a difficult balancing act of apparently conflicting interests. Publishers want to retain and enhance profitability. Electronic availability of journals is not relieving the cost to libraries. Electronic journals are often treated as a value-added service, rather than a replacement technology. Thus the library budget appears to be shrinking for the same amount of information resource. Meanwhile, user demand for more digital content direct to desktops continues to grow. Purchase of a digital product is likely to mean less money for a paper-based one, and thus the balancing of costs against opportunity has arguably never been harder. As important as it is to monetise the increasing costs of print versus electronic journals, there are wider economic and international issues, such as information inequalities, that electronic journals can address given new pricing structures and the opportunities possible in the digital arena. Traditional publishing and distribution mechanisms do not deliver information products in an equitable way because a library in an economically developing country just cannot afford the same level of information provision as one in a rich country.

Digital resources, by breaking the relationship between the cost of production and distribution from that of intellectual property charges, offer an opportunity to deliver more equitable information services. To take advantage of the new economic possibilities of digital resources, the World Health Organisation has negotiated a deal with publishers of approximately 1000 leading medical and scientific journals to offer electronic subscriptions at 'free or deeply-reduced rates to institutions in the developing world' for an initial three-year period. It is clear this is an enormous information benefit to the developing world. It also offers economic benefits to all parties that are only possible in the digital arena. Digital distribution costs to the publishers are virtually nothing, but they gain significant market knowledge and customer loyalty in a new and developing world market. The opportunity for cooperation and central or consortia negotiation enables bodies, such as the World Health Organisation, to predict costs against significant benefits and to manage these effectively in a predictable way with easily apparent value.

6

Hypermedia

Multimedia presentations can make very powerful learning aids, and it would be a very useful facility if we could build multimedia presentations from the stored information. These presentations might be requested by some client, built at the library from the latest materials available, and then delivered to the site of learning. But who is to build these presentations? Librarians are certainly overworked, and anyway manual authoring of these presentations is not practical, except in special cases where the end value of the product is intrinsically high. Articles, books and multimedia presentations built in response to user queries would be good examples of the sort of value add that digital libraries can provide. We refer to them as bundles. There are two stages to the creation of a bundle; the first involves the user interacting with the user catalogue in order to specify the set of documents to bundle, and the second, the creation of the hypertext, is undertaken automatically.

In order to help locate suitable documents from the resource catalogue we are prototyping three tools. The first of these tools is the *classification tool,* which allows the user to view the classification hierarchy (e.g. Dewey Decimal) as a tree, and to select that sub-tree or branch which contains the set of documents to be placed in the intermediate results list. The second tool is the *attribute tool,* which is a form based query tool, which displays all the document attributes from the catalogue, and allows the user to specify the attributes of the set of documents to be placed in the intermediate results list.

These attributes are such items as the author, the title and keywords. The third tool is an *information retrieval tool* which allows the user to enter a free text query. The tool then locates that set of documents having the best match to the query, using an algorithm developed by Li based upon that suggested by Salton . The tool compares the frequency of terms in the query with the frequency of terms in the documents, as held in pre-prepared indexes.

At present this tool only works with text based documents, but we envisage that at a later date we will incorporate the results of work in the Multimedia Research Group in the area of media based content retrieval. Once the initial query has been made, a list of suitable documents will appear in the intermediate results list box. From this list, the user may elect to keep all, or a selection, of the documents retrieved.

Documents that are marked for keeping will appear in the final list of results, regardless of any subsequent queries. The user may now elect to refine the query, or add further results to the list. This is achieved by running any one of the query tools again, with a new query.

Automatic construction of hypertexts from a collection of linear documents is one of the holy grails of the hypermedia research community. However, when a document has explicit structure, it is usually possible to produce usable hypertexts automatically. Most work in the area has concentrated on using features such as tables of contents and indexes to construct the hypermedia links. In this case we have a much coarser grained table of contents, namely the library catalogue, and in place of indexes, we have attributes such as keywords. The hypertext system that we have used for these experiments has been Microcosm which has certain key advantages for acting as such an experimental workbench, not least because of the fact that it was developed at Southampton, so we have access to all its API's, but also because it supports multiple methods of locating information.

Microcosm produces hypertext applications which have a bias towards querying and information retrieval, rather than the simple "button pushing" hypertext that we have come to expect from some of the more popular authoring packages. This quality of hypertext lends itself to this application.

Microcosm: A Tool for Hypermedia Link

The first method of access to the information uses the *classification information*. This is the information that that is held in the Document Management System (DMS) and is almost exactly equivalent to the information that is held in a library catalogue. It contains the position(s) within the document hierarchy that the file will be located, and it contains all the attributes, such as title, author, date of creation, physical media type and keywords.

This information is very high quality, as it provides specific information about documents, and Microcosm provides tools for traversing the subject hierarchy, and for querying the documents by attributes such as keywords. The second method of access is *hypermedia link following*. It is generally supposed that hypermedia links are manually authored in order to indicate some relationship between the two items at each end of the link. Such links are of very high value, but creating them requires considerable manual effort. However, the Multimedia Research Group at Southampton always considered that the reduction of this effort, and the automation of link creation, was an important research issue. One of the earliest results of this research was the introduction of *generic links*, which are links with a fixed end point, but which may start at any point where the source object is located.

Typically this means any place where a particular text string is located. The third method of data access is text based information retrieval. The interface to this functionality requires the user to make a selection of text from some document, or else to type in some text, and then choose "compute links" from the menu. The information retrieval engine will consult its indexes, and return a list of documents with the most similar vocabulary to the query.

Academic libraries, in particular, are now generally highly computerised in their basic housekeeping processes and in presenting themselves via on-line public access catalogues (OPACs). One of the strengths of the traditional libraries is that many large collections of books and materials in other media are catalogued with great care and attention to bibliographic detail and accuracy using standard cataloguing rules such as Anglo-American Cataloguing Rules (AACR2). As Howard Rheingold points out 'Librarians and other specialists have a toolkit and syntax for dealing with well-known problems that people encounter in trying to make sense of large bodies of information. However even key libraries such as the Library of Congress are constantly having to review their strategies and approaches to alternative methods of cataloguing such as copy cataloguing and minimal cataloguing in order to dramatically bring down their backlogs.

On-line journal abstracting databases also traditionally provide very thorough bibliographic detail created by professional graduate level staff. The combination of a variety of materials from different sources may provide a variety of classification schemes and types of subject headings. These can be added to the bundle's hierarchies. Although at the document level the classification may not easily convey a sufficient level of separation, nevertheless it can be used in the way a library user traditionally browses a library shelf.

On the World Wide Web we see subject catalogues such as the WWW Virtual Library being developed to give a useful alternative way to access a huge amount of information. At the same time Internet Yellow Pages directories, while they become obsolete fairly quickly, still sell because they provide an overview of accessible items which is not yet so easily scanned from today's computer screen. The options for locating information are varied and different ones will suit different users at different times and also the same users at different levels of understanding.

The level of a item - who it is intended for- has less frequently been emphasised in the past. It may perhaps be highlighted by a pointer such as a treatment code or a readership category, but this may become more important in the future with the enormous volumes generated by both paper and electronic publication. The catalogue entries produced by the information specialist may give a degree of rigour to the information retrieval process. However, a multimedia bundle will frequently contain documents produced by and often further modified by the authors, particularly in the academic environment, which do not have the advantage of such in-depth indexing.

One way to compensate for this might simply be to provide or point to a glossary or dictionary which helps the searchers choose their terms. The linking mechanisms of Microcosm do, in any case, give considerable help in retrieving relevant items. Free text terms used by the author are often more up to date in style and therefore more akin to the searcher's own vocabulary. The art is in balancing the effort required versus the result, particularly as terminology can change dramatically as one moves forwards or backwards in time.

Collection Management Issues

The late twentieth century saw the beginning of the age of digital information in corporate archives, the creative arts, financial markets, medical information, and scholarship, among other venues. How the United States chooses to preserve and manage its digital information affects core issues in key industries-from medical textbook publishing to entertainment and to future scholarship in science, technology, and the arts and humanities. It profoundly affects how the future will come to know our present and is, therefore, integral to the nation's identity, now and to come.

In this terrain, the Library of Congress (LC) has chosen to open its investigations with a series of probes into six principal areas in which the LC faces collection-management issues: large Web sites, electronic books, electronic journals, digitally recorded sound, digital film, and digital television. The scope of the effort was defined to encompass material that is "born digital," that is, objects that have been created in digital form rather than converted from analog to digital.

Historic film or news footage may be embedded in a newly created digital educational project. Re-release of entertainment products partly or wholly in digital form, either as new editions of older works or as reused elements in an otherwise-new work, further blurs the distinction. The production process itself is not hermetically sealed analog or digital. "Materials collected or generated for a television show," wrote the team from the WGBH Educational Foundation, "may consist of a great threaded mesh of digital and analog components, so tightly bound together that, at any point in their life cycle, one may serve as surrogate for another."

A similar case can be made for radio broadcasts, and many persons in the recording industry agree that preservation of a digitally recorded sound product should include its packaging-the notes, artwork, and photograph of the artist, for example. Even on the Web, many sites offer digitised versions of print works; for this reason, archiving the Web itself can be seen as encompassing both born-digital and digitised materials. One publishing executive argued that "digital" should be thought of as a medium in which content was both created and made accessible to the public. However, another publisher cautioned that the distinction between "digitised" and "born digital" is very important because it relates to the concept of completeness, and that accompanying that concept are notions of "copies," "versions," and other ideas critical to managing works and their associated rights.

The notion of scope arose at many levels, from the definition of the object to the extent of the effort. Several people inside and outside the library community urged planners to consider the scope of the effort carefully, including such factors as what was selected for the collection (even if it were a single collection), its longevity (10, 100, or 1,000 years), and its purpose (preservation, limited access, or public access).

From a practical point of view, given the sizes of the resources, selection seems particularly important in film, television, and the Web. The Web is complicated by the fact that only part of it is publicly accessible and by unresolved issues over rights. It is not clear, for example, that a Web site may be "harvested" for purposes of preservation without the knowledge and permission of the various rights holders.

Several people in both the technical and the arts communities urged attention to "ephemera" as well as to "published" works (the definition of "publication" is being contested). Others believed the effort would do well to focus on published materials subject to copyright and to which the LC has a clear mandate.

A number of respondents in film, television, and sound noted that again, the distinction between publication and ephemera is blurred. For example, a historic radio broadcast that is captured by the listener may contain aural information that reflects its relatively poor reception at the time; retaining that quality goes to the traditional mandate of preserving the experience, which might not be reflected in the script or in a studio recording. Similarly, only a very small percentage of the material shot is actually used in the commercial release of a film, yet digital video disc (DVD) releases have provided new life for outtakes and other associated production materials.

The relative utility of material changes over the cultural life of a film or a performance; the first public release does not necessarily capture all of its aesthetic or future scholarly value. There is a substantial economic incentive, since enhancing a DVD release is one strategy for combating piracy. The notion of scope also surfaced at the level of the artifact or item.

Discussions of Web sites, e-books, e-journals, and digital television make clear the difficulty of drawing boundaries among these items. Within the Web itself are emerging distinctions between the "surface" Web and the "deep" Web. E-books and e-journals download content from the Web to their respective formats and include hyperlinks to the Web for ancillary augmentation.

The advent of interactive television also invites new forms of multimedia that combine resources built for the Web with those created for broadcasting in digital form. Moreover, an item that appears seamless to the user is frequently a composite document. Formats as well understood as electronic scholarly journals are built as multimedia objects in which the constituent elements may include text, images, animation, or advertisements, each of which may be encoded in a different format.

Finally, several people from the arts communities emphasized the importance of collecting the version of the object that the creator (e.g., the director of a film) considered final in the format that he or she considered final. There are complexities to notions of "authorship"; many of these are not new to digital but are magnified by the circumstances under which digital products may be distributed and used. These complexities are related to the complicated intellectual property considerations that surround digital information. Even in a format as carefully studied as is that of electronic scholarly journals, creation and deposit can involve numerous stakeholders, and the number of interested parties multiplies in sound, television, and film, in which individuals and entities have traditionally had rights in the processes of creation and distribution.

Frank Romano points out that the e-books world is witnessing changes in traditional roles and functions; for example, writers can self-publish and thus become distributors, while software companies can behave like publishers. Similar shifts and realignments can be seen in some metadata discussions, where, as Peter Lyman notes, both computer scientists and librarians are putting forth different yet overlapping views of how the systems might work.

Technical Issues in Long-term Storage

One of the technical experts cautioned planners not to "underestimate" the importance of and differences among formats. There was, nonetheless, a consensus around the basic issues, if not necessarily around solutions. The issues, which include technical obsolescence and standards, metadata, information security, and the overall architecture of the system, are by no means discrete.

Standards affect creation as well as preservation. As one scholar of film and new media pointed out, the evolution of his organisation's Web site represented a patchwork of changing and evolving standards. Several writers pointed out that the issue is not only making sure that bits survive but also ensuring the preservation of a technical environment that will permit future retrieval of the information, the work as envisioned by the author or creator, and the experience of the user. The longevity of the storage medium was a consistent concern, as was signal degradation and software obsolescence.

One technical expert urged that degradation be compared with the process by which a photograph ages. The image fades; the medium on which the image is printed also disintegrates. There are methods for error detection; however, at some point, there is concern that the integrity of the digital object is compromised. One solution is migration from one medium to another. When a digital work is migrated, perhaps in very short order given the rapid development of the technology, what is the original work? In the case of recorded sound, would improvements to fidelity resulting from more sophisticated software technology compromise the integrity of the original, since it is no longer truly the artist's treatment of a work and misrepresents the recording technology of the time? At least one technical expert did not consider this to be a serious problem but did acknowledge that the rules for the successive formats must be retained.

On the other hand, the team from the WGBH Educational Foundation noted that while standard archival practices call for refreshing the data through migration and emulation, these strategies might be inadequate for "handling the intricacies, interdependencies, and sheer volume of television content." For film and television, this has resulted in attention to selection and collection policies inside traditional libraries as well as other organisations and has highlighted the importance of metadata as a management tool. Playback-usually associated with the equipment or software that enables users to re-create the performance of a film, for example-was seen to be a particular problem for e-books as well as for digitally recorded sound and film. Certain early tapes are no longer accessible because the equipment to read them no longer exists or is hard to find. Playback affects any effort to enable future users to re-create the work (however defined) as it was originally experienced.

Issues associated with playback can be expanded to operating systems, browsers, and so on. Solutions vary from emulation to maintaining collections of relevant hardware and software so that an archive or archiving system of digital content can imply preservation of certain kinds of equipment as well. Particularly for e-books, where so much of the design is predicated on screen size, re-creating the experience for future users implies access to the device that was intended to display the content.

The rapid obsolescence of some formats, as well as the plethora of standards, was widely considered to be a barrier both to creation and to preservation. Those who had opinions on open versus proprietary standards favored the former because they were believed to facilitate management of the archive and its content. This applies to a broad range of issues, from operating systems to markup language, compression, and fonts. Before September 11, 2001, few people consulted had strong opinions on information security, but those who did thought that it was important as a guarantor of trust.

One technical expert did not see the information security needs of an archive as being different from its general needs, or that, for example, the mission of the archive added a layer of concern. One example that was offered was the information typically provided on copyright registration concerning the authors, who might use a pseudonym or who might wish to keep their own addresses, or the addresses of their agents, from general use. There are overlaps between this kind of information and the information included in metadata. At least one person cautioned against excessive restriction, arguing that too many restrictions inhibit accountability. Those who addressed technical issues tended to favor distributed rather than centralised systems, because the former would accommodate a high degree of "local" variation within shared protocols.

There were also calls for interoperability, which would make it possible for information to be shared across platforms and among vendors. Two architectural approaches were set forth: one for e-journals, which has been fleshed out in some detail, and a more rudimentary approach that looks at the problem of preservation from a broad perspective in which the LC is one of many entities that might be involved. But, as one technical expert noted, the technology is likely to be developed outside of the traditional library community by other interests. The LC has an important role as "stimulator of initiatives and a consumer of successful technologies," but it does not have the money or expertise to dictate an outcome.

Metadata, or "data about data," are simultaneously a standard, a management and access tool, and a feature of the system architecture. Moreover, as pointed out by Lyman in his study of archiving the Web, the metadata discussions reveal the different visions of archiving as embodied by the library and computer science communities. He writes, "The librarian tends to look at the content of the Web page as the object to be described and preserved. The computer scientist tends to look at the Web as a technology for linking information, thus looks at the Web as a system of relationships." One of the functions of metadata, as the various schemes have evolved since 1995, is outlining the terms and conditions of use-that is, access.

Few failed to identify intellectual property rights (IPR) management and fair use as key issues. The complexity of this set of issues varies across media. Thus, questions of international law hang heavily over the Web and any products that are distributed through the Web, while changing perceptions of who is or is not a public figure and the layered rights associated with recorded sound, film, and television figure prominently in discussions of those formats. Some arose from unfamiliarity with the distinction that is common among traditional preservation circles in which use of rare objects, for example, can be calibrated and surrogates used in their stead.

Finally, there is an inherent tension in the entertainment and publishing industries: the value of a digital asset lies in providing access to it, but unauthorised access and duplication can reduce its value. While there was near unanimity on the importance of managing intellectual property responsibly, no voices called for some version of complete lockout. Indeed, one representative from a major company with interests in several areas thought that the most important issues were both protection of intellectual property rights and ease of use. There was widespread acknowledgment of the need to find a balance between the economic needs of the creators and distributors and the legitimate uses of the works, but there was a range of opinion as to what that meant.

Some suggested ways to handle management of intellectual property "behind the scenes" through technological means, which could be coupled with pricing that discouraged inappropriate use. Other proposals revolved around ways to use time, such as restricting access on the basis of estimates of time during which the owner expected to extract the economic value. However, product cycles of reuse would complicate that approach. Several people felt that existing laws were sufficient: what is required, they maintained, is appropriate enforcement. Others believed that there was a need to clarify the law.

Given that the Web is an international phenomenon, attention to international law is particularly important. As of this writing, terms such as "copy," "publication," "performance," and "public figure," whose definitions were once widely agreed on, had become subject to discussion.

Still others pointed to misperceptions that were clouding the discussion in several contradictory ways: people think that information in digital form has both more value and far less value than does information in analog form. A number of people, particularly in the film and entertainment industries, noted that the inflamed environment in which the discussions are taking place makes reasonable attempts at compromise very difficult.

Several people pointed out that copyright as a mechanism, which had arisen in the context of print, had already begun to fray under the stress of its application to media other than text, and that it was becoming increasingly unwieldy. In film, the multiplicity of rights and permissions that affect distribution and reuse of material had derailed educational projects because it was simply impossible to unravel the layers. Recorded sound has similar layers of rights.

Retrospective conversion of printed documents into digital forms is an increasingly necessary and desirable task facing those building digital libraries. Networked access technologies like the World Wide Web (WWW) allow remote use of digital collections and a variety of new methodologies for interaction and manipulation. Digital conversion efforts along these lines are becoming commonplace, with hundreds of projects underway around the world to capture existing printed monographs, serials, and special-format items with digital technologies. Digital imaging technology is inexpensive and can provide high resolution and color representations, but images cannot by themselves be indexed or rapidly searched for content.

7 Electronic Texts

Today the authors have tended to concentrate on those types of electronic text which, to a greater or lesser extent, represent a transcription of a non-electronic source, rather than the category of electronic texts which are primarily composed of digitised images of a source text. However, there are a growing number of electronic textual resources which support both these approaches; for example some projects involving the digitisation of rare illuminated manuscripts combine high-quality digital images with electronic text transcriptions. Creating and processing electronic texts was one of the earliest areas of computational activity, and has been going on for at least half a century.

When combined with an intimate knowledge of the non-electronic source material, readers should be able to decide for themselves which approach—and thus which combinations of hardware and software, techniques and design philosophy—will be most appropriate to their needs and the needs of any other prospective users. Although every functional aspect of computers is based upon the distinctive binary divide evidenced between 1's and 0's, true and false, presence and absence, it is rarely so easy to draw such clear distinctions at the higher levels of creating and documenting electronic texts. Readers should not assume that any course of action recommended here will necessarily be the 'best' approach in any or all given circumstances; however everything the authors say is based upon our understanding of what constitutes good practice—and results from almost twenty-five years of experience running the Oxford Text Archive. Conversely, if you are hoping to produce an electronic text that will have broad functionality and appeal, and the original source contains presentational features which might be considered worthy of note, then you should be attempting to create a very different object - perhaps one where visual fidelity is more important than the absolute accuracy of any transcription.

Deciding to create an electronic text is just like deciding to begin any other type of construction project. While the desire to dive right in and begin building is tempting, any worthwhile endeavour will begin with a thorough planning stage. In the case of digitised text creation, this stage is called document analysis. Document analysis is literally the task of examining the physical object in order to acquire an understanding about the work being digitised and to decide what the purpose and future of the project entails. The digitisation of texts is not simply making groups of words available to an online community; it involves the creation of an entirely new object. This is why achieving a sense of what it is that you are creating is critical. The blueprint for construction will allow you to define the foundation of the project. It will also allow you to recognise any problems or issues that have the potential to derail the project at a later point. Document analysis is all about definition - defining the document context, defining the document type and defining the different document features and relationships. At no other point in the project will you have the opportunity to spend as much quality time with your document. This is when you need to become intimately acquainted with the format, structure, and content of the texts.

One of the first tasks to perform in document analysis is to define the goals of the project and the context under which they are being developed. This could be seen as one of the more difficult tasks in the document analysis procedure, as it relies less upon the physical analysis of the document and more upon the theoretical positions taken with the project. This is the stage where you need to ask yourself why the document is being encoded. It is also important to take into consideration the external influences on the project. Often the bodies that oversee digitisation projects, either in a funding or advisory capacity, have specific conditions that must be fulfilled. They might for example have markup requirements or standards (linguistic, TEI/SGML, or EAD perhaps) that must be taken into account when establishing an encoding methodology.

Also, if you are creating the electronic text for scholarly purposes, then it is very likely that the standards of this community will need to be adhered to. Again, it must be remembered that the electronic version of a text is a distinct object and must be treated as such. Just as you would adhere to a publishing standard of practice with a printed text, so must you follow the standard for electronic texts.

The most stringent scholarly community, the textual critics and bibliographers, will have specific, established guidelines that must be considered in order to gain the requisite scholarly authority. Therefore, if you were creating a text to be used or approved by this community their criteria would have to be integrated into the project standards, with the subsequent influence on both the objectives and the creative process taken into account.

If the digitisation project includes image formats, then there are specific archiving standards held by the electronic community that might have to be met—this will not only influence the purchase of hardware and software, but will have an impact on the way in which the electronic object will finally be structured.

External conditions are easily overlooked during the detailed analysis of the physical object, so be sure that the standards and policies that influence the outcome of the project are given serious thought, as having to modify the documents retrospectively can prove both detrimental and expensive.

While you cannot satisfy each desire, trying to evaluate what information might be the most important to your audience will allow you to address the needs and concerns you deem most appropriate and necessary. Also, if there are specific objectives that you wish users to derive from the project then this too needs to be established at the outset. If the primary purpose for the texts is as a teaching mechanism, then this will have a significant influence on how you choose to encode the document.

Conversely, if your texts are being digitised so that users will be able to perform complex thematic searches, then both the markup of content and the content of the markup will differ somewhat. Regardless of the decision, be sure that the outcome of this evaluation becomes integrated with the previously determined project objectives.

You must also attempt to assess what tools users will have at their disposal to retrieve your document. The hardware and software capabilities of your users will differ, sometimes dramatically, and will most likely present some sort of restriction or limitation upon their ability to access your project. SGML encoded text requires the use of specialised software, such as Panorama, to read the work.

Even HTML has tagsets that early browsers may not be able to read. It is essential that you take these variants into consideration during the planning stage. There might be priorities in the project that require accessibility for all users, which would affect the methodology of the project. However, don't let the user limitations stunt the encoding goals for the document.

Hardware and software are constantly being upgraded so that although some of the encoding objectives might not be fully functional during the initial stages of the project, they stand a good chance of becoming accessible in the near future.

The first stage of document analysis is not only necessary for detailing the goals and objectives of the project, but also serves as an opportunity to examine the context of the document. This is a time to gather as much information as possible about the documents being digitised.

The amount gathered varies from project to project, but in an ideal situation you will have a complete transmission and publication history for the document. There are a few key reasons for this. Firstly, knowing how the object being encoded was created will allow you to understand any textual variations or anomalies. This, in turn, will assist in making informed encoding decisions at later points in the project.

The difference between a printer error and an authorial variation not only affects the content of the document, but also the way in which it is marked up. Secondly, the depth of information gathered will give the document the authority desired by the scholarly community. A text about which little is known can only be used with much hesitation.

While some users might find it more than acceptable for simply printing out or reading, there can be no authoritative scholarly analysis performed on a text with no background history. Thirdly, a quality electronic text will have a TEI header attached. The TEI header records all the information about the electronic text's print source. The more information you know about the source, the more full and conclusive your header will be—which will again provide scholarly authority.

Lastly, understanding the history of the document will allow you to understand its physicality. The physicality of the text is an interesting issue - and one on which very few scholars fully agree. Clearly, an understanding of the physical object provides a sense of the format, necessary for a proper structural encoding of the text, but it also augments a contextual understanding.

While the physical object has trained readers to follow a more linear narrative, the electronic document will provide you with an opportunity to develop the variant branches found within the text. Depending upon the decided project objectives, you are free to highlight, augment or furnish your users with as many different associations as you find significant in the text. Yet to do this, you must fully understand the ontology of the texts and then be able to delineate this textuality through the encoding of the computerised object. It is important to remember that the transmission history does not end with the publication of the printed document. Tracking the creation of the electronic text, including the revision history, is a necessary element of the encoding process. The fluidity of electronic texts precludes the guarantee that every version of the document will remain in existence, so the responsibility lies with the project creator to ensure that all revisions and developments are noted. While some of the documentation might seem tedious, an electronic transmission history will serve two primary purposes.

One, it will help keep the project creator(s) aware of what has developed in the creation of the electronic text. If there are quite a few staff members working on the documents, you will be able to keep track of what has been accomplished with the texts and to check that the project methodology is being followed. Two, users of the documents will be able to see what emendations or regularisations have been made and to track what the various stages of the electronic object were.

Defining the document type is a critical part of the digitisation process as it establishes the foundation for the initial understanding of the text's structure. At this point you should have an idea of what documents are going to be digitised for the project. Even if you not sure precisely how many texts will be in the final project, it is important to have a representative sample of the types of documents being digitised.

Examine the sample documents and decide what categories they fall under. The structure and content of a letter will differ greatly from that of a novel or poem, so it is critical to make these naming classifications early in the process. Not only are there structural differences between varying document types but also within the same type.

Deciding upon document type will give you an initial sense of the shape of the text. There are basic structural assumptions that come with classification: looking for the stanzas in poetry or the paragraphs in prose for example. Having established the document type, you can begin to assign the texts a more detailed structure. Without worrying about the actual tag names, as this comes later in the process, label all of the features you wish to encode.

For example, if you are digitising a novel, you might initially break it into large structural units: title page, table of contents, preface, body, back matter, etc. Once this is done you might move on to smaller features: titles, heads, paragraphs, catchwords, pagination, plates, annotations and so forth. One way to keep the naming in perspective is to create a structure outline. This will allow you to see how the structure of your document is developing, whether you have omitted any necessary features, or if you have labelled too much.

Once the features to be encoded have been decided upon, the relationships between them can then be examined. Establishing the hierarchical sequence of the document should not be too arduous a task—especially if you have already developed a structural outline. It should at this point be apparent, if we stick with the example of a novel, that the work is contained within front matter, body matter, and back matter.

Within front matter we find such things as epigraphs, prologues, and title pages. Within the paragraphs can be found quotations, figures, and notes. This is an established and understandable hierarchy. There is also a sequential relationship where one element logically follows another.

Using the above representation, if every body has chapters, paragraphs, and notes, then you would expect to find a sequence of <chapter> then <paragraph> then <note>, not <chapter>, <note>, then <paragraph>. Again, the more you understand about the type of text you are encoding, the easier this process will be. While the level of structural encoding will ultimately depend upon the project objectives, this is an opportune time to explore the form of the text in as much detail as possible.

Having these data will influence later encoding decisions, and being able to refer to these results will be much easier than having to sift through the physical object at a later point to resolve a structural dilemma. The analysis also brings to light any issues or problems with the physical document. Are parts of the source missing? Perhaps the text has been water damaged and certain lines are unreadable? If the document is a manuscript or letter perhaps the writing is illegible? These are all instances that can be explored at an early stage of the project.

While these problems will add a level of complexity to the encoding project, they must be dealt with in an honest fashion. If the words of a letter are illegible and you insert text that represents your best guess at the actual wording then this needs to be encoded. The beauty of document analysis is that by examining the documents prior to digitisation you stand a good chance of recognising these issues and establishing an encoding methodology.

The benefit of this is threefold: firstly, having identified and dealt with this problem at the start you will have fewer issues arise during the digitisation process; secondly, there will be an added level of consistency during the encoding stage and retrospective revision won't be necessary; thirdly, the project will benefit from the thorough level of accuracy desired and expected by the scholarly community.

This is also a good time to examine the physical document and attempt to anticipate problems with the digitisation process. Fragile spines, flaking or foxed paper, badly inked text, all will create difficulties during the scanning process and increase the likelihood of project delays if not anticipated at an early stage. This is another situation that requires examining representative samples of texts.

It could be that one text was cared for in the immaculate conditions of a Special Collections facility while another was stored in a damp corner of a bookshelf. You need to be prepared for as many document contingencies as possible. Problems not only arise out of the condition of the physical object, but also out of such things as typography. OCR digitisation is heavily reliant upon the quality and type of fonts used in the text.

OCR software is optimised for laser quality printed text. This means that the older the printed text, the more degradation in the scanning results. These types of problems are critical to identify, as decisions will have to be made about how to deal with them - decisions that will become a significant part of the project methodology.

The final stage of document analysis is deciding which features of the text to encode. Once again, knowing the goals and objectives of the project will be of great use as you try to establish the breadth of your element definition. You have the control over how much of the document you want to encode, taking into account how much time and manpower are dedicated to the project.

Once you've made a decision about the level of encoding that will go into the project, you need to make the practical decision of what to tag. There are three basic categories to consider: structure, format and content. In terms of structure there are quite a few typical elements that are encoded. This is a good time to examine the structural outline to determine what skeletal features need to be marked up.

In most cases, the primary divisions of text - chapters, sections, stanzas, etc.—and the supplementary parts—paragraphs, lines, pages—are all assigned tag names. With structural markup, it is helpful to know how detailed an encoding methodology is being followed. As you will discover, you can encode almost anything in a document, so it will be important to have established what level of markup is necessary and to then adhere to those boundaries.

Some of the common elements relate to attributes such as bold, italic and typeface. Then there are other aspects that take a bit more thought, such as special characters. Format issues also include notes and annotations (items that figure heavily in scholarly texts), marginal glosses, and indentations. Elements of format are easily forgotten, so be sure to go through the representative documents and choose the visual aspects of the text that must be carried through to the electronic object.

The third encoding feature concerns document content. This is where you will go through the document looking for features that are neither structural nor format based. This is the point where you can highlight the content information necessary to the text and the user. Refer back to the decisions made about textual relationships and what themes and ideas should be highlighted.

If, for example, you are creating a database of author biographies you might want to encode such features as author's name, place of birth, written works, spouse, etc.

Having a clear sense of the likely users of the project will make these decisions easier—and perhaps more straightforward. This is also a good time to evaluate what the methodology will be for dealing with textual revisions, deletions, and additions—either authorial or editorial.

Again, it is not so critical here to define what element tags you are using but rather to arrive at a listing of features that need to be encoded. Once these steps have been taken you are ready to move on to the digitisation process.

Digitisation - Scanning, OCR, and Re-keying

Digitisation is quite simply the creation of a computerised representation of a printed analog. There are many methods of digitising and varied media to be digitised. Digitising other formats, audio and video for example, there are many thorough analyses of procedure. In other words, recommendations for digitising are constantly changing. As hardware and software develop, so does the quality of digitised output. The price cuts in storage costs allow smaller projects to take advantage of archival imaging standards. The digitisation chain is a concept expounded by Peter Robinson in his aforementioned publication. The idea is based upon the fundamental concept that the best quality image will result from digitising the original object. If this is not an attainable goal, then digitisation should be attempted with as few steps removed from the original as possible. Therefore, the chain is composed of the number of intermediates that come between the original object and the digital image - the more intermediates, the more links in the chain. Each link attains a level of importance so that if one piece of the chain were to break, the entire project would fail. Regardless of the technology utilised by the project, the results will depend, first and foremost, on the quality of the image being scanned. Scanning a copy of a microfilm of an illustration originally found in a journal is acceptable if it is the only option you have, but clearly scanning the image straight from the journal itself is going to make an immeasurable difference in quality.

This is one important reason for carefully choosing the hardware and software. If you know that you are dealing with fragile manuscripts that cannot handle the damaging light of a flatbed scanner, or a book whose binding cannot open past a certain degree, then you will probably lean towards a digital camera. If you have text that is from an 18th-century book, with fading pages and uneven type, you will want the best text scanning software available. Knowing where your documents stand in the digitisation chain will influence the subsequent imaging decisions you will make for the project. The first step in digitisation, both text and image, is to obtain a workable facsimile of the page. To accomplish this you will need a combination of hardware and software imaging tools. This is a somewhat difficult area to address in terms of recommending specific product brands, as what is considered industry (or at least the text creation industry) standard is subject to change as technology develops.

There are quite a few methods of image capture that are used within the humanities community. The equipment ranges from scanners (flatbed, sheetfed, drum, slide, microfilm) to high-end digital cameras. In terms of standards within the digitising community, the results are less than satisfactory. Projects tend to choose the most available option, or the one that is affordable on limited grant funding. However, two of the most common and accessible image capture solutions are flatbed scanners and high-resolution digital cameras. Flatbed scanners have become the most commonplace method for capturing images or text. Their name comes from the fact that the scanner is literally a flat glass bed, quite similar to a copy machine, on which the image is placed face down and covered. The scanner then passes light-sensitive sensors over the illuminated page, breaking it into groups of pixel-sised boxes. It then represents each box with a sero or a one, depending on whether the pixel is filled or empty.

The importance of this becomes more apparent with the discussion of image type below. As a result of their lowering costs and widespread availability, the use of quality flatbeds ranges from the professional digital archiving projects to the living rooms of the home computer consumer. One benefit of this increased use and availability is that flatbed scanning technology is evolving continually. This has pushed the purchasing standards away from price and towards quality. In an attempt to promote the more expensive product, the marketplace tends to hype resolution and bit-depth, two aspects of scanning that are important to a project but are not the only concerns when purchasing hardware. While it is not necessarily the case that you need to purchase the most expensive scanner to get the best quality digital image, it is unlikely that the entry-level flatbeds will provide the image quality that you need. However, while it used to be the case that to truly digitise well you needed to purchase the more high-end scanner, at a price prohibitive to most projects, the advancing digitising needs of users have pushed hardware developers to create mid-level scanners that reach the quality of the higher range. As a consumer, you need to possess a holistic view of the scanner's capabilities. Not only should the scanner provide you with the ability to create archival quality images but it should also make the digitisation process easier. Many low-cost scanners do not have high-grade lenses, optics, or light sources, thereby creating images that are of a very poor quality. The creation of superior calibre images relates to the following hardware requirements:

— the quality of the lens, mirrors, and other optics hardware;

— the mechanical stability of the optical system;

— the focal range and stability of the optical system;

— the quality of the scanning software and many other hardware and software features.

Also, many of the better quality scanners contain tools that allow you to automate some of the procedures. This is extremely useful with such things as colour and contrast where, with the human eye, it is difficult to achieve the exact specification necessary for a high-quality image. Scanning hardware has the ability to provide this discernment for the user, so these intelligent automated features are a necessity to decrease task time. One of the disadvantages of a flatbed scanner is that to capture the entire image the document must lie completely flat on the scanning bed. With books this poses a problem because the only way to accomplish this is to bend the spine to the breaking point. It becomes even worse when dealing with texts with very fragile pages, as the inversion and pressure can cause the pages to flake away or rip.

A solution to this problem, one taken up by many digital archives and special collections departments, is to digitise with a stand-alone digital camera. Digital cameras are by far the most dependable means of capturing quality digital images. The ability to digitise with variant lighting is a significant benefit as it won't damage the make-up of the work, a precaution which cannot be guaranteed with flatbed scanners. The high resolution and heightened image quality allows for a level of detail you would expect only in the original. As a result of these specifications, images can be delivered at great sise. A good example of this is the Early American Fiction project being developed at UVA's Electronic Text Center and Special Collections Department. The Early American Fiction project, whose goal is the digitisation of 560 volumes of American first editions held in the UVA Special Collections, is utilising digital cameras mounted above light tables. They are working with camera backs manufactured by Phase One attached to Tarsia Technical Industries Prisma 45 4x5 cameras on TTI

Reprographic Workstations. This has allowed them to create high quality images without damaging the physical objects. As they point out in their overview of the project, the workflow depends upon the text being scanned, but the results work out to close to one image every three minutes.

While this might sound detrimental to the project timeline, it is relatively quick for an archival quality image. The images can be seen at such a high-resolution that the faintest pencil annotations can be read on-screen. There are a few tools that are commonly seen in use with many digitisation projects. Regardless of the brand of software purchased, the project will need text scanning software if there is to be in-house digitisation of text and an image manipulation software package if imaging is to be done. There are a wide variety of text scanning softwares available, all with varying capabilities. As this software is optimised for laser quality printouts, projects working with texts from earlier centuries need to find a package that has the ability to work through more complicated fonts and degraded page quality. While there is no standard, most projects work with Caere's OmniPage scanning software. In terms of image manipulation, there are more choices depending upon what needs to be done.

For image-by-image manipulation, including converting TIFFs to web-deliverable JPEGs and GIFs, Adobe Photoshop is the more common selection. However, when there is a move towards batch conversion, Graphic's DeBabelizer Pro is known for its speed and high quality. If the conversion is being done in a UNIX environment, the XV operating system is also a favourite amongst digitisation projects. Electronic text creation primarily involves the digitisation of text and images. Apart from re-keying, the best method of digitising text is Optical Character Recognition (OCR). This process is accomplished through the utilisation of scanning hardware in conjunction with text scanning software. OCR takes a scanned image of a page and converts it into text. Similarly, image capture also requires an image scanning software to accompany the hardware. However, unlike text scanning, image capture has more complex requirements in terms of project decisions and, like almost everything else in the digitisation project, benefits from clearly thought out objectives. The first decision that must be made regarding image capture concerns the purpose of the images being created. The reason for this is simple: the higher quality the image need be, the higher the settings necessary for scanning. There are four main types of images: 1-bit black and white, 8-bit greyscale, 8-bit colour and 24-bit colour. A bit is the fundamental unit of information read by the computer, with a single bit being represented by either a '0' or a '1'. A '0' is considered an absence and a '1' is a presence, with more complex representations of information being accommodated by multiple or gathered bits.

A 1-bit black and white image means that the bit can either be black or white. This is a rarely used type and is completely unsuitable for almost all images. The only amenable image for this format would be printed text or line graphics for which poor resulting quality did not matter. Another drawback of this type is that saving it as a JPEG compressed image—one of the most prevalent image formats on the web—is not a feasible option. 8-bit greyscale images are an improvement from 1-bit as they encompass 256 shades of grey. It is often used for non-colour images and provides a clear image rather than the resulting fuzz of a 1-bit scan. While greyscale images are often considered more than adequate, there are times when non-colour images should be scanned at a higher colour because the finite detail of the hand will come through distinctly.

Also, the consistent recommendation is that images that are to be considered preservation or archival copies should be scanned as 24-bit colour. 8-bit colour is similar to 8-bit greyscale with the exception that each bit can be one of

256 colours. The decision to use 8-bit colour is completely project dependent, as the format is appropriate for web page images but can come out somewhat grainy. Another factor is the type of computer the viewer is using, as older ones cannot handle an image above 8-bit, so it will convert a 24-bit image to the lower format. However, the factor to take into consideration here is primarily storage space. An 8-bit image, while not having the quality of a higher format, will be markedly smaller. If possible, 24-bit colour is the best scanning choice.

This option provides the highest quality image, with each bit having the potential to contain one of 16.8 million colours. The arguments against this image format are the size, cost and time necessary. Again, knowing the objectives of the project will assist in making this decision. If you are trying to create archival quality images, this is taken as the default setting. 24-bit colour makes the image look more photo-realistic, even if the original is greyscale. The thing to remember with archival quality imaging is that if you need to go back and manipulate the image in any way, it can be copied and adjusted. However, if you scan the image as a lesser format then any kind of retrospective adjustments will be impossible. While a 24-bit colour archived image can be made greyscale, an 8-bit greyscale image cannot be converted into millions of colours.

The second concern relates to the resolution of the image. The resolution is determined by the number of dots per inch (dpi). The more dots per inch in the file, the more information is being stored about the image. Again, this choice is directly related to what is being done with the image. If the image is being archived or will need to be enlarged, then the resolution will need to be relatively higher. If, when using an imaging software program, you click on the 'save as' function to finalise the capture, you will see that there are quite a few image formats to choose from. In terms of text creation there are three types fundamental to the process: TIFF, JPEG, and GIF. These are the most common image formats because they transfer to almost any platform or software system.

TIFF (Tagged Image File Format) files are the most widely accepted format for archival image creation and retention as master copy. More so than the following formats, TIFF files can be read by almost all platforms, which also makes it the best choice when transferring important images. Most digitisation projects begin image scanning with the TIFF format, as it allows you to gather as much information as possible from the original and then saves these data. This touches on the only disadvantage of the TIFF format - the size of the image. However, once the image is saved, it can be called up at any point and be read by a computer with a completely different hardware and software system. Also, if there exists any possibility that the images will be modified at some point in the future, then the images should be scanned as TIFFs.

JPEG (Joint Photographic Experts Group) files are the strongest format for web viewing and transfer through systems that have space restrictions. JPEGs are popular with image creators not only for their compression capabilities but also for their quality. While a TIFF is a lossless compression, JPEGs are a lossy compression format. This means that as a filesize condenses, the image loses bits of information. However, this does not mean that the image will markedly decrease in quality. If the image is scanned at 24-bit, each dot has the choice of 16.8 million colours - more than the human eye can actually differentiate on the screen. So with the compression of the file, the image loses the information least likely to be noticed by the eye. The disadvantage of this format is precisely what makes it so attractive - the lossy compression. Once an image is saved, the discarded information is lost. The implication of this is that the entire image, or certain parts of it, cannot be enlarged. Additionally, the more work done to the image, requiring it to be re-saved, the more information is lost. This is why JPEGs are not recommended for archiving - there is no way to retain all of the information scanned from the source. Nevertheless, in terms of viewing capabilities and storage size, JPEGs are the best method for online viewing.

GIF (Graphic Interchange Format) files are an older format that are limited to 256 colours. Like TIFFs, GIFs use a lossless compression format without requiring as much storage space. While they don't have the compression capabilities of a JPEG, they are strong candidates for graphic art and line drawings. They also have the capability to be made into transparent GIFs - meaning that the background of the image can be rendered invisible, thereby allowing it to blend in with the background of the web page. This is frequently used in web design but can have a beneficial use in text creation. There are instances, where it is possible that a text character cannot be encoded so that it can be read by a web browser. It could be inline images (a head-piece for example) or the character is not defined by ISOLAT1 or ISOLAT2.

TIFFs would not be used for online delivery, but if you want your images to have any future use, either for archiving, later enlarging, manipulation, or printing, or simply as a master copy, then there is no other format in which to store the images. In terms of online presentation, then JPEGs and GIFs are the best method. JPEGs will be of a better calibre and smaller filesize but cannot be enlarged or they will pixelate. Yet in terms of viewing quality their condition will almost match the TIFF. How you use GIFs will depend on what types of images are associated with the project. However, if you are making thumbnail images that link to a separate page which exhibits the JPEG version, then GIFs are a popular choice for that task. Preservation imaging is defined as 'high-speed, 1-bit (simple black and white) page images shot at 600 dpi and stored as Group 4 fax-compressed files'. The results of this are akin to microfilm imaging. While this does preserve the text for reading purposes, it ignores the source as a physical object. Archiving often presupposes that the objects are being digitised so that the source can be protected from constant handling, or as an international means of accessibility.

However, this type of preservation annihilates any chance of presenting the object as an artefact. Archiving an object has an entirely different set of requirements. Yet, having said this, there is also a prevalent school of thought in the archiving community that the only imaging that can be considered of archival value is film imaging, which is thought to last at least ten times as long as a digital image. Nonetheless, the idea of archival imaging is still discussed amongst projects and funding bodies and cannot be overlooked. There is no set standard for archiving, and you might find that different places and projects recommend another model. However, the following type, format and resolution are recommended:

— *24-bit*: There really is little reason to scan an archival image at anything less. Whether the source is colour or greyscale, the images are more realistic and have a higher quality at this level. As the above example shows, the filesize of the subsequently compressed image does not benefit from scanning at a lower bit-size.

— *600 dpi*: This is, once again, a problematic recommendation. Many projects assert that scanning in at 300 or 400 dpi provides sufficient quality to be considered archival. However, many of the top international digitisation centres recommend 600 dpi as an archival standard - it provides excellent detail of the image and allows for quite large JPEG images to be produced.

The only restrictive aspect is the filesize, but when thinking in terms of archival images you need to try and get as much storage space as possible. Remember, the master copies do not have to be held online, as offline storage on writeable CD-ROMs is another option.

— *TIFF*: This should come as no surprise given the format discussion above. TIFF files, with their complete retention of scanned information and cross-platform capabilities are really the only choice for archival imaging. The images maintain all of the information scanned from the source and are the closest digital replication available. The size of the file, especially when scanned at 24-bit, 600 dpi, will be quite large, but well worth the storage space. You won't be placing the TIFF image online, but it is simple to make a JPEG image from the TIFF as a viewing copy.

This information is provided with the caveat that scanning technology is constantly changing for the better. It is more than likely that in the future these standards will become passé, with higher standards taking their place. The goal of recognition technology is to re-create the text and, if desired, other elements of the page including such things as tables and layout. Refer back to the concept of the scanner and how it takes a copy of the image by replicating it with the patterns of bits - the dots that are either filled or unfilled. OCR technology examines the patterns of dots and turns them into characters. Depending upon the type of scanning software you are using, the resulting text can be piped into many different word processing or spreadsheet programs.

Caere OmniPage released version 10.0 in the Autumn of 1999, which boasts the new Predictive Optical Word Recognition Plus+ (POWR++) technology. As the OmniPage factsheet explains, POWR++ enables OmniPage Pro to recognise standard typefaces, without training, from 4 to 72 point sizes. POWR++ recognises 13 languages (Brazilian Portuguese, British English, Danish, Dutch, Finnish, French, German, Italian, Norwegian, Portuguese, Spanish, Swedish, and U.S English) and includes full dictionaries for each of these languages. However, OCR software programs (including OmniPage) are very up-front about the fact that their technology is optimised for laser printer quality text. The reasoning behind this should be readily apparent. As scanning software attempts to examine every pixel in the object and then convert it into a filled or empty space, a laser quality printout will be easy to read as it has very clear, distinct, characters on a crisp white background - a background that will not interfere with the clarity of the letters.

However, once books become the object type, the software capabilities begin to degrade. This is why the first thing you must consider if you decide to use OCR for the text source is the condition of the document to be scanned. If the characters in the text are not fully formed or there are instances of broken type or damaged plates, the software will have a difficult time reading the material. The implications of this are that late 19th and 20th-century texts have a much better chance of being read well by the scanning software. As you move further away from the present, with the differences in printing, the OCR becomes much less dependable. The changes in paper, moving from a bleached white to a yellowed, sometimes foxed, background creates noise that the software must sift through. Then the font differences wreak havoc on the recognition capabilities. The gothic and exotic type found in the hand-press period contrasts markedly with the computer-set texts of the late 20th century.

It is critical that you anticipate type problems when dealing with texts that have such forms as long esses, sloping descenders, and ligatures. Taking sample scans with the source materials will help pinpoint some of these digitising issues early on in the project. While the advantages of exporting text in different word processing formats are quite useful if you are scanning in a document to print or to compensate for an accidentally deleted file, there are a few issues that should take priority with the text creator. Assuming you are using a software program such as OmniPage, you should aim for a scan that retains some formatting but not a complete page element replication. In terms of text creation, and the long-term preservation of the digital object, you want to be able to control this markup. If possible, scanning at a setting that will retain font and paragraph format is the best option. Scanning at a mid-level of formatting will assist you if you have decided to use your own encoding.

Unfortunately for the text creator, there are still many situations where the documents or project preclude the use of OCR. If the text is of a poor or degraded quality, then it is quite possible that the time spent correcting the OCR mistakes will exceed that of simply typing in the text from scratch. The amount of information to be digitised also becomes an issue. Even if the document is of a relatively good quality, there might not be enough time to sit down with 560 volumes of texts (as with the Early American Fiction project) and process them through OCR. The general rule of thumb, and this varies from study to study, is that a best-case scenario would be three pages scanned per minute - this doesn't take into consideration the process of putting the document on the scanner, flipping pages, or the subsequent proofreading. If, when addressing these concerns, OCR is found incapable of handling the project digitisation, the viable solution is re-keying the text. Once you've made this decision, the next question to address is whether to handle the document in-house or out-source the work. Deciding to digitise the material in-house relies on having all the necessary hardware, software, staff, and time.

There are a few issues that come into play with in-house digitisation. The primary concern is the speed of re-keying. Most often the re-keying is done by the research assistants working on the project, or graduate students from the text creator's local department. The problem here is that paying an hourly rate to someone re-keying the text often proves more expensive than out-sourcing the material. Also, there is the concern that a single person typing in material tends to overlook keyboarding errors - and if the staff member is familiar with the source material, there is a tendency to correct automatically those things that seem incorrect. So while in-house digitisation is an option, these concerns should be addressed from the outset. Again, as with most steps in the text creation process, the answers to these questions will be project dependent. The decisions made for a project that plans to digitise a collection of works will be markedly different from those made by an academic who is creating an electronic edition.

It reflects back, as always, to the importance of the document analysis stage. You must recognise what the requirements of the project will be, and what external influences (especially staff size, equipment availability, and project funding) will affect the decision-making process.

Proprietary and Non-proprietary Markup Lanugage

As the name implies, presentational markup is concerned with the visual structure of a text. Depending upon what processing software is being used, the markup explains to the computer how the document should appear. So if the work should be seen in 12 point, Tahoma font, the software dictates a markup so that this happens. Presentational markup is concerned with structure only insofar as it relates to the visual aspect of the document. It does not care whether a heading is for a book, a chapter or a paragraph - the only consideration is how that heading should look on the page. Most proprietary language formats tend to focus solely on presentational issues. To move into descriptive markup would require that the software provide the document creator with the ability to formulate their own tags with which to encode the structure and presentation of the work. In other words, descriptive markup relates less to the visual strategy of the work and more to the reasons behind the structure. It allows the creator to encode the document with a markup that more clearly shows how the presentation, configuration, and content relate to the document as a whole. Once again, the beneficial effects of thorough document analysis can be seen. Having a holistic sense of the document, having the detailed listing of critical elements in the document, will exemplify how descriptive markup advances a project. In this case, a non-proprietary language will be the most beneficial, as it will allow the document creators to arrive at their own tagsets, providing a much needed level of control over the encoding development.

In 1985, Adobe Systems created a programming language for printers called PostScript. In so doing, they produced a system that allowed computers to 'talk' to their printers. This language describes for the printer the appearance of the page, incorporating elements like text, graphics, colour, and images, so that documents maintain their integrity through the transmission from computer to printer. PostScript printers have become industry standard with corporations, marketers, publishing companies, graphic designers, and more. Printers, slide recorders, imagesetters - all these output devices utilise PostScript technology. Combine this with PostScript's multiple operating system capability and it becomes clear why PostScript has become the standard for printing technology. PostScript language can be found in most printers - Epson, IBM, and Hewlett-Packard just to name a few - almost guaranteeing that a high standard of printing can be found in both the home and office.

Portable Document Format (PDF) was created by Adobe in 1993 to complement their PostScript language. PDF allows the user to view a document with a presentational integrity that almost resembles a scanned image of the source. This delivery of visually rich content is the most attractive use of PDF. The format is entirely concerned with keeping the document intact, and, to ensure this, allows any combination of text, graphics and images. It also has full, rich colour presentation and is therefore often used with corporate and marketing graphic arts materials. Another enticing feature, depending on the quality of the printer, is that when a PDF file is printed out, the hard copy output is an exact replication of the screen image. PDF is also desirable for its delivery strengths. Not only does the document maintain its visual integrity, but it also can be compressed. This compression eases on-line and CD-ROM transmission and assists its archiving opportunities. PDF files can be read through an Acrobat Reader application that is freely available for download via the web. This application is also capable of serving as a browser plug-in for online document viewing. Creating PDF files is a bit more complicated than the viewing procedure. To write a PDF document it is necessary to purchase Adobe software.

PDFWriter allows the user to create the PDF document, and the more expensive Adobe Capture program will convert TIFF files into PDF formatted text versions. If the user would like the document to become more interactive, offering the ability to annotate the document for example, then this functionality can be added with the additional purchase of Acrobat Exchange, which serves an editorial function. Exchange allows the user to annotate and edit the document, search across documents and also has plug-ins that provide highlighting ability.

HyperText Markup Language

HyperText Markup Language (or HTML as it is commonly known) is a non-proprietary format markup system used for publishing hypertext on the World Wide Web. To date, it has appeared in four main versions (1.0, 2.0, 3.2, 4.0), with the World Wide Web Consortium (W3C) recommending 4.0 as the markup language of choice. HTML is a derivative of

SGML - the Standard Generalised Markup Language. SGML allows you to create your own markup language but provides the rules necessary to ensure its processing and preservation. HTML is a successful implementation of the SGML concepts, and, as a result, is accessible to most browsers and platforms. Along with this, it is a relatively simple markup language to learn, as it has a limited tagset. HTML is by far the most popular web-publishing language, allowing users to create online text documents that include multimedia elements (such as images, sounds, and video clips), and then put these documents in an environment that allows for instant publication and retrieval.

There are many advantages to a markup language like HTML. As mentioned above, the primary benefit is that a document encoded with HTML can be viewed in almost any browser - an extremely attractive option for a creator who wants documents which can be viewed by an audience with varied systems. However, it is important to note that while the encoding can cross platforms, there are consistently differences in page appearance between browsers. While W3C recommends the usage of HTML 4.0, many of its features are simply not available to users with early versions of browsers. Unlike PDF which is extremely concerned with keeping the document and its format intact, HTML has no true sense of page structure and files can neither be saved nor printed with any sense of precision.

Besides the benefit of a markup language that crosses platforms with ease, HTML attracts its many users for the simple manner with which it can be mastered. For users who do not want to take the time to learn the tagset, the good news is that conversion-to-HTML tools are becoming more accessible and easier to use. For those who cannot even spare the time to learn how to use HTML-creation software, of which there are a limited quantity, they can sit down with any text creation program (Notepad for example) and author an HTML document. Then by using the 'Open File'; tool in a browser, the document can immediately be viewed.

In contrast, the concise guidelines to HTML that are available on-line (and usually as a "help" option from the menu of a Web client) are a good introduction to some of the basic SGML concepts. This is of real value to the user. The notion of marking up a text is quite often an overwhelming concept. Most people do not realise that markup enters into their life every time they make a keystroke in a word processing program. So for the uninitiated, HTML provides a manageable stepping-stone into the world of more complex encoding. Once this limited tagset is mastered, many users find the jump into an extended markup language less intimidating - and more liberating.

However, one of the drawbacks to this easy authoring language is that many of the online documents are created without a DTD. A DTD is the abbreviation for a document type definition, which outlines the formal specifications for an SGML encoded document. Basically, a DTD is the method for spelling out the SGML rules that the document is following. It sets the standards for what markup can be used and how this markup interacts with others. So, for example, if you create an HTML document with a specific software program, say HoTMetaL PRO, the resulting text will begin with a document type declaration stating which DTD is being used. As it stands now, web browsers require neither a DTD nor a document type declaration. Browsers are notoriously lax in their HTML requirements, and unless something serious is missing from the encoded document it will be successfully viewed through a Web client.

The impact of this is that while HTML provides a convenient and universal markup language for a user, many of the documents floating out in cyberspace are permeated with invalid code. The focus then moves away from authoring documents that conform to a set of encoding guidelines and towards the creation of works that can be viewed in a browser. This problem will become more severe with the increased use of Extensible Markup Language, or XML as it is more commonly known. This markup language, which is being lauded as the new lingua franca, combines the visual benefits of HTML with the contextual benefits of SGML/TEI. However, while XML will have the universality of HTML, the web clients will require a more stringent adherence to markup rules. While documents that comply with the rules of an HTML DTD will find the transition relatively simple, the documents that were constructed strictly with viewing in mind will require a good deal of clean up prior to conversion.

This is not to say that HTML is not a useful tool for creating online documents. As in the case of PostScript and PDF, the choice to use HTML should be document dependent. It is the perfect choice for static documents that will have a short shelf-life. If you are creating course pages or supplementary materials regarding specific readings that will not be necessary or available after the end of term, then HTML is an appropriate choice. If, however, you are concerned about presentational and structural integrity, the markup of document content and/or the long-term preservation of the text, then a user-definable markup language is a much better choice.

The late 1970s and early 1980s saw a consensus emerging that descriptive markup languages had numerous advantages over other types of text encoding. A number of products and macro languages appeared which were built around their own descriptive markup languages - and whilst these represented a step forward, they were also constrained by the fact that users were required to learn a new markup language each time, and could only describe those textual features which the markup scheme allowed (sometimes extensions were possible, but implementing them was rarely a straightforward process).

The International Standards Organisation (ISO) also recognised the value of descriptive markup schemes, and in 1986 an ISO committee released a new standard called ISO 8879, the Standard Generalised Markup Language (SGML). This complex document represented several years' effort by an international committee of experts, working together under the Chairmanship of Dr Charles Goldfarb (one of the creators of IBM's descriptive markup language, GML).

Since SGML was a product of the International Standards process, the committee also had the benefit of input from experts from the numerous national standards bodies associated with the ISO, such as the UK's British Standards Institute (BSI).

A great deal of largely unjustified mystique surrounds SGML. You do not have to look very hard to find instances of SGML being described as 'difficult to learn', 'complex to implement', or 'expensive to use', when in fact it is none of these things. People all too frequently confuse the acronym, SGML, with SGML applications - many of which are indeed highly sophisticated and complex operations, designed to meet the rigorous demands of blue chip companies working in major international industries (automotive, pharmaceutical, or aerospace engineering).

It should not be particularly surprising that a documentation system designed to control and support every aspect of the tens of thousands of pages of documentation needed to build and maintain a battleship, fix the latest passenger aircraft, or supplement a legal application for international recognition for a new advanced drug treatment, should appear overwhelmingly complex to an outsider.

In fact, despite its name, SGML is not even a markup language. Instead, it would be more appropriate to call SGML a 'metalanguage'. In a conventional markup language, such as HTML, users are offered a pre-defined set of markup tags from which they must make appropriate selections; if they suddenly introduce new tags which are not part of the HTML specification, then it is clear that the resulting document will not be considered valid HTML, and it may be rejected or incorrectly processed by HTML software (e.g. an HTML-compatible browser).

SGML, on the other hand, does not offer a pre-defined set of markup tags. Rather, it offers a grammar and specific vocabulary which can be used to define other markup languages (hence 'metalanguage'). SGML is not constrained to any one particular type of application, and it is neither more nor less suited to producing technical documentation and specifications in the semiconductor industry, than it is for marking up linguistic features of ancient inscribed tablets of stone.

In fact, SGML can be used to create a markup language to do pretty well anything, and that is both its greatest strength and weakness. SGML cannot be used 'out-of-the-box', so to speak, and because of this it has earned an undeserved reputation in some quarters as being troublesome and slow to implement. On the other hand, there are many SGML applications, which can be used straightaway, as they offer a fully documented markup language which can be recognised by any one of a suite of tools and implemented with a minimum of fuss.

SGML provides a mechanism for like-minded people with a shared concern to get together and define a common markup language which satisfies their needs and desires, rather than being limited by the vision of the designers of a closed, possibly proprietary markup scheme which only does half the job.

SGML offers another advantage in that it not only allows (groups of) users to define their own markup languages, it also provides a mechanism for ensuring that the rules of any particular markup language can be rigorously enforced by SGML-aware software. For example, within HTML, although there are six different levels of heading defined there is no requirement that they should be applied in a strictly hierarchical fashion; in other words, it is perfectly possible for a series of headings in an HTML document to be marked up as <H1>, then <H3>, followed by <H5>, followed in turn by <H2>, <H4>, and <H6> - all to achieve a particular visual appearance in a particular HTML browser.

By contrast, should such a feature be deemed important, an SGML-based markup language could be written in such a way that suitable software can ensure that levels of heading nest in a strictly hierarchical fashion (and the strength of this approach can perhaps become even more evident when encoding other kinds of hierarchical structure, e.g. a <BOOK> must contain one or more <CHAPTER>s, each of which must in turn contain one or more <PARAGRAPH>s, and so on).

There is one final, crucial, difference between SGML-based markup languages and other descriptive markup languages: the process by which International Standards are created, maintained, and updated. ISO Standards are subject to periodic formal review, and each time this work is undertaken it happens in full consultation with the various national standards bodies. The Committee which produced SGML has guaranteed that if and when any changes are introduced to the SGML standard, this will be done in such a way as to ensure backwards compatibility.

This is not a decision which has been undertaken lightly, and the full implications can be inferred from the fact that commercial enterprises rarely make such an explicit commitment (and even when they do, users ought to reflect upon the likelihood that such a commitment will actually be fulfilled given the considerable pressures of a highly competitive marketplace).

The essential difference has been characterised thus: the creators of SGML believe that a user's data should belong to that user, and not be tied up inextricably in a proprietary markup system over which that user has no control; whereas, the creators of a proprietary markup scheme can reasonably be expected to have little motivation to ensure that data encoded using their scheme can be easily migrated to, or processed by, a competitor's software products.

The SGML standard gives a very rigid definition as to what constitutes an 'SGML document'. Whilst there is no need for us to consider this definition in detail at this stage, it is worthwhile reviewing the major concepts as they offer a valuable insight into some crucial aspects of an electronic text.

Perhaps first and foremost amongst these is the notion that an SGML document is a single logical entity, even though in practice that document may be composed of any number of physical data files, spread over a storage medium (e.g. a single computer's hard-disk) or even over different types of storage media connected together via a network.

As today's electronic publications become more and more complex, mixing (multilingual) text with images, audio, and image data, it reinforces the need to ensure that they are created in line with accepted standards. For example, an article from an electronic journal mounted on a website may be delivered to the end-user in the form of a single HTML document, but that article (and indeed the whole journal), may rely upon dozens or hundreds of data files, a database to manage the entire collection of files, several bespoke scripts to handle the interfacing between the web and the database, and so on.

SGML operates on the basis of there being three major parts which combine to form a single SGML document. Firstly, there is the SGML declaration, which specifies any system and software constraints. Secondly, there is the prolog, which defines the document structure. Lastly, there is the document instance, which contains what one would ordinarily think of as the document. Whilst this may perhaps appear unnecessarily complicated, in fact it provides an extremely valuable insight into the key components which are essential to the creation of an electronic document.

The SGML declaration tells any software that is going to process an SGML document all that it should need to know. For example, the SGML declaration specifies which character sets have been used in the document (normally ASCII or ISO 646, but more recently this could be Unicode, or ISO 10646). It also establishes any constraints on system variables (e.g. the length of markup tag names, or the depth to which tags can be nested), and states whether or not any of SGML's optional features have been used.

The SGML standard offers a default set-up, so that, for example, the characters < and > are used to delimit markup tag names - and with the widespread acceptance of HTML, this has become the accepted way to indicate markup tags - but if for any reason this presented a problem for a particular application (e.g. encoding a lot of data in which < and > were heavily used to indicate something else), it would be possible to redefine the delimiters as @ or #, or whatever characters were deemed to be more appropriate.

The SGML declaration is important for a number of reasons. Although it may seem an unduly complicated approach, it is often these fundamental system or application dependencies which make it so difficult to move data around between different software and hardware environments. If the developers of wordprocessing packages had started off by agreeing on a single set of internal markup codes they would all use to indicate a change in font, the centring of a line of text, the occurrence of a pagebreak etc., then users' lives would have been made a great deal easier; however, this did not happen, and hence we are left in a situation where data created in one application cannot easily be read by another.

Furthermore, by supplying a default environment, the average end-user of an SGML-based encoding system is unlikely to have to familiarise him- or herself with the intricacies of the SGML declaration. Indeed it should be enough simply to be aware of the existence of the SGML declaration, and how it might affect one's ability to create, access, or exploit a particular source of data.

The next major part of an SGML document is the prolog, which must conform to the specification set out in the formal SGML standard, and the syntax given in the SGML declaration. Although it is hard to discuss the prolog without getting bogged down in the details of SGML, suffice it to say that it contains (at least one) document type declaration, which in turn contains (or references) a Document Type Definition (or DTD).

The DTD is one of the single most important features of SGML, and what sets it apart from - not to say above - other descriptive markup schemes. Although we shall learn a little more about the process in the following section, the DTD contains a series of declarations which define the particular markup language which will be used in the document instance, and also specifies how the different parts of that language can interrelate (e.g. which markup tags are required and optional, the contexts in which they can be used, and so on).

Often, when people talk about 'using SGML', they are actually talking about using a particular DTD, which is why some of the negative comments that have been made about SGML are erroneous, because such complaints should properly be directed at the DTD rather than at SGML in general.

Other than some of the system constraints imposed by the SGML declaration, there are no strictures imposed by the SGML standard regarding how simple or complex the markup language defined in the DTD should be. Whilst the syntax used to write a DTD is fairly straightforward, and most people find that they can start to read and write DTDs with surprising ease, to create a good DTD requires experience and familiarity with the needs and concerns of both data creators and end-users.

A good DTD nearly always reflects a designer's understanding of all these aspects, an appreciation of the constraints imposed by the SGML standard, and a thorough process of document analysis and DTD-testing. In many ways this situation is indicative of the fact that the creators of the SGML standard did not envisage that individual users would be very likely to produce their own DTDs for highly specific purposes.

Rather, they thought (or perhaps hoped), that groups would form within industry sectors or large-scale enterprises to produce DTDs that were tailored to the needs of their particular application. Indeed, the areas in which the uptake of SGML has been most enthusiastic have been operating under exactly those sorts of conditions - for example, the international Air Transport Authority seeking to standardise aircraft maintenance documentation, or the pharmaceutical industry's attempts to streamline the documentary evidence needed to support applications to the US Food and Drug Administration.

However, as a general rule, if users wish to write their own DTDs, or tweak an SGML declaration, they are entirely free to do so (within the framework set out by the SGML standard) - but the vast majority of SGML users prefer to rely upon an SGML declaration and DTD created by others, for all the benefits of interoperability and reusability promised by this approach.

This brings us to the third main part of an SGML document: namely, the document instance itself. This is the part of the document which contains a combination of raw data and markup, and its contents are constrained by both the SGML declaration, and the contents of the prolog (especially the declarations in the DTD).

Clearly from the perspective of data creators and end-users, this is the most interesting part of an SGML document - and it is common practice for people to use the term 'SGML document' when they are actually referring to a document instance. Such confusion should be largely unproblematic, provided these users always remember that when they are interchanging data (i.e. a document instance) with colleagues, they should also pass on the relevant DTD and SGML declaration.

Having identified the features you wish to encode, you will need to find a DTD which meets your requirements. Rather than trying to write your own DTD from scratch, it is usually worthwhile investing some time to look around for existing public DTDs which you might be able to adopt, extend, or adapt to suit your particular purposes.

There are many DTDs available in the public domain, or made freely available for others to use, but even if none of these match your needs, some may be worth investigating to see how others have tackled common problems. Although there are some tools available which are designed to facilitate the process of DTD-authoring, they are probably only worth buying if you intend to be doing a great deal of work with DTDs, and they can never compensate for poor document analysis.

Once again, there are many useful tools available to help convert from one markup scheme to another, but if your target format is SGML this may have some bearing on the likelihood of success (or failure) of any conversion process. As we have seen, SGML lends itself most naturally to a structured, hierarchical view of a document's content (although it is perfectly possible to represent very loose organisational structures, and even non-hierarchical document webs, using SGML markup) and this means that it is much simpler to convert from a proprietary markup scheme to SGML if that scheme also has a strong sense of structure (i.e. adopts a descriptive markup approach) and has been used sensibly.

However, if a document has been encoded with a presentational markup scheme which has, for example, used codes to indicate that certain words should be rendered in an italic font - regardless of the fact that sometimes this has been for emphasis, at other times to indicate book and journal titles, and elsewhere to indicate non-English words - then this will dramatically reduce the chances of automatically converting the data from this presentation-oriented markup scheme into one which complies with an SGML DTD.

It is probably worth noting at this point that these conversion problems primarily apply when converting from a non-descriptive, non-SGML markup language into SGML; the opposite process, namely converting from SGML into another target markup scheme, is much more straightforward (because it would simply mean that data variously marked-up with, say, <EMPHASIS>, <TITLE>, and <FOREIGN> tags, had their markup converted into the target scheme's markup tags for <ITALIC>).

It is also worth noting that such a conversion might not be a particularly good idea, because you would effectively be throwing information away. In practice it would be much more sensible to retain the descriptive/SGML version of your material, and convert to a presentational markup scheme only when absolutely required for the successful rendering of your data on screen or on paper.

Indeed, many dedicated SGML applications support the use of stylesheets to offer some control over the on-screen rendition of SGML-encoded material, whilst preserving the SGML markup behind the scenes. If you are creating SGML documents from scratch, or editing existing SGML documents there are several factors to consider. It is essential that you have access to a validating SGML parser, which is a software program that can read an SGML declaration and a document's prolog, understand the declarations in the DTD, and ensure that the SGML markup used throughout the document instance conforms appropriately.

In many commercial SGML- and XML-aware software packages, a validating parser is included as standard and is often very closely integrated with the relevant tools (e.g. to ensure that any simple editing operations, such as cut and paste, do not result in the document failing to conform to the rules set out in the DTD because markup has been inserted or removed inappropriately).

It also possible to find freeware and public domain software which have some understanding of the markup rules expressed in the DTD, while also allowing users to validate their documents with a separate parser in order to guarantee conformance. So for the purposes of creating valid SGML documents, we have seen that there are a number of tools which you may wish to consider.

Producing valid SGML files which conform to a DTD, is in some respects only the first stage in any project. If you want to search the files for particular words, phrases, or marked-up features, you may prefer to use an SGML-aware search engine, but some people are perfectly happy writing short scripts in a language like Perl. If you want to conduct sophisticated computer-assisted text analysis of your material, you will almost certainly need to look at adapting an existing tool, or writing your own code.

Having obtained your SGML text, whether as complete documents or as fragments resulting from a search, you will need to find some way of displaying it. You might choose to simply convert the SGML markup in the data into another format (e.g. HTML for display in a conventional web browser), or you might use one of the specialist SGML viewing packages to publish the results - which is how many commercial SGML-based electronic texts are produced.

An SGML-based markup language usually offers a number of advantages over other types of markup scheme, especially those which rely upon proprietary encoding. However, although SGML has met with considerable success in certain areas of publishing and many commercial, industrial, and governmental sectors, its uptake by the academic community has been relatively limited.

We can speculate on why this might be so - for example, SGML has an undeserved reputation for being difficult and expensive to produce -because it imposes prohibitive intellectual overheads, and because the necessary software is lacking. While it is true that peforming a thorough document analysis and developing a suitable DTD should not be undertaken lightly, it could be argued that to approach the production of any electronic text without first investing such intellectual resources is likely to lead to difficulties.

The apparent lack of readily available, easy-to-use SGML software, is perhaps a more valid criticism - yet the resources have been available for those willing to look, and then invest the time necessary to learn a new package (although freely available software tends to put more of an onus on the user than some of the commercial products). However, what is undoubtedly true is the fact that writing a piece of SGML software (e.g. a validating SGML parser), which fully implements the SGML standard, is an extremely demanding task - and this has been reflected in the price and sophistication of some commercial applications.

Whilst SGML is probably more ubiquitous than many people realise, HTML - the markup language of the World Wide Web - is much better known. Nowadays, the notion of 'the Web' is effectively synonymous with the global Internet, and HTML plays a fundamental role in the delivery and presentation of information over the Web. The main advantage of HTML is that it is a fixed set of markup tags designed to support the creation of straightforward hypertext documents.

Although HTML was not originally designed as an application of SGML, it soon became one once the designers realised the benefits to be gained from having a DTD. However, this meant that the HTML DTD had to be written retrospectively, and in such a way that any existing HTML documents would still conform to the DTD - which in turn meant that the value of the DTD was effectively diminished! This situation led to the release of a succession of different versions of HTML, each with their own slightly different DTD.

Nowadays, the most widely accepted release of HTML is probably version 3.2, although the World Wide Web Consortium (W3C) released HTML 4.0 on 18th December 1997 in order to address a number of outstanding concerns about the HTML standard. It is perfectly possible to deliver SGML documents over the Web, but there are several ways that this can be achieved and each has different implications.

In order to retain the full 'added-value' of the SGML markup, you might choose to deliver the raw SGML data over the Web and rely upon a behind-the-scenes negotation between your web-server and the client's browser to ensure that an appropriate SGML-viewing tool is launched on the client's machine. This enables the end-user to exploit fully the SGML markup included in your document, provided that s/he has been able to obtain and install the appropriate software.

Another possibility would be to offer a Web-to-SGML interface on your server, so that end-users can access your documents using an ordinary Web browser whilst all the processing of the SGML markup takes place on the server, and the results are delivered as HTML. Alternatively, you might decide to simply convert the markup into HTML from whatever SGML DTD has been used to encode the document (either on-the-fly, or as part of a batch process) so that the end-user can use an ordinary Web browser and the server will not have to undertake any additional processing.

Meanwhile, delivering electronic text marked-up according to another SGML DTD meant that end-users were obliged to obtain suitable SGML-aware tools, and very few of them seemed willing to do this. The creators of XML adopted the following design goals:

1. XML shall be straightforwardly usable over the Internet.
2. XML shall support a wide variety of applications.
3. XML shall be compatible with SGML.
4. It shall be easy to write programs which process XML documents.
5. The number of optional features in XML is to be kept to the absolute minimum, ideally zero.
6. XML documents should be human-legible and reasonably clear.
7. The XML design should be prepared quickly.
8. The design of XML shall be formal and concise.
9. XML documents shall be easy to create.
10. Terseness in XML markup is of minimal importance.

They sought to gain the generic advantages offered by supporting arbitrary SGML DTDs, whilst retaining much of the operational simplicity of using HTML. To this end, they 'threw away' all the optional features of the SGML standard which make it difficult (and therefore expensive) to process.

At the same time they retained the ability for users to write their own DTDs, so that they can develop markup schemes which are tailored to suit particular applications but which are still enforceable by a validating parser. Perhaps most importantly of all, the committee which designed XML had representatives from several major companies which develop software applications for use with the Web, particularly browsers, and this has helped to encourage a great deal of interest in XML's potential.

SGML has its roots in a time when creating, storing, and processing information on computer was expensive and time-consuming. Many of the optional features supported by the SGML standard were intended to make it cheaper to create and store SGML-conformant documents in an era when it was envisaged that all the markup would be laboriously inserted by hand, and megabytes of disk space were extremely expensive.

Nowadays, faster and cheaper processors, and the falling costs of storage media (both magnetic and optical), mean that the designers and users of applications are less worried about the concerns of SGML's original designers. On the other hand, the ever growing volume of electronic information makes it all the more important that any markup which has been used has been applied in a thoroughly consistent and easy to process manner, thereby helping to ensure that today's applications perform satisfactorily.

XML addresses these familiar concerns, whilst taking advantage of modern computer systems and the lessons learned from using SGML. For example, now that the cost of storing data is of less concern to most users (except for those dealing with extremely large quantities of data), there is no need to offer support for markup short-cuts which, while saving storage space, tend to impose an additional load when information is processed.

Instead, XML's designers were able to build-in the concept of 'well-formed' data, which requires that any marked-up data are explicitly bounded by start- and end-tags, and that all the tagged data in a document nest appropriately (so that it becomes possible, say, to generate a document tree which captures the hierarchical arrangement of all the data elements in the document). This has the added advantage that when two applications (such as a database and a web server) need to exchange data, they can use well-formed XML as their interchange format, because both the sending and receiving application can be certain that any data they receive will be appropriately marked-up and there can be no possible ambiguity about where particular data structures start and end.

XML takes this approach one stage further by adopting the SGML concept of DTDs, such that an XML document is said to be 'valid' if it has an associated DTD and the markup used in the document has been checked (by a validating parser) against the declarations expressed in that DTD. If an application knows that it will be handling valid XML, and has an understanding of and access to the relevant DTD, this can greatly improve its ability to process that data - for example, a search and retrieval application would be able to construct a list of all the marked-up data structures in the document, so that a user could refine the search criteria accordingly.

Knowing that a vast collection of XML documents have all been validated against a particular DTD will greatly assist the processing of that collection, as valid XML data is also necessarily well-formed. By contrast, while it is possible for an XML application to process a well-formed document such that it can derive one possible DTD which could represent the data structures it contains, that DTD may not be sufficient to represent all the well-formed XML documents of the same type.

There are clearly many advantages to be gained from creating and using valid XML data, but the option remains to use well-formed XML data in those situations where it would be appropriate. Today's Web browsers expect to receive conformant HTML data, and any additional markup included in the data which is not recognised by the browser is usually ignored.

The next generation of Web browsers will know how to handle XML data, and while all of them will know how to process HTML data by default, they will also be prepared to cope with any well-formed or valid XML data that they receive. This offers the opportunity for groups of users to come together, agree upon a DTD they wish to adopt, and then create and exchange valid XML data which conforms to that DTD.

Thus, a group of academics concerned with the creation of electronic scholarly editions of major texts could all agree to prepare their data in accordance with a particular DTD which enabled them to markup the features of the texts which they felt to be appropriate for their work. They could then exchange the results of their labours safe in the knowledge that they could all be correctly processed by their favourite software.

Text Encoding Initiative (TEI)

The Text Encoding Initiative (TEI) began with a planning conference convened by the Association for Computers and the Humanities (ACH), gathering together over thirty experts in the field of electronic texts, representing professional societies, research centers, and text and data archives. The importance of the modularity and extensibility of the TEI's DTD cannot be over-stated. In the same way every implementation of the TEI DTD must have certain standard components (e.g. header information and the core tag set), one of the eight base tag sets, to which can then be added any combination of the additional tag sets or user-defined application-specific extensions.

Although SGML was released as an ISO standard in 1986, its usage has grown steadily rather than explosively, and uptake has tended to occur within the documentation departments of major corporations, government departments, and global industries. This is in dramatic contrast to XML, which was released as a W3C Recommendation in 1998 but was able to build on the tremendous level of international awareness about the web and HTML. However, it is also important to remember that XML (like SGML), is only one amongst a family of related standards, and that these XML-related standards are developing and changing very rapidly - so you should remember to visit these sites regularly, or risk making the wrong decisions on the basis of out-dated information. Keeping up-to-date with the Text Encoding Initiative is a much more straightforward matter.

8
Archival Collections

The advent of new technology has suggested to many that the document was nearing the end of its influential reign. To fully assess the document's evolving role requires a broad understanding of both old and new documents.

Seeing documents as the means to make and maintain social groups, not just the means to deliver information, makes it easier to understand the utility and success of new forms of document. This social understanding of documents should better explain the evolution of Web as a social and commercial phenomenon. As new technologies take us through major transformations in the way we use documents, it becomes increasingly important to look beyond the conduit image. We need to see the way documents have served not simply to write, but also to underwrite social interactions; not simply to communicate, but also to coordinate social practices. The sociologist Anselm Strauss explored the way new forms of document allowed new forms of community to come into existence. His work predates the proliferation of computers and so provides an interesting view of the way other developing technologies supported social relations in new ways.

In particular, new media allowed small communities to form though their members were often few, and those few spread over large distances. These groups can look surprisingly like modern equivalents of the scholarly communities that formed throughout the world in the Renaissance. These too were held together by common interests and shared communications.

The letters circulating among the Fellows of the Royal Society in England formed the prototype for scientific journals, which still bind intellectual communities together. And indeed Strauss's initial observations were based on the new ways scholars were building communities of interest with the support of new communications technologies and may help understand the future of scholarly communities in the digital age. Photocopiers, faxes, and other forms of cheap reproduction have allowed not only scholars, but other groups of people with shared interests to form a "social world" with relative ease and autonomy. Neither capital nor authorisation was needed.

From political undergrounds connected only by samizdat journals to wind-surfers, DeLorean owners, and beekeepers, people with shared interests use communications technologies to help form themselves into self-created and self-organising groups. To a significant degree, these are held together by documents circulating among members, keeping each conscious of being a member and aware of what others are up to. One of the most astounding recent examples has been the spread of "zines" — cheaply produced newsletters. Needing little more than a typewriter or word processor, a photocopier and stapler, and the Post Office or a fax, zines are often put together at home by one or two people and are "mid-cast" among small groups.

The practice began with fans of particular television programs and rock groups. Consequently, these documents were known as "fan-zines" and now just "zines." One estimate reckons that these "Xeroxed, hand-written, desktop-published, sometimes printed, and even electronic" documents have produced some 20,000 titles in the past couple of decades. Consequently, scattered groups of people unknown to one another, rarely living in contiguous areas, and sometimes never seeing another member, have nonetheless been able to form robust social worlds. The role of documents in linking people this way helps explain the particular enthusiasm of small, widely scattered interest groups for the Internet, where electronic zine publishing, which at the margin is even cheaper than conventional zines, is developing rapidly. The Internet now has over 600 e-zine titles, and growth will almost certainly outstrip the twenty percent of the paper form.

Once again, people can first recognise and then develop shared interests through their access to shared documents. The growth in zine titles, both on and off the Internet, may also indicate how much more volatile new documents make social worlds. The key to forming a new group is starting a new publication to help hold it together. Consequently, as publication costs come down, formation becomes much easier. This allows people to test the "market" for a new group quite cheaply. In the past, the cost of starting a new sub-group undoubtedly put limits on dissent. As the costs descend, forming a splinter group becomes easier. Low-inertia resources inevitably make both worlds and sub-worlds correspondingly labile.

Old paper forms may, then, have been a resource for stability. And the volatility allowed by newer forms may help account for the large number of "404" dead links on the Internet, marking zine sites that have already been abandoned by groups, some of which might all along have been more imaginary than either real or virtual. Strauss's argument helps illustrate the importance of documents to the formation of communities. It doesn't necessarily, however, undermine the idea of the document as a dart rather than a more sociable object.

Where an imaginary community does not exist, an imagined one exists on too large a scale to be known in any other way. And the central way they can be imagined is through the documents they share.In the case of the American revolution, newspapers, the first mass-produced and mass-consumed objects, were crucial in making their dispersed readers aware of Anderson's "communion" across space and time. The proliferation of daily newspapers, pamphlets, journals, and tracts made each reader aware that what he or she was doing thousands and possibly tens of thousands of others were doing at the same time and with the same interests.

Ideas of cultural objects not just connecting, but coordinating social performance help explain the social life of various documents. Radio and television programs and movies, all different types of document, have provided a similar and yet more extensive sense of social coordination. In the morning at work people would discuss what they had seen at home the night before, again with an implicit sense of coordinated practice. To some degree, in the United States network broadcasts took over some of this ritual role from the nineteen fifties on. Newscasters, for instance, began to assume a central role in the daily ritual. In this way, document forms both old and relatively new have underwritten a sense of community among a disparate and dispersed group of people.

As newspapers recede before broadcast and on-line communication, and as the multiplication of television channels disrupts schedulers' control over what is seen when, the strong feeling of coordinated performance provided by these documents is changing. One possible result may be that the loss of simultaneous practice will reinforce the need and desire for common objects — the wish at least to see the same thing, if not at the same time. Here the Internet is a particularly powerful medium for providing access to the same thing for people more widely dispersed than ever before. Moreover, the reach of the Internet is increasing a sense of simultaneity as ideas emerging on one side of the world can almost instantaneously be picked up through the Internet and absorbed into the local context by communities on the other. Creative use of new documents no longer involves direct challenges to old ones, with on-line forms replacing hard-copy predecessors. Rather, these new forms appear to reinvigorate the old, extending their useful social life not ending it.

Thus, as another example, on-line library catalogues providing abstracts, indexing, and in some cases full texts for print journals have reinforced these journals rather than undermined them. The journals still remain the best social filter for the flood of writing available on any topic as well as the best repositories of the development of ideas and attitudes. In these realms, digital media, as yet, do not compete. The electronic resources, however, have made using print journals much easier than during the Gutenberg era. There are differences between internal communication — where the stripped down zine, often uninterpretable to outsiders, has proved uniquely powerful — and external communication — which requires more explicit documents like contracts and business letters.

Intercommunal and intracommunal documents are not, however, necessarily two quite different sorts of document. More usually, they involve two different practices built around the same documents. Within communities, documents face the challenge of gaining attention of community members. Between communities they face that challenge and the difficulty of coordinating practice despite different interpretive strategies.

The central issue here is for the intended audience to be able to recognise documents intended for them. Faced with similar problems, and realising that books were not universal documents but addressed different audiences, book designers long ago developed numerous strategies that help readers distinguish different kinds of books.

Consequently, books use far more than their title to engage certain audiences and tell others to pass by. In an increasingly crowded attention economy, the challenge of reaching an intended audience accounts for the demand for sophisticated Web-page designers and the importance of autonomous agents on the net that can plant links in strategic sites.

Despite this work, with most links and pages, it's still very hard even to make even a reasonable guess at the intended audience. This difficulty may reflect an implicit assumption by many that documents have universal appeal or that content alone will marshal an audience. Yet if the overall form appears unclear, few will linger over the content, especially given the ease with which links allow people to pass by. Documents that pass successfully between communities need to be able to engage two interpretive strategies and to survive where the recipients can no longer be assumed to share the interpretive assumptions of the members of the originating community.

Within a community highly condensed forms of communication, which rely on the shared assumptions of the community, work well. Between communities these must be elaborated, often to the exasperation of the original community, whose members can see the elaboration as redundant. Anyone who has used the Internet much has probably come across the different approaches. Most ftp sites, which are usually constructed primarily for use within a known community, are almost completely inscrutable — a collection of files with semiliterate names. Successful web sites designed to engage people from different communities have, by contrast, a much more public face.

In passing between communities, documents play an important role, bringing people from different groups together to negotiate and coordinate common practices. Such negotiations are particularly significant in institutions, such as bureaucracies and corporations, that comprise many different communities. Here the direction of the institution as a whole depends on the successful outcome of negotiations among its constituent groups, all of whom have particular interests at stake. Both the means and a willingness to come to a shared understanding are vital to the effectiveness of such institutions.

Because documents passing between communities face different interpretive strategies in each one, the challenge of coordinating practice around them is always theoretically and often practically problematic.One result of frequent intercommunal communication may be cross-border communities, groups of people who are, collectively, capable of dealing with the codes of both worlds and of talking a common language among themselves. These groups are essentially bilingual in terms of the two dominant communities their members come from. Institutions can strive to create such groups, but the more effective ones tend to emerge.

But intercommunal communication isn't only a matter of comprehension and coordination. Documents are also used to patrol and control. In the first case, documents can patrol community boundaries rather than cross them. Strange formats, unexplained generic conventions, jargon, abbreviations, allusions, as well as private languages are all examples of ways in which documents keep people out as much as bring them in. More simple than obfuscation, of course, is simple secrecy. Documents are kept from certain eyes. Encryption, blind "carbon" copies, restricted access and so forth, make secrecy quite as prevalent on the Internet as it has been in the world of paper documents. Many Internet sites simply restrict access to registered users.

Intercommunal documents can both promote and retard institutional development, depending on whether boundary objects lead to collaboration or control. Understanding the potential for both is thus particularly important for large institutions. The issue of documents as instruments of power and control is an important one. Much debate around this issue, however, tends to argue that document technologies determine certain social processes — either for good or for ill.

While document technology is undoubtedly linked to both, neither of these accounts gives the whole picture. And neither result is inevitable. This argument surely holds for the Internet, too. Some argue it will fulfill social democratic ideals, others that it will undermine civil, political, and economic institutions. Each outcome is no doubt feasible, but the technology alone guarantees neither. The outcome of contemporary social-technological pressures for change, whether for good or for ill, will be the result of social struggle and negotiation. Consequently, the means of negotiation are particularly important. Here, the Internet and related technologies are intriguingly both the forum and the topic of debate.

Changes in documentary forms have lead some to foresee a shift from "objects" to "performance." The journalist John Perry Barlow, for instance, points out that recordings of rock bands are rapidly losing value because they can so easily be pirated. Cheap analog recording devices like the conventional tape recorder produced such poor copies of originals that for most fans it was worth paying to buy a professionally cut disc. Similarly, with print documents it has usually been easier to buy than to copy. But now digital technology makes the production of copies indistinguishable in all essentials from the original, making copying often the cheaper and easier choice.

Simultaneously, some claim that written documents are moving from the permanence of old forms to the performance of new ones. Certainly, notions of "real-time response," "collaborative work," "multi-authored hypertexts," "shared documents," "relational databases," "on-line editing," "continuous up-dates," "interlinked data," "live video links," and other properties suggest that their malleability makes new documents significantly different from old ones. Those who struggled for years with stencils and White Out undoubtedly appreciate the shift from fixed to a different sense of fluid. Nevertheless, it's important not to ignore some counterpressures developing within the new technologies themselves. While many technologies strive to achieve the immediacy of the conversation, the phone call, and other live links, people occasionally use new technologies to achieve the opposite: to escape that very immediacy.

For instance, e-mail and faxes may be used to overcome the delay of "snail mail." But people also use them for messages that could be delivered by the more conversational phone call. While voice mail allows us to leave messages for people we cannot reach, occasionally people use it to avoid reaching someone they would prefer not to talk to. Similarly, people allow an answering machine to pick up and announce "I'm not here, now," even though "I" is indeed "here" and listening in, just to add a little delay between message and response. Practices like these are not simply desperate responses to the burdensome pressures of modern life or information overload. They are as much innovative ways to reintroduce time and physical traces into what would otherwise be immediate and ephemeral exchanges.

At the very least, they suggest that delay and fixity may be just as important to all of us as immediacy, mutability, and indivisibility. While everyone can benefit from technology capable of overcoming separations of space and time and the convergence of producer and consumer, it seems people are beginning to appreciate how important these distinctions can be. New technologies help us to transcend burdensome barriers of space and time. But, in part through the improvisations of users, the same technologies are also valued for their ability to reinject both space and time into communication. Written forms have long done this. In general, new technologies have minimised the technological separation of producer and consumer. It is a shift of some significance that the computer we read on is also the one we write on, whereas the book we read is very different from the manuscript we write. This single medium makes the intertextual relationship of reading and writing more than an abstruse intellectual concept.

Changes in technology make it clear that we can no longer take for granted a correspondence between social purpose and technological resources. Now a trace may appear where it wasn't expected, or disappear when it was taken for granted. This change doesn't insist we simply leap from product to performance, renounce fixity and embrace transience, become digital where once we were material. Rather, it suggests that we should consider a symbiosis between the two.

Moreover, we should consider not only the fascinating possibilities presented to us by the digital document, but also the importance of the immutable and the transient to central social practices from preserving great works to signing contracts and cashing checks. From this point of view, the fixed, immutable "document" is best understood not as an inferior and outdated alternative to conversation or other types of unmediated and immediate communication, but, in appropriate places, as an object that plays valuable social roles because it mediates and temporises, records traces and fixes spaces, and demands institutions as well as technologies of distribution.

Attempts to introduce time stamps, hash marks, and other forms of electronic version identification stress how important to social and particularly legal institutions the idea of a fixed state of a document is. Being able to talk about the "same" document, for all the Hereclitan conundrums, is extremely useful.

If the utility of both the fixed and the fluid is recognised, the Web may develop much of its innovative power from the possibility of producing documents that combine both fixity and fluidity. Already, many documents retain a constant text while their links are continually changed. As the social roles of continuity and change, of areas of stasis and areas open to dynamic revision, are better understood, social institutions may develop around this joint capacity in intriguing ways, much as libraries developed their usefulness out of the juxtaposition of fixed individual texts combined to an ever expanding collection and a continually revised set of interlinked catalogues. This interplay between fixity and fluidity, formerly possible only on the scale of collections may now become a central feature of individual documents.

Metadata Collection

Metadata facilitates the discovery and retrieval of information, it provides for resource presentation and navigation, and it contains the information needed to preserve digital data files. While several digital collections of books have been created for the Internet, it is only recently that libraries and archives have begun to digitise archival collections for Web delivery.

The first major challenge associated with the Barren Lands project centred on how to represent archival material within an online environment. A search of the Internet for similar archival projects revealed that online archival collections were most often presented in one of two ways: as an online exhibition or as a simple database of independent archival documents. Following the "exhibition" method, institutions presented archival collections online in much the same way as they would present an exhibition of physical materials; narrative descriptions or transcriptions of items were presented with links to digital representations of those items. These Web sites tended to be small in size and highlighted materials that were considered important. The second approach followed by many institutions was to create a database-driven Web site with basic search and browse techniques. In these digital repositories, each archival document was treated as a separate entity and basic descriptive metadata elements such as title, author, and date were given for each item. Although the Barren Lands project team found aspects of both methods of delivery appealing, they decided that neither approach was fully compatible with their vision of the project.

While the "exhibition" approach provided an abundance of narrative contextual information, this method was deemed impracticable for the size of the digital collection. Similarly, a strict database approach was also not favoured, as it did not retain the contextual linkages between the documents. Instead, the Barren Lands project team decided to create two levels of descriptive metadata to provide the necessary contextual information for the archival materials and to allow for comprehensive searching.

Descriptive Metadata

In most digital collections, each book, article, map, etc. is considered to be an independent digital object. The Barren Lands project was different in that the archival collection consisted of many documents that were inter-related with each other. For example, in the case of J.B. Tyrrell's correspondence, the meaning and significance of an individual letter can only be understood if it is read within the context of a series of letters. It was essential that these natural connections be retained within the digital environment. At the same time, it was necessary that each document remain an independent digital object for the purpose of resource discovery and retrieval. The solution to this problem was to adopt a two-tiered approach to the creation of descriptive metadata—one tier to describe the archival materials as a collective unit and another to describe each digital object.

Tier 1—Describing Archival Collections

Although paper-based finding aids and item listings for some of the materials did exist for the J.B. Tyrrell and James W. Tyrrell collections, the project team was unable to use this information in the construction of the online collection. Problems with the pre-existing descriptive metadata were three-fold: first, the metadata was not in electronic format; second, the metadata did not contain all of the necessary descriptive information; and third, the archival materials were not described consistently according to archival descriptive standards. Because of these problems, the project team decided to re-describe both collections according to the Canadian descriptive standard, the Rules for Archival Description (RAD).

Once the descriptive metadata was complete, it was necessary to encode this information in a standard data structure. In order to retain the relationships between archival materials, the project team adopted the Encoded Archival Description (EAD) data structure standard, which is jointly administered by the Society of American Archivists and the Library of Congress. EAD is a non-proprietary standard in the form of a Standard Generalised Markup Language (SGML) and Extensible Markup Language (XML) Document Type Definition (DTD). Developed specifically for archival finding aids, the EAD standard has the ability to accurately represent the multilevel nature of archives in a machine-readable format. Consequently, the EAD standard facilitates access by allowing users to "drill down" into an archival finding aid, beginning at the fonds or collection level description down to the descriptions of individual items.

Tier 2—Item Level Description

Since no existing data structure standard contained all of the features needed for the item level descriptions, the decision was made to create a customised XML DTD based on the Text Encoding Initiative (TEI).

Not all features of the TEI DTD were needed for the project; in fact, only the elements contained within the TEI Header and the paragraph <p> and page break <pb> elements were included in the DTD. Furthermore, as the structure and features of the online collection became more defined, it was clear that many of the descriptive metadata elements in the DTD would need to be customised for the Barren Lands project. The customised DTD contains many of the standard fields found in descriptive metadata schema such as title, author, extent, subject, and others that facilitate in the discovery and retrieval of information.

Features that make the metadata schema unique are attributes to determine whether records are published or not, as well as attributes to identify the various types of notes and subject heading standards that are used in the item level record. The DTD also enables linking between documents—users can link from an item level record to the EAD encoded finding aid—as well as between item-level records, if a relationship has been defined.

File Naming Systems

Another significant metadata challenge with archival materials is how to incorporate different document types into an online collection. The problems associated with multiple media collections do not generally lie in the presentation of various media, but rather in their preparation for online delivery. The Barren Lands project consists of a variety of documentary forms, all of which needed to be handled in a slightly different manner. For example, published reports required OCR, manuscript letters and newspaper clippings needed to be manually re-keyed, and no additional work was required for maps and photographs. To simplify the development of the digital collection, it was necessary to create a method for quickly identifying the document type for each digital object. As a form of structural metadata, the file naming structure was used to distinguish between documentary forms. Directories were created for each type of document, such as letters, diaries, published text, maps, photographs, and so on. Then, as each archival document was scanned, a unique identifier, containing a letter to identify the documentary form followed by a five-digit number, was recorded in a relational database.

Structural Metadata

Once the images were scanned and item level descriptions complete, the final challenge was to create the linkages between the two. Collecting an adequate amount of structural metadata is critical to this linking process. In the Barren Lands project, structural information such as unique identifiers, page sequence numbers, page numbers as stated on the document, special features such as tables of contents and indexes, and other relevant information was collected in a relational database at the point of scanning. Some descriptive metadata relating to individual pages of the digital object, such as titles of maps or illustrations and content dates were also recorded in the database.

Administrative Metadata

In addition to descriptive and structural metadata, the Barren Lands project team also captured administrative or technical metadata during the scanning process. As each image was scanned, information relating to the source type, file format, scanning date, and scanner was captured in a relational database.

Other types of administrative metadata, such as file compression format, image resolution, and image height and width were captured in the TIFF tags associated with each image. Although this administrative information was not used in the construction of the digital collection, it was important to capture this technical information just in case it was needed in the future.

Archiving Portable Document Format

Adobe Portable Document Format (PDF) is a widely used standard for electronic document distribution worldwide in many institutional settings. Much of its popularity comes from its ability to faithfully encode both the text and the visual appearance of source documents, preserving their fonts, formatting, colors, and graphics. PDF files can be viewed, navigated, and printed with a free Adobe Acrobat Reader, available on all major computing platforms.

PDF has many applications and is commonly used to publish government, public, and academic documents. Many of the electronic journals and other digital resources acquired by libraries are published in PDF format. As libraries grow more dependent on electronic resources, they need to consider how they can preserve these resources for the long term. Many libraries retain back runs of print journals that are over 100 years old, and which are still consulted by researchers. No digital technology has lasted nearly that long, and many data formats have already become obsolete and not easily readable in a much shorter time period.

PDF is a platform-independent document format developed by Adobe as a follow-up to its Postscript language. Although Postscript was designed specifically for printing, PDF is meant to support on-line, secure, interactive use, as well as printing. PDF combines attributes of structured text formats and traditional image formats, so that a document can be used both in terms of its text and in terms of its "look" on-screen or on the page. This allows PDF readers not only to display and print documents, but also to carry out text-oriented operations such as searching for text strings, or cutting-and-pasting. Like Postscript, PDF is, at its heart, a page description language. However, unlike Postscript, it is more of a declarative than a procedural language. This makes PDF easier to manipulate and analyse than Postscript.

As with Postscript, the specification of PDF is openly and freely published, but Adobe controls its development. Three revisions of PDF have been published to date, with PDF 1.3 the latest version for which specifications are published. So far, all of the revisions for which specifications have been published are backward-compatible. Because the basic standard is public, Adobe does not have a monopoly on PDF tools, and third parties have developed tools that also work with PDF. However, because the standard is complex, and changes from time to time, much of the support for the format, as well as the tools that are considered to set the standard for PDF use, comes from Adobe. A typical PDF document consists of a sequence of pages, each of which includes data that indicates what should be "drawn" on a particular page. This data includes text, font specifications, margins, layout, graphical elements, and background and text colors.

A PDF file does not always contain the full glyph specification of characters in the document, but at least includes the name of the fonts used and specifies the space all characters will occupy. PDF includes metadata on the document, specifying things such as page size, page numbering, and a structured table of contents. Add-ons, such as hyperlinks, forms, and even pieces of scripting code in Java or Postscript that control dynamic displays or the user interface, can also be included.

Not all PDF documents encode the text of a document directly. It is possible to embed images of a page in PDF, so that a picture of text is encoded but not the text itself. Some scanners, for instance, can output this "uninterpreted" form of PDF. Such uninterpreted PDF files tend to be much larger than PDF files that encode text directly as characters, and text-oriented operations such as searching and textual copying and pasting are not supported by these files. Still, some libraries have produced these large, uninterpreted PDF files for their users as a way of quickly and inexpensively distributing scans of print materials. For applications such as electronic reserves, where scanned copies are typically not kept beyond a semester or two, this form of PDF can be acceptable.

PDF was originally designed for 8-bit character sets (which can support at most 256 characters). Some limited support for Unicode also exists, but the format has not yet taken full advantage of Unicode's capabilities. One consequence of this design is that some multilingual documents may be represented by switching between different, sometimes customised, 256-character sets. Alternatively, some "exotic" characters may be represented as small images, rather than as text. Unlike XML, PDF was not originally designed for arbitrary structural annotations, although the last revision of PDF includes some facilities for user-defined structural markup.

PDF is a less efficient format for text analysis than purely text-based formats such as XML or HTML, and readers have noted that searching for words within a PDF viewer can be noticeably slower than searching for words in an HTML viewer. The central role that appearance plays in PDF is both a strength and a weakness; it allows publishers to specify exactly how they want a document to look, but it also makes it difficult for users to reformat or repaginate the document if that would be better for them. PDF includes facilities for encrypting content, or directing that a document not be printable. It is possible to use encryption so that a document cannot be decrypted without a password. However, once the document is decrypted, it is possible, in theory, to make an unlocked copy that can be freely copied, read, or printed. Even if it is technically possible to do so, though, legal and practical restrictions to doing so may still exist.

As data formats go, PDF is particularly likely to be supported for a long time, and to spawn migration paths. This has been the case with Adobe's Postscript, which is now an industry standard, and for which PDF itself can be seen as the next step in migration. Adobe is highly invested in the success of PDF, but even if Adobe fails or abruptly changes course, a community of third-party tools for handling PDF has started to emerge. PDF is used widely by many well-funded bodies so there should be widespread support for using and migrating PDF, should Adobe fail to provide adequate support for the format. Even so, it is likely that PDF will one day be superseded by another format. It may be a successor format, or it may be a completely different format that users prefer over PDF. Hence, it is necessary to have migration strategies planned for PDF. Currently, there is no other format that can encompass all of the features of PDF in a form that standard tools can interpret. However, it is possible to easily migrate two important aspects of PDF documents: the page images and the text. These aspects may be sufficient for the types of preservation that libraries require.

Any program that displays or prints PDF files in effect converts PDF pages into static page images. Most page image formats are pixel-oriented, where pictures are encoded using a grid with each grid cell (known as a pixel) associated with a particular color. Some image formats, including PDF and Postscript, are stroke-oriented, encoded with instructions about lines to plot, regions to color, and text to place. They can also include instructions to embed pixel-oriented images at specified locations. Pixel-oriented formats have a well-understood mathematical representation, making them easy to migrate.

Stroke-oriented image formats are not so standardised. They can encode information about the structure of a picture, such as the lines that are drawn in it, that can only be approximated to a certain resolution in purely pixel-oriented formats. On the other hand, since pixel-oriented formats can typically accommodate very fine resolutions, an image converted from a stroke-oriented format to a pixel-oriented format at fine enough resolution can be visually indistinguishable from its original.

Third-party software exists to turn PDF both into Postscript, and into pixel-oriented image formats. Converting from PDF to most image formats loses direct encoding of the text. Structural information and other PDF extras would also be lost in such a conversion.

PDF can also be converted into text, at least when the text (rather than pictures of the text) has been directly encoded in PDF files. Formatting and layout information would be lost in a straight text conversion, and the text conversion of certain pages with complex layout may not always be read in "logical" reading order, without human intervention. For example, if a PDF encoding of a two-column page first renders the left column and then the right, a simple text extraction from the PDF will yield a readable text transcription.

On the other hand, if the PDF encoding goes back and forth between the two columns, or renders the right column before the left column, programs may have a much more difficult time reconstructing the text in the order it was meant to be read. Different PDF-generating programs may be more or less accommodating about rendering PDF text in a logical reading order.

A straight text conversion would also lose structural information and other PDF extras, as well non-textual items such as pictures, diagrams, and possibly equations. However, it is possible to write conversions to HTML or XML that would include a "table of contents" header that incorporated the structure of the PDF document, and that would preserve certain types of PDF hyperlinks. Text in non-European languages may also be difficult to migrate correctly, because of the previously-described limitations of PDF's support for Unicode, unless a standard set of well-defined fonts, with widely available specifications, is used to represent non-European characters. Although it is possible to migrate the appearance of PDF files, or the text, migrating both of them into a single document would be more difficult.

The only other formats commonly used to specify both the text and the appearance of documents are word-processor formats, and those tend to be proprietary, system-dependent, and more ephemeral than PDF itself is likely to be. Converting to these formats may also lead to subtly different appearances, depending on the implementation of the word processing program. RTF (Rich Text Format) may be the best target for word-processor-oriented conversions at this time, though it is far from a perfect choice. Even if it is infeasible to migrate both the text and the look of PDF into a single document, it may still be possible to migrate PDF documents into a presentation that allows one to switch between text-oriented and image-oriented views of the same document. In theory, it is possible to convert all of the information in a PDF file into an XML format with appropriate tags and attributes. However, at present there is no standard XML format used for representing PDF-like documents.

Unless such a format were standardised, and then supported with software, converting to XML might be largely an academic exercise, since no software currently exists to interpret such a format, and software developed especially to interpret the new XML format could probably just as easily interpret the information in its original PDF form. On the other hand, an XML-based form of PDF might be easier for existing XML-based search and analysis software to process. Interactive features of PDF would be harder to migrate, and Postscript, JavaScript, or other scripting snippets may be impractical to migrate on a large scale, because it is much harder to migrate program code than data. Libraries may want to avoid committing to preserving these "extra" features of PDF files, except in carefully limited cases.

Certain preservation techniques, such as integrity checks and backups, are necessary to preserve any type of digital information. Beyond those basic requirements, institutions need three things to reliably preserve PDF-format documents so that they can be reused in perpetuity:

1) A specification of exactly what an institution is committing to preserve.

   Easiest to commit to:

— Static images of the PDF document pages

A bit harder, but still important:

— Static images with exact replication of original fonts

— The text encoded in the PDF document

— The table-of-contents structure encoded in the PDF document

Much more difficult:

— Dynamic, script-dependent, or other auxiliary attributes of a PDF document. Specific attributes, such as normal Web hyperlinks, may be preservable if a commitment is made up-front to preserve them.

2) Quality control over the PDF documents acquired, to ensure that the format specifications match the archiving institution's guidelines.

Institutions that create PDF files meant for archiving, or who receive them from publishers, need to employ policies that ensure that the PDF they acquire is easy to migrate. In particular:

- — For PDF files where the text encoding should be preserved, all text should be encoded as characters, using standard character sets. Unicode is preferred for multilingual documents or documents not in European languages. The pages and text encodings should appear in the document in logical reading order.
- — Embedded scripting should be avoided, where possible, and especially when it affects the static appearance of the page.
- — Documents should be received in unencrypted form, or with the encryption undone immediately on receipt.
- — Documents should use a version of PDF that is publicly documented, and preferably which has an ample set of third-party tools available.

In addition to establishing standards for acquired PDF files, institutions may also find it useful to have tools to automatically check incoming PDF files and warn of any unexpected PDF constructs appearing in them. Such automated checks could be used to automatically flag malformed PDF files, or files that failed to meet institutional encoding standards, while avoiding expensive manual checks on all incoming files. However, writing such tools, or buying suitable tools developed by third parties, may also be nontrivial. Institutions with a common interest in preserving PDF may wish to collaborate on the development of such tools.

3) Tools and procedures for migrating PDF into other formats.

> Some software tools exist for extracting text and images from PDF files, and can be used for migration. Especially useful are tools that can be invoked automatically without human interaction. Examples in the free software world include Ghostscript for image migration, and Pstotext or Prescript for text migration. Some commercial conversion tools exist as well. Further research and development may be necessary to ensure that these conversion tools will correctly migrate all of the PDF files of interest to institutions.

At present, image-based conversion does not appear difficult to complete and verify, but automatic extraction of text, due to the nature of text layout, may not always be perfect. One possible technique for increasing the reliability of automatically extracted text would be similar to the "double-keying" principle for data entry: run two independently developed text extractors against the same PDF file, and flag points where the extractors yield different text in a different order. It remains to be seen how useful this technique would be in practice. It may be useful to run migration routines on new PDF files as soon as they are acquired, even if migrated files are not yet required.

After the migration is attempted, checks could be run to see if any problems were detected in the process. Institutions do not necessarily have to keep migrated copies of the files, as long as they have verified that migration works, and they preserve the original PDF files and the programs that will perform the migration. If one were being especially careful, though, it may be advisable to save alternative forms immediately, not just in digital form, but also in print form. Although such practices would further decrease the probability of total loss of PDF documents, they also may substantially increase the per-volume cost of preserving these documents. It is probably sufficient to have trusted methods of backup, integrity checking, mirroring, and migrating. Dynamic electronic journals are often defined as e-journals in which the content changes frequently. In reality, this is not yet happening much. E-journals may publish articles as they are ready, without waiting for a whole issue's worth of articles, but this change is sequential addition.

Dynamic e-journals can be defined as those that contain moving elements or make elements move. Moving elements include, for example, audio and video clips as well as animations. Because moving elements are not printable, libraries can no longer rely on printing the e-journals as a primary preservation strategy. Microfilm and microform are likewise static and cannot accommodate moving elements either. We will refer to these as "dynamic elements." E-journals that can make elements move typically include embedded software that enables movement, or scripts and programs that render content on the fly. We will refer to this sort of dynamism as functionality.

Because one cannot print dynamic e-journals to preserve them, the task at hand is to define new ways of preserving content that makes no sense without these constituent, dynamic aspects. While we know how to catalog, index, and retrieve moving files, we must refine this cataloging since the elements are embedded in more readily cataloged articles.

Cataloging, indexing, and retrieving the kind of content that cannot be rendered without interactive functionality are particularly vexing hurdles, especially if the content changes with every user's instantiation of that content.

Dynamic electronic journals are a natural outgrowth of Internet and Web technologies. The electronic journals were born in Web environments and are meant to be rendered and displayed in current Web environments. However we preserve them, for the time being they must also be Web accessible. In the future, it is likely that electronic material will be rendered in other digital (and perhaps even non-digital) environments.

Of course, besides dynamic elements and functionalities, dynamic e-journals contain text and other intellectually significant elements. The following list delineates several categories of "preservables" about which decisions of inclusion or exclusion must be made at the outset of the archiving process in order to know what to ask publishers to submit to the archive:

— *Content* — intellectual content, including research and so-called supplementary materials
— *Structure* — the relationship among items and all of their embeddings
— *Processes* — basic Web functionalities
— *Visual Aspects* — look and feel, layout, etc., in contrast to dynamic files like audio, video, and animated content
— *Linkages* — internal and external hyperlinks which raise important structural questions as well as copyright issues
— *Interactivity* — dynamic functionality

What we archive must be accompanied by the requisite types of metadata that will make it possible for future generations of scholars and researchers to obtain access to the archived materials: descriptive, representational, technical, and administrative metadata at the very least.

The long-term preservation of e-journals will require a large repository, replete with ingest functions, search engine, and display mechanisms. In order for a digital store of this magnitude and complexity to be accessed many years from now, it would have to be exercised, that is, put to use to verify the data's integrity, to insure the functioning of all mechanisms and the usefulness of the metadata, etc.

Preservation Strategies

Archives may preserve bits "blindly" and rely on digital archaeologists of the future to piece documents and software back together. To address some of the risks data run — such as fragility and decay — data refreshing from time to time seems essential. Unfortunately, the unpredictable timing of software and hardware obsolescence, among many other unforeseeable risks and events, spells doom for most material early on in its history. This solution is hardly proactive and begs for alternatives.

Avoiding this archaeological approach leads to thinking more in depth about emulation and migration as more viable preservation strategies. Emulation entails imitating or recreating a software environment so that programs and preserved data appear to run natively. This preservation strategy would appear to lend itself to capturing the dynamic nature of the electronic journals, but at this time the long-term feasibility of emulation is hotly contested. Still, given the dynamic specificities of the content at issue in dynamic e-journals, it may be necessary to investigate further the precise ways in which emulation can and cannot be used to preserve dynamic functionality, if not dynamic elements.

Migration currently seems to be the preservation strategy of choice, principally because it is the only and last-resort method in actual use. This approach is recommended for all digital objects one wants to prevent from falling into disuse. Ideally, a migration policy lays out when and how to transfer data, but knowing when and how to migrate data is only the first in a series of challenges in managing data migration over the long term.

The most important downside of migration as a preservation strategy is inevitable data loss. In addition, each digital archiving system will have to document its history and processes, create metadata, and otherwise track the many and constantly growing numbers of versions of any give file or dataset. The urgency of solving the nexus of versioning problems will emerge with the first series of migrations. All the same, since the interruption of vendor support is a common trigger for migrating data, as are software and hardware obsolescence, migration seems suitable to trying to ensure bit streams survive. It is questionable, however, if migration will be enough to maintain usable environments upon which dynamic functionalities rely to render content usable

Changing Landscape

Authors want more and more to take advantage of what the Web can offer in the way of functionality. Scientists, for example, devise software to carry out and report on their experiments, so it is not surprising to find them asking publishers with increasing frequency to publish software that is incorporated into their articles, software that must be used to understand the research at hand. If not preserved the science it helps report will also be partially lost.

E-publishers engaged in providing Web instantiations of their print journals report being reluctant to incorporate dynamic functionalities which are expensive propositions in large measure because of their discipline-based varieties. Publishers also appear reluctant to go down this path until print versions become a thing of the past. They indicate they would do away with print except that librarians insist they not dismiss it until we know better how to preserve electronic publications.

Editorial Process

Most e-journals, precisely because they are born of an all-print environment, remain tied to print preparation processes. They rely on well-established procedures to take an article through its life cycle, from its authoring to its publication. By now many publishers have introduced email as the primary means of communicating and transferring data, but few use the Web as an administrative-editorial platform. Those who do tend to be electronic-only publishers and they are instituting new and exciting new practices.

JIME, the Journal of Interactive Media Education, has been a pioneer in several regards.JIME's primary audience comprises education technologists and it uses their disciplinary expertise to develop the e-journal site. For the JIME editors, "knowledge construction" is an iterative and collaborative process. Inasmuch, the scholarly debate does not start with publication but early in the peer review process. To this end, JIME developed and implemented the Digital Document Discourse Environment (D3E), software enabling a document-discussion-anchored publication to emerge. The decision to use this software as a backbone has broad ramifications that reach beyond the process-oriented exigencies it satisfies technologically.

Working at any stage on the e-journal site, authors, editors and reviewers invoke the Web's capacity to streamline the editorial and review processes by relying on its dynamic, functional interactivity. It is worth noting that while e-journals and other scholarly e-community sites have generally failed in their attempts to establish threaded discussions, JIME appears to have a critical mass of such activity, owing in part to its enabling interactive software. This e-journal is available at no cost.

Audio, Video, and Multimedia

The use of thumbnails (small image files) as clickable links to still images is common in many disciplines. The thumbnail serves several functions. Perhaps most importantly, a thumbnail graphic can be transmitted to a browser far more efficiently than its larger counterpart.

Secondly, a thumbnail provides both a tease and a glimpse of what the authors have to display with their texts.

The prevalence of thumbnails and the myriad ways they are used can be gleaned from glancing at any number of e-journals. Architronic: The Electronic Journal of Architecture, Conservation Ecology, and Earth Interactions illustrate the varieties of visuals that appear as thumbnails: pictures, graphs, pie charts, data tables, drawings, etc. Alan Dodson's "Performance and Hypermetric Transformation: An Extension of the Lerdahl-Jackendoff Theory" appears in Music Theory Online. Viewable with or without frames, access to images and audio clips are easy and numerous.

The Interactive Multimedia Electronic Journal of Computer-Enhanced Learning is, not surprisingly given its purpose, replete with examples of static and dynamic visuals of all sorts. To know at a glance what each article might include in the way of non-text media, scroll through any article: iconic indicators with short captions appear in the right-hand margin. In some electronic journals, dynamic non-text elements often end up as "supplementary material." Since one cannot print film and audio clips or multimedia of any sort, supplementary materials typically grace e-journals with print editions. The decision to include multimedia as a separate file provides the publisher an opportunity to highlight multimedia content and thereby promote and market the e-journal as desired.

A simple example of this occurs at Optics Express. The e-journal's home page teases the reader with an animated image and a caption that includes a link to information about a current related article. By following the link, the reader can then access both a PDF version of the text of the article and the separately presented multimedia element. Since 1998, a subscription to the Computer Music Journal, published by the MIT Press, includes an annually produced CD-ROM of music and sound related to the articles the e-journal has published in the course of the year. One can also purchase the CD-ROM separately.

The e-journal itself seems devoid of music and sound files. In the humanities and the arts especially, readers may come across multimedia applications that offer artistic depth or breadth in support of the content at hand, sometimes nearly stealing the show! Such is the case in one Postmodern Culture article on filmmaker Dziga Vertov's Kino-Eye. A pulsing eye-camera lens greets the reader with visual echoes of the topic at hand. The image's caption reads, "Animated image constructed by author using Man With a Movie Camera production stills."

The Journal for MultiMedia History, published by the Department of History at the University of Albany, is a most interesting example of multimedia-enhanced research because its practice demonstrates how paradigms can shift rather easily and to useful ends. JMMH did not adopt the publish-as-needed model that Web technologies make possible and that most electronic-only journals embrace. Instead, it publishes a single issue per year; it also breaks with the traditional article or text-centered approach to journal publishing.

Personalisation Tools

Some customisation tools can serve several purposes. Tools such as alerting services that send emails with news about newly published articles and other content-related events promote the use of the e-journal's site, but do not directly influence content delivery or usability. Other tools affect the content more directly and beg for ways to be preserved.

The Internet Journal of Chemistry (IJC) explores the potential Web technologies offer. The journal's files are not stored as PDF or HTML files, but instead are served up dynamically or on-the-fly. It offers the most straightforward and unencumbered testing ground for researching on-the-fly generation of scholarly content. In addition, approximately seventy-five percent of the articles contain interactive elements. IJC editor Steven Bachrach, who engages the help of students to manage conversions and production, likes authors to be able to submit materials in their preferred formats, thereby increasing the likelihood that readers will have to download appropriate plug-ins to ensure that all content can run as intended.

In addition to lifting constraints on authors who may want to take full advantage of new technologies, IJC offers readers an extensive range of customisation preferences that complicate the task of preserving content. IJC includes tools for readers to control layout, fonts, and color schemes. Readers can decide where to display footnotes (low on the page or in a floating window); they can create annotations and then decide whether to view these annotations within the document's frame or in a floating window. Readers can also personalise formats to view chemical structures a number of different ways: as standard GIF/JPEG images, using links to a data file, as embedded objects, or other options.

The IJC is not alone in offering annotation tools and preferences, but IJC annotations are private. In contrast, the Journal of Universal Computer Science (JUCS) offers readers not only public annotation and comment features but also labeling options.

9

Digital Cataloguing

Cataloguing in some form or other is still the key to access - indeed it is even more important if users are to find the knowledge and information they need amongst the tidal wave of raw data. However, cataloguing is an expensive business, and the economic pressures will be made worse by the increase in publishing in both digital and print formats.

This will force the even wider re-use of records than is already occurring, but efficient re-use is only possible if records are prepared to common standards. The Web and digital publishing communities have realised the importance of standards, and there is a flurry of activity to develop them. Unfortunately there is a multiplicity of standards in development, and it can be difficult to find one's way through the maze.

Cataloguing standards -leaving aside communications and catalogue search protocols such as Z39.50 -can be categorised as:

— data dictionaries (lists of data elements)

— formats (how the data are carried)

— identifiers (to uniquely identify documents, authors etc)

— cataloguing rules (by which data are presented consistently to facilitate retrieval).

The data dictionaries with greatest significance for libraries are Dublin Core, which originated at a conference hosted by OCLC in Dublin Ohio, and ONIX (Online Information eXchange) which has emerged from the book trade as a subset of the wider EPICS (EDItEUR Product Information Communication Standards) data dictionary. EItEUR is the international organisation concerned with developing standards to support trade applications, but who are also keen to ensure collaboration with the library sector.

In the formats category we have MARC (MAchine Readable Cataloguing), which has been building up its capability to accommodate records for digital documents. Meanwhile the new kid on the block is XML (eXtensible Mark-up Language) with its specially designed metadata format, the Resource e-scription Framework (RDF) for embedding records in XML documents.

Identifiers are important to uniquely identify an item to facilitate the reuse of common components and to minimise data traffic. The library world has through the International Federation of Library Associations (IFLA) been working towards a standard identifier to allow the unique identification of persons and the re-use of accurate name authority data packages. However, this requires name authority registries in each country, and there has not been the resource to achieve that. Meanwhile in the trade sector rights management is a hot topic.

Publishers, authors and other rights holders naturally want to derive revenue from the electronic market in their digital documents, and the unique identification of rights holders is essential to support this. The potential profits from this marketplace could mean that the network of registries foreseen by IFLA might be funded by trade organisations. This convergence of purpose is useful to illustrate what may become an increasingly familiar phenomenon.

The final component of the information architecture is the cataloguing codes used to provide the intellectual structure for the data. Without that structure the data loses much of its meaning was originally developed for resource discovery of digital documents on the Web. It comprises 15 data elements and is meant to be simple and cheap to apply, especially by the originators of the documents. The ONIX subset emerged from the Association of American Publishers discussions on how to get e-commerce applications under way in the trade sector. It is driven in particular by the needs of on-line booksellers where rich metadata, e.g. reviews, blurbs, extracts and images, is necessary to make up for the inability of customers to browse the books in the flesh. ONIX is implemented in XML.

Version 2.0 has been published, which can accommodate multimedia publications and e-books. ONIX is being adopted by an increasing number of trade bodies, for example in the US, UK, Germany and Latin America, and by international bodies like the ISBN network and the International OI Foundation as their preferred metadata standard for descriptive data associated with the International Standard Book A study was commissioned recently to examine the potential for ONIX to be used in the library sector.

The fact that ONIX is based on the IFLA Functional Requirements for Bibliographic Records model means that there is basic compatibility with library applications. Indeed the trade sector can be commended for not trying to reinvent the wheel and for drawing on the best of what the library world can offer. Librarians who were consulted as part of the study were enthused by the potential for trade-library collaboration, and saw ONIX as having tremendous potential for acquisitions functions and for enriching catalogue records. Indeed some foresaw ONIX as having the potential eventually to replace MARC as the format for carrying cataloguing data. Obviously extension to wider library applications will require more data elements, e.g. preservation data, but the format is expansible. This raises the question for libraries -which data dictionary does one choose? Are Dublin Core and ONIX competing or complementary? For a time there was concern that they were competing. However, the messages one hears more recently are of convergence, e.g. with the adoption of qualifiers by DC, and of dialogue between the communities. Which one predominates in the library sector will depend on the capabilities of library systems, on the availability of records in the different formats and on the investment that is put in to developing the systems and schemes.

In this situation it is obvious that interoperability will be paramount, and that realisation is gaining ground. The preexisting format in widespread use in libraries is MARC. It is well established in the library sector, but not so well in the trade sector. This makes cross sector collaboration more difficult.

The main drawback of MARC is the number of national variants and the apparent competition between UNIMARC and MARC21. The difficulties of exchanging records are pushing countries like the UK and organisations like LIBER to pursue harmonisation of formats.

The predominance of the US in research -and to a degree in publishing -means that the target format of choice is becoming MARC21. The UK is almost certainly going to harmonise its UKMARC format with MARC21, provided the role for non-US organisations in the governance of MARC21 satisfies the UK community. XML, the major new format that carries out the same function as MARC in a digital environment, grew out of the Standard Generalised Mark-up Language (SGML) originally developed to support computer typesetting, and the Hyper-text Mark-up Language (HTML) developed for writing Web pages. Combined with Java script XML is an even more powerful web authoring language.

If libraries were to invest in changing their systems to MARC21 only to find that within a few years MARC is replaced, say, by ONIX or Dublin Core records encoded in the XML format. One leading light, closely involved with developing the MARC format, saw MARC lasting at least 15 years in to the future and probably longer, because of the huge investment by libraries in systems and data. Crosswalks between formats were seen as the way of achieving interoperability, and continuing development of the format would accommodate new applications and data types.

Rules for Cataloguing

Cataloguing rules are the area where there is arguably the least international standardisation. This could be a barrier that remains when format issues etc are resolved. The Anglo-American Cataloguing Rules (AACR) is the most widely used code, but its influence is confined largely to the English-speaking world.

However, the growing interest in AACR from other regions, including LIBER members, has prompted a review by the Committee of Principals for AACR, which is looking at internationalisation of the code's development and governance. The virtual library environment means that not only must cataloguing rules cope with digital documents, but they must be also be capable of facilitating access to items from a collection that now expands well beyond the physical confines of one institution.

Another area of change being considered is whether one continues to catalogue the work in hand (currently prescribed by AACR) or the intellectual work, where the physical manifestation acquired by the library is recorded at a secondary level. This has been characterised as the "content versus carrier" debate. The FRBR favours a tiered approach working from the intellectual work at the highest level, as does ONIX, since it has adopted the FRBR model. So work is well advanced to adapt at least one major cataloguing code to a hybrid print and digital environment.

What's more, provided AACR does increase its international appeal by being more welcoming to non-English speaking communities, it may offer a common code in which catalogue data can be more readily exchanged. However, the difficulty of overcoming cultural differences between national codes should not be underestimated. Cataloguing is often singled out for scrutiny in trying to pare costs. Cataloguing has adapted to these pressures by collaboration, and there are many success stories, e.g. OCLC, the Research Libraries Group and the Consortium of European Research Libraries. However, even more collaboration will be needed to contain costs in the digital environment. Indeed, as libraries try to cope with constrained acquisitions and operating budgets, collaboration becomes a major driver in itself.

For instance in the UK university and national library sectors much work is being devoted to developing collaborative acquisition, retention and preservation schemes, and cataloguing systems need to be able to cope with the demands this collaboration places upon them. Collaboration is also a major force in the trade sector. Book publishers, music publishers and video companies want to ensure their products are readily available from the on-line retailers. So they, too, are collaborating. For collaboration to work interoperability is paramount.

The trade does not want to have to re-key data between applications. Nor do libraries want to convert records between formats as they exchange records. Lastly, but of greatest importance for a service industry, are the users and their needs. Users want a hybrid library; they don't want to search separate catalogues for print and digital documents. Neither are they interested in the distinction between what their library holds locally and what is on Web. So they are driving libraries towards providing seamless services, where again interoperability is the key.

There are a number of issues for the library community that also have to be taken into account when weighing up the answers to the questions about the future. The first is the systems support for the new formats. We are seeing hybrid systems beginning to emerge from some of the larger vendors. Support for XML will improve as the database management systems that underpin many of the library vendors packages improve their XML support.

There is all the technical data that has to be captured, which is essential for access to the electronic texts and for preservation. Indeed the ideal time to make preservation decisions is at the time of cataloguing, so that the decisions can be recorded. Then there are the time penalties of having to load digital documents, especially from DVD, CD-ROM etc, in order to discover the technical and descriptive data. All this slows the process. Record transfer and other forms of collaboration have already been mentioned as a way of minimising and sharing those costs. Another parallel strategy is the creation of productivity tools to gather the information automatically. An example of this approach is the range of productivity tools developed and being refined as part of the CORC (Cooperative Online Resource Catalogue) programme initiated and led by OCLC.

Another issue for libraries are what records are available, at what cost and whether they are of useful quality. A traditional problem at the trade/library interface has been the quality of records produced by publishers, whose staff in many cases do not have appropriate training. This is still an issue to a degree, but, whatever one thinks about the descriptive cataloguing data provided by publishers, there is still value in capturing the rich additional data produced by them. And, of course, the increasing role of commercial bibliographic agencies is helping to provide cleaner descriptive data, too.

The last major issue, especially if common standards prove an elusive goal between different sectors, is the interoperability of standards, in particular the availability of crosswalks. It is encouraging to note that these are being developed, for instance between MARC and ONIX. The assembly of materials from many different sources and of many different formats is a challenge to techniques of bibliographic control developed in the context of static, print-based collections.

Digital resources can be created with no information about their provenance, change location or disappear without warning, have content which changes rapidly and lack any kind of quality control. Some more familiar media found in digital libraries also pose problems, such as still and moving images, which are especially difficult to describe for effective retrieval. Unfortunately, providing access to information remains a sophisticated task not amenable to automation. There are two levels at which cataloguing of digital libraries might be considered.

10

Technology Access

Digital technologies open a world that paradoxically is simultaneously more complex and, in some ways, simpler. It is more complex because now the same document or document format may intrinsically be represented in different media for different purposes, forcefully motivating the need to distinguish carefully between the format and the medium. Furthermore, different media may be used interchangeably for different stages of document handling, that is, for capture, storage, access, distribution, and use. To complicate the situation even more, the documents may be encoded in a myriad of ways at each of these stages. And yet, separation of the format and the medium—and treating each stage of document handling separately—may open up a more logical structure free from traditional constraints. In this sense, digital technologies may simplify certain aspects of librarianship. Digital technologies present many new challenges, however, that must be considered. For example, although these varying formats may be decoded and translated back and forth among each other, many fear that the means of decoding may become lost as a result of technological obsolescence, conceivably making digitally stored documents inaccessible.

There are also many who question the longevity of the physical media used in digital technologies. Others suggest that the appropriate way to address both of these problems—as well as to take advantage of the declining costs of computer storage and of increasing storage densities—may well be to copy stored documents periodically onto new media. Indeed the main advantage of the world of digital technologies, namely that they represent a kind of "esperanto" of mutually comprehensible and interchangeable formats, may, if not properly managed, also represent their biggest weakness, because of the rapidity of change and obsolescence, and because of the wide range of choices available at any given time.

Periodic recopying onto new media represents a whole new approach for libraries to the operation and financing of "inventory management". The implications could be quite extensive. Librarians tend to think in terms of periods of centuries rather than having to recopy every few years. Such considerations may either hinder the adoption of digital technologies for preservation or other purposes or eventually cause some rethinking of the underlying economics of librarianship. The incentive for such potential reevaluation, however, is not limited to the preservation of older materials, nor is the influence of technology the only driving factor. The underlying stimulus is a gradual transition over the centuries—perhaps spurred by the exponential growth of recorded knowledge and information—from documents with associated physical or conceptually useful lifetimes, times between new editions, or, more generically, times between "instances", that can be measured in decades or centuries; to documents with associated times between instances measured in much shorter units of time—even, in the case of "active documents", measured in minutes or seconds. The financial and other implications of this could undoubtedly be far-reaching for libraries, introducing into the library milieu unfamiliar concepts associated with continuous processes or processes with relatively short lifetimes, such as "depreciation" and "lifecycle costing."

These are concepts that are familiar to the world of digital electronic processing and quite normal outside of universities, but that have been avoided in worlds—such as research libraries—that depend to a greater or lesser extent upon irregular gifts or grants of varying or unpredictable size, donations directed to the purchase and immediate storage of documents, but not to their maintenance. Indeed, one of the most serious questions facing librarians in the future may be how to effect a match between the changing economic demands of "continuous processes" and the traditional nature of many funding sources. Yet the potential of digital technologies and of the flexibility they offer is boundless.

Over the coming decades, these technologies may open up vistas of ever-increasing storage densities to where entire libraries can be electronically stored in the space of a single room; of blinding access and distribution speeds allowing whole documents to be moved almost instantly across the nation's (and indeed the world's) data networks, leading to the concept of the "distributed library;" of ease of replication at very modest cost (another cause for alarm, particularly to those concerned with protection of intellectual property); of "print-on-demand" where paper copies of documents are only printed "just in time" and not inventoried in advance of need; of accessibility at a distance away from where the "digital document" or preservation copy was created or is stored; and of intelligent automated document analysis. Indeed, the means of creation and production of documents have already been revolutionised by these technologies. These technologies also open up horizons for totally new document formats, such as active documents whose contents may combine different media such as text, sound, video or voice; or whose contents may change dynamically with time, what Harvey Wheeler called "the fungible book."

The preservation of these new "active" formats is not of direct interest to the subject of preservation of more traditional formats, but is of indirect interest because digitally preserved traditional documents can be incorporated into such active documents. Some view the introduction of digital technologies into the world of libraries as likely to cause a revolution as far-reaching as that caused by the printing-press: a massive paradigm shift. Others view the introduction with concern, an intimidating perturbation that disturbs an equilibrium and modalities of scholarship that have served well for many decades or even for centuries. Either way, digital technologies cannot be ignored.

The next twenty years are likely to be times of extraordinary change. Our libraries—indeed our universities, colleges, and our scholarly communities—may well be remade by the consequences of this technological revolution. And yet—in spite of technology's impact and of the revolutionary consequences of that impact—it must be recognised that technology itself is not the ultimate driving force. It is the inexorable pressure caused by the exponential growth of recorded knowledge, and the ever-increasing complexity, costs, and other problems associated with the storage and distribution of, and access to, such information. Technology can provide some solutions: it is not an end in itself. Furthermore—for many reasons too numerous to detail here—the "digital library" is not about to replace the "paper library." Both will need to coexist in a shifting environment, at least for the foreseeable future. This in itself will present librarians with many economic, organisational, social, technical, and other challenges. Between the eager apostles of technology and those who approach change with extreme caution lies the mass of professionals who are trying to understand and grapple with the potential of this shifting environment, many of them implementing prototype activities designed to elucidate greater insight, many working to close the gap between promise and reality.

The rash of new information technology has raised major problems for librarians and archivists, faced with a flood of new kinds of media such as audio and video tape or computer disks. Most of these technologies were designed and manufactured without permanence as a prime consideration. A worse problem is the short life of the reading devices; even the less than permanent tapes or disks often do not deteriorate until long after the machines to read them become unavailable.

Digital preservation thus depends upon copying, not on the survival of the physical media. Librarians and archivists must prepare for reformatting as a regular step in information management. In this, they must join with computer center managers, individual computer owners, and all others who need to keep machine-readable data for more than a few years.

Computer-based Archives

There is great economy of scale in maintaining new media—not so much the devices, but in sharing the expertise. Cooperation is essential for libraries to manage. Not only will standard formats help a great deal, but copying digital information is much easier than generating it. Particularly where lots of intellectual effort is required it makes no sense for different groups to work on the same file. It will be much easier for libraries to obtain updated versions from central sources than for each library to manage all its own reformatting. A cooperative program for converting digital information would be appropriate. It should involve both maintaining records of who has what, seeing that conversions are done only once, and seeing to it that important materials are kept in more than one place. There are a great many existing computer-based archives.

Efforts should be made to find funding to put archives of this sort on a firm footing. In the long run, it will be cheaper to have sites of responsibility for particular materials than to attempt to duplicate expertise in specialised records conversion.

Furthermore, sites of this form will function in the traditional way to link scholars working in the same area, even if these links are now via electronic mail rather than by physical travel to the site. Most of the computer-based archives above are textually oriented. Support is needed to extend computer-based archives in the multimedia areas, and also in the areas of numerical data and programs. Some attention is also needed to ways of indexing the material in these archives, as there is no straightforward way to locate information, particularly non-textual information, in machine-readable form. Bibliographic guides will have to be developed, and even the format these should take is not clear. Industrial and government computing groups have often had the problem of maintaining old tape files, and have stimulated much of the work in records management for machine-readable files. Unfortunately the history here is often poor: it is said that we know more about the 1860 census than the 1960 census, which was written on a very early form of computer tape and which no one realised in time should be copied to newer media.

Copyright rules may pose a severe problem. The copyright life of much material greatly exceeds the technological life of the media it is recorded on. A library may well be able to preserve something only by copying it, but may have difficulty obtaining permission to do that. With luck the original issuer will publish the material in a new format, but as the devotees of old records and movies can testify, this does not always happen. Leaving aside the question of how it is accomplished, through either amendment or court interpretation, the concept of "fair use" should be extended to include the copying to new media of a publication which is no longer available for sale, and the distribution of the copy to other libraries. At the moment, there is an exemption for copying of a publication that a library already owns, but not for distribution to libraries that do not own the original being copied.

The law may also pose problems even for information where the copyright law does not bar conversion. A library or archives might wish to store information derived from old, copyright-expired publications; or from public domain sources; or from publications of the university to which it belongs. However, it is doubtful that a copyright can be asserted in a straightforward transcription to machine-readable form of a non-copyrighted document or audiotape. The rule that a copyright can only be claimed for the result of creative activity is somewhat unclear. It has recently been interpreted to say that (a) collecting and alphabetising names into a telephone book is not copyrightable but at the very least (b) numbering the pages in a Government-provided text is copyrightable. Although measuring the creativity in these publications is like arguing whether a concrete block is more or less intelligent than a 2x4, the legal uncertainty causes all vendors of electronic information to require specific contracts limiting the use of the purchased data, imposing administrative burdens on everyone.

Libraries and archives, depending on the circumstances, might be on either side of this issue. Presumably, the ability to enforce a copyright in a converted text will encourage someone to do a conversion. On the other hand, if the issuer then disappears, it becomes difficult to get permission to do the next conversion when that becomes necessary. Again, it would be useful to have a rule that the copyright lasts only as long as someone is willing to sell the protected item. The copyright law also affects the question of multiple copies. The United States is developing a very high speed digital network which will soon provide 45 Mbits/second between major sites and should be at 1 Gbit/second before the end of the decade. Thus, libraries and archives may well feel that there is no need to have their own copy of something, since the delay in getting it remotely may be negligible.

But, depending on copyright rules and the developing business practices in the electronic information industry, it may be difficult to arrange access permission. On the other side, it would be unfortunate if the existence of the network meant that important documents were kept in only one copy which was at risk of disappearing. Finally, the insertion of copy-protection into sound recordings acts against the interests of libraries and long-term permanence of the original material. Deposit of an unprotected copy in some trustworthy institution is probably the best solution, but not something the industry is pursuing.

OI Usability

We have identified the commercially available online information resources (OI) which are relevant to digital libraries as online databases, CD-ROMs and bulletin boards. This definition is dictated in part by the association of these resources within the literature, and in part by the interdependent nature of the technologies that comprise them. New and existing OI resource providers are variously constrained and enabled in their efforts to take advantage of advances in data transfer (like fiber-optics), processing (like massively parallel architectures) and information storage (like terabyte hard drives and CD-ROM.) These technological components define an accessibility baseline of OI resource usability. Digital libraries which contain OI products and services must at least facilitate physical connection to these resources. Beyond this point, there are many aspects to usability that make using OI resources more enjoyable, less expedient, more expensive, less effective, and so on.

The aspects of OI usability can be classified into four major categories:

1. HCI Usability,
2. Content Usability,
3. Organisational Usability and
4. Interorganisational Usability.

HCI Usability involves issues of individual access and individual resource usage on a personal level or within working groups. It highlights human-computer interaction with the OI resource interface, but also takes into consideration how individuals might need to coordinate resource usage in a work group setting.

Content Usability involves characteristics of the information itself. It addresses issues of information relevance, information awareness, information retrieval methods, and expertise.

Organisational Usability involves the situated use of OI and OI resources. A library or organisation may provide training and support staff to help people use the available resources, or it may not. The information itself may be used collaboratively among working groups or symbolically as post-decision support.

Interorganisational Usability involves use of OI and OI resources within interorganisational networks. This may entail uses of OI to achieve competitive advantage, or to coordinate professionals of the virtual organisation.

OI Users

Non-scholarly users of OI resources in the digital library may be today's consumers of commercial OI services. Martha E. Williams has been accumulating and analysing the statistics of the online database industry for a number of years. Her classifications of "users" are at the institutional level: academics, information brokers, government, industry, legal institutions, medical institutions, not-for-profits and libraries. Levy and Marshall also confirm that digital libraries are "users" of OI resources. The people searching these databases are also called "users", and they are often segmented on the basis of their information usage into two groups: end-users and intermediaries. Intermediaries are usually associated with libraries or corporate information centers. They search the OI resources at their disposal on behalf of others who will use the information retrieved in decision-making or other tasks. Aumente quotes 1987 DIALOG usage statistics as 80% by search intermediaries. End-users are commonly considered to be individuals who use the information they retrieve directly in their own work tasks.

There has been a significant amount of research attention paid to the end-user. However, some researchers have found it difficult to segregate the intermediary from the end-user in situated use. They have concluded that in their studies all individual OI resource users were essentially intermediaries because "the work practices of their settings led them to share their search results with others, either by request or on their own initiative". Who the user is and what the user does has been the quintessentially interesting research question of the OI resource provider and the digital library architect. However, as was demonstrated by the videotext fiasco, the providers and architects are not always willing or able to perform the research and evaluate the results before constructing or marketing the resources. When empirical usability research does not exist or cannot be done because the technologies under construction have no current equivalent, OI resource providers in industry and academia rely on theoretical perspectives that are widely espoused by respected members of their communities to guide them.

One perspective on OI usability is widely and tenaciously held. It can be characterised as optimistically rational, and it is espoused as a complex array of social, political and organisational strategies which emphasize the importance of information, information resources and information technology for economic survival and social progress. These strategies call be called as "informational imperatives." They guide organisations and individuals to adopt more information-intensive practices, and they set expectations for particular socio-technical results.

OI Reserach

Currently, most empirical studies indicate that the use of online databases in particular, and the use of libraries and information resources in general, has not been integrated into decision-making and strategic planning activities to the degree that informational imperatives might project. Explanations of why this may be so are guided by identifiable themes. The dominant perspective is rationalist, but strong currents of institutionalism, human relations theory, critical theory and postmodernism run through the discourse on many OI usability aspects.

Rational Utility

HCI Usability: It involves issues of access and resource usage on an individual level or within working groups. It highlights human-computer interaction with the OI resource interface, but also takes into consideration how individuals might need to coordinate resource usage in a work group setting. Rationalist discussions of online database usage begin with the assumption that an individual will naturally want to conduct his or her own search. So, providing quick and easy access to OI resources is their primary concern. Their solutions to problems of usability focus on the human-computer interface—usually the computer screen or application presentation layer. They may suggest adding "richer", multimedia formats or the development of natural language interfaces. Michael Eisenberg discusses some studies which tried to measure the effectiveness of bibliographic database searching by untrained users. For the most part, these studies were conducted as experiments on undergraduate and graduate students. They all seem to conclude that anyone can search effectively, given the right interface, although the only researcher to report situated results was somewhat baffled: "Results were surprising in that the online searches resulted in few references in the students' bibliographies" Rationalists expect the aggregate use of OI resources by working groups to yield productivity benefits and stimulate additional use.

Content Usability. Content Usability involves characteristics of the information itself. It addresses issues of information relevance, information awareness, information retrieval methods, and expertise. Rationalists believe that when individuals learn about OI resources, they will recognise the potential value of OI contents and use them accordingly. If OI resources are not being used, then it must be because people just don't know enough about them. They believe, as Jon Kaye does, that "to take full advantage of on-line database services, the threshold of awareness of the value of information must be raised. Users are still not understanding the value of information as a strategic tool".

However, rationalists working with content usability understand that establishing awareness is only one facet of the problem. Once access and awareness have been established, there are still issues of information retrieval and information overload. Some researchers, like Ray R. Larson, try to resolve both of these problems simultaneously by developing online systems which use techniques derived from information retrieval research. Recognising that users sometimes just "give up" when their queries don't return relevant results immediately, Larson attempts to cluster the data into meaningful classifications that, when coupled with statistical ranking mechanisms, can "reduce the cognitive load on the user in selecting relevant documents".

Organisational Usability. It involves the situated use of OI and OI resources. An organisation may provide training and support staff to help people use the available resources, or it may not. The information itself may be used collaboratively among working groups or symbolically as post-decision support. One of the reasons why rationalist managers of an organisation may choose not to provide technical support or training on OI resources is because it costs too much. Researchers like Michael Koenig seek to convince them otherwise by extrapolating from economic theory to affirm that organisations systematically underinvest in OI support services and libraries. He then goes on to assert that the existence of these organisational infrastructures enhances the free-flow of information throughout the organisation, and leads directly to productivity gains and improved decision-making, but his studies do not identify the mechanism by which they do so.

Along with providing OI resource usage support, rational organisations in the Information Age are expected to develop formal organisational strategies to guide the optimised use of both internal and external information available through these resources. But a survey of IS managers by King and Grover found that "[n]early 55% reported either 'irregular' or 'no formal process', suggesting that analyses dealing with information technology and information as a strategic resource have not yet become a routine and regular part of the planning process". King and Grover suggest that, in order to successfully 'mine' online databases for potentially powerful information, organisations should adopt a model of competitive advantage like those developed by rationalists concerned with interorganisational OI usability.

Interorganisational Usability. Marchand and Horton adopt the view that efficiently functioning markets are the highest good. And, for rationalists, healthy competition is the hallmark of efficiently functioning markets.

Interorganisational Usability involves use of OI and OI resources within interorganisational networks. This may entail uses of OI to achieve competitive advantage, or to coordinate professionals of the virtual organisation. According to Marchand and Horton, managers must learn to use information strategically, in order to correctly assess environmental changes in their own industries and to spot potential opportunities in heretofore "other" industries. To do this, managers will have to realign the organisational structure with TQM-like methodologies.

The profitability and efficiency concerns of corporate information consumers may not be motivating concepts for digital library planners, but an interorganisational usability awareness may allow them to consider that "outsourcing" organisations may take advantage of publicly available digital libraries. Rational perspectives which encourage efficiency and the attainment of competitive advantage rarely consider the consequences of shifting the productivity burden to public institutions.

Human Resourcefulness

A preponderant proportion of the OI usability literature reflects a rational point of view. But, within the HCI community, there is a large contingent of researchers who are interested not only in enhancing productivity but also in designing OI resources which enhance the work experience.

HCI Usability. While rationalists assume that OI resource access naturally leads to use, human relations (HR) theorists seek to broaden the definition of accessibility. Mary Culnan has personalised the access question by breaking it down into three behaviorally oriented components: physical access (i.e. finding a terminal), interface access (i.e. using a query command language) and informational access (i.e. displaying data.) We have classified the last two components as aspects of Content

Usability, largely on Culnan's findings that "physical access to the terminal used to access the system and access to the actual information system are independent dimensions". Furthermore, on the physical access dimension, she suggests that physical accessibility does not necessarily lead to use. Contrary to rationalist expectations, she finds that experience with a resource improves perceptions of accessibility and potential usefulness of the information attainable through that resource.

HR theorists researching at the group level are also very different from rationalists in one important respect—their expectations incorporate a notion of equity. Unlike Flores et al., who suggest that efficient control is the answer to group work coordination problems, Grudin suggests that a balance in terms of who does the work and who benefits from that work would go further to alleviate coordination issues. Although Grudin's work focuses on internal OI resources, like scheduling systems; his concepts can be seen to apply to external OI resources and digital libraries as well—especially when research functions are organisationally segmented.

Content Usability. HR theorists do not approach OI resource content usability from a perspective which assumes that mere awareness of the potential usefulness of a resource is enough to ensure use. In fact, Nicholas and Erbach conclude their examination of end-user searching in four commercially available OI resources with an important observation. They find that the services are dissimilar, the pricing structures are divergent, downloading speeds are highly variable independent of baud rates, and in-depth knowledge about even a small set of OI services is difficult for any one person to obtain and maintain. Their findings are based on end-user observations and are motivated by a concern for lowering the frustration level of the end-user by identifying user behaviors which are not well-accommodated by the OI resources in the study. Nicholas and Erbach make numerous suggestions for improving these existing resources, which if followed, would lead to a standard approach to OI resource design. However, they do not explicitly make this recommendation. Pfaffenberger agrees that there are a great many obstacles to end-user searching in OI resources. He points out that equal opportunity of information access was rhetoricised as the inevitable by-product of technologically enhanced information networks. But he identifies inequity of expertise as the most serious threat to equity of access. Pfaffenberger suggests that online databases will only attract end-users who are highly educated and are able to judge the significance of the material they encounter online. Much of his discussion takes on a critical theory perspective, especially when he refers to the decline in public education quality and the proletarianisation of the white collar work force, but we have included it here because his suggestion to restructure the online information formats so they are more accessible to end-users is a human-factors solution to the problem of expertise.

Organisational Usability. HR guided researchers are nearly unanimous in their advocacy of training and support infrastructures for OI resource usage. They may suggest that an organisation provide basic skills training and technical support for its OI workforce, or they may suggest a kind of self-help system which blends humans and technology into a single package. Mark S. Ackerman describes how one such system has been developed to combine information sharing with expertise sharing. His system is not merely a factual repository, it is a device for growing organisational memory, and so it encourages managers to reorganise work—especially how expertise is captured and how it is made available to all levels of the workforce.

Mintzberg takes a different tack. Rather than suggesting a technological solution to information access, he concentrates his attention on intermediaries and collaboration. While trying to answer the question: "Why do managers not use information as they apparently should?", he focuses on identifying how managers work. He suggests that organisational impediments to OI resource usage arise from dysfunctional goal setting and the nature of managerial work and advancement. Mintzberg also encourages the reorganisation of work to alleviate the problem, but he states that "[m]anagers need broad-based formal information systems, in large part independent of the computer...There is reason to believe that the best filters and pattern recognisers are intelligent human beings—bright specialists (and alter egos) who can stand between the manager and mass of data out there".

Interorganisational Usability. The Human Relations perspective usually focuses on issues of job satisfaction and worker productivity, so there is not much HR literature which addresses OI resource usability at an interorganisational level. One notable exception is a report issued in 1982 by the United Nations Centre on Transnational Corporations. The UN was worried that the "information gap" between developed and developing countries had been widening and lessening the potential for real competition by developing countries in world markets. They commissioned this study which suggested two organisational solutions to level the playing field: build human resource infrastructures in the developing countries, like the Mexican information center, or establish search centers in the information-rich countries. Whereas the rationalist is interested in allowing markets to function and information to flow, researchers with an HR view are more interested in removing barriers to entry and leveling the playing field.

The digital library community has taken many of the guiding principles of the public service library community to heart, and it strongly embraces the concepts of HR theorists. But concerns for equity of access, fairness in the distribution of work and advocacy for adequate training in distributed, multi-organisational environments should be guided by an awareness of these non-academic contexts of use in addition to traditional academic contexts.

Institutionalised Use

A small but significant body of the OI usability literature reflects an institutional perspective. These researchers are interested in how organisational and institutional environments constrain or enable use of OI resources and their contents. Although, institutionalists may recommend technological fixes to OI resources, they are more likely to recommend policy or procedural modifications that are within an organisation's power to change.

HCI Usability. Institutional discussions of OI resource usage do not assign an active, rational decision-making role to the individual. They are more likely to present OI resource user choices as a complex set of constraints set up by the various organisations and institutions which provide and administer OI services. Aumente presents a historical overview of the videotext and online database industry, with an accent on HCI usability aspects. He finds fault with the usability of videotext formats and the communication exchange capabilities of the medium, but notes that similarly constrained services, like online databases, have been successful. He looks to see where the technological constraints have been overcome within the videotext arena, for example France's Minitel, and identifies the external political factors as key enablers. Aumente's set of recommendations for the establishment of usable and viable OI resources involves technological enhancements which are tightly coupled with political support for developing a national OI infrastructure. Wanda Orlikowski has examined the introduction of groupware databases which served as digital libraries throughout a large, geographically dispersed organisation. Her study found that the groupware had been developed expressly for collaborative use. For those groups within her organisation who shared information in a cooperative mode, the system was usable. But for the consultants, who worked in a competitive, non-information sharing mode, the system was largely unusable. They did not have any established norms for sharing information through digital libraries.

Furthermore, they had real economic incentives not to share, but to retain and obtain as much expertise for themselves as possible. Orlikowski does not assume that everyone will want to use the resource, and she does not assume that equal access brings with it any incentives to use. She locates the implementation problem of her study outside the technological infrastructure, within the competitively-focused organisational incentive structures for the consultants, and suggests that modifications will have to be made here before the OI resource usage practices of the consultants can be expected to change.

Content Usability. Institutionalist information retrieval approaches try to acknowledge the taken-for-granted ways of doing things that can be discerned in particular organisations or environments. Oddy et al. have tried to incorporate situational information into OI retrieval systems. They attempt to generate generic research scripts and to match search processes with markers in the script so that the system will "know" where the searcher is in his or her research project. Oddy et al. believe that "[p]eople engaged in empirical work can be viewed as members of a community: they complete similar tasks, espouse shared social and technical norms, and operate within a unique reward structure". So knowing where a researcher is in a research project can help a search intermediary determine what is the most relevant information. Oddy et al. were able to identify some important patterns along these lines, but their study results suggest that "both users and intermediaries are constrained by their expectations about current systems and by their views of their own roles in the search process".

Organisational Usability. Kling and Elliott have investigated how the organisational environment can influence the use of OI resources and have made some suggestions for organisational support of the use of OI resources in digital libraries. They focus attention on how these systems can be effectively integrated into the work practices of specific organisations. They suggest that the systems could be more organisationally usable if they were designed to include the infrastructure necessary to support and accommodate people as they learn to maintain and use these resources. However, Kling and Elliott recognise that their advice may be ignored by OI systems designers and digital library architects who make assumptions about how their systems will be used which are based on the taken-for-granted concepts of their own cultural and organisational ways of doing things.

Organisational use of OI resources is often associated with a library or an information center. Research services may be provided to an entire organisation by a small group of information specialists who make use of OI resources, and print information resources, on behalf of others. This confounds the issue of who is actually the "user"—someone who performs the OI search, or someone who uses the information retrieved by the searcher. In cooperative work settings, identifying the end-user of the information as someone separate from the information intermediary becomes even more difficult. O'Day and Jeffries have concluded that, in the organisations they studied, virtually everyone functioned as an intermediary in some fashion; either by updating team members, consulting, broadcasting or putting the information into a shared archive.

Although rationalists might suggest that the intermediary represents an inefficiency in the system of getting relevant information directly and quickly to the end-user, O'Day and Jeffries show that modes of work which involve information sharing, as opposed to intensive, individualised use, are prevalent. While informational imperatives may encourage intensive information gathering practices, not all the information gathered is actually used in decision making. In fact, Feldman and March suggest that information gathering is largely a symbolic act of the decision making process. They cite studies which show that little systematic relation can be established between the time of receiving the results of an information search and the time of making a decision. However, these studies do find that when the intrinsic quality of a decision is difficult to assess, the signals generated by information gathering during the decision making process may impart a legitimacy that affects the perceived quality of that decision. So, when managers cannot show that their decision is "correct", they can at least build confidence by showing that they have followed accepted practice in formulating it. With respect to OI resources, the conclusions of Feldman and March would suggest that organisational decision makers might be more likely to use them in a "scanning" mode when decision criteria are ambiguous, performance measures are vague or when decision quality requires a long period to become established.

Interorganisational Usability. There are a number of environmental constraints on OI resource use at individual, group and organisational levels. When a resource is constructed expressly for use at the interorganisational level, the reasons for its underutilisation may be attributed to these constraints and to additional environmental influences. Francois Libmann's study of European online technology transfer databases shows that reasons for OI resource implementation failure can be linked to cultural concepts. He finds that "[n]o one has sought to create synergies between databases and other elements in the world of technology transfer (interpersonal networks for example)...databases are on the whole little or inefficiently used to optimise innovatory process. This is a cultural problem and should be dealt with as such, and is one which is not exclusive to technology transfer databases". Libmann suggests that national policy must be modified to address this need. US policy makers have encouraged the construction of digital libraries, and have stressed the importance of their educational support functions. But organisations on the periphery of academia, such as Libmann's who are promoting university/industry technology transfer efforts, are also interested in constructing or using digital library services. Digital libraries may serve these organisations, or may be embedded within them, depending on how central or supplemental the research function is to their core organisational processes.

Postmodern Perspective

A recent and growing body of OI literature assumes a postmodern perspective. The philosophical discourse of postmodernists is suffused with an awareness of the power of language and the malleability of 'the text.' They see network technologies, digital libraries and OI resources as important components of the postmodern condition, and variously discuss online databases as new structures of domination and electronic writing as another level of reality—"textuality" or "hyperreality"

HCI Usability. Postmodern views of OI usability do not fall neatly into the admittedly rationalist framework. According to Amiran, Unsworth and Chaski, "There is no psycholinguistic evidence that the process of reading suddenly changes when it is conducted in a different medium" But they do find significant differences in the malleability of electronic texts, and suggest that a shift toward electronic scholarly publications may encourage a reinterpretation of the concepts of authorship, ownership and scholarship at individual and institutional levels.

Content Usability. Usability of 'the text', according to Timothy W. Luke, lies in its ability to serve as a site of shared cultural consciousness . Luke examines Baudrillard's concept of 'hyperreality' and presents it, not as a future capability, but as an extension of existing social and political simulations which use current implementations of electronic media. He suggests that simulation and the shared cultural consciousness it can achieve are important contributions to the social infrastructure. Luke and postmodernists see fiction and simulation as preceding and defining reality for those residents involved—that's hyperreality. Although this perspective takes environmental and institutional factors into account, the postmodern view of content usability differs greatly from the institutional view, which is focused on how OI resources are manipulated by users. Postmodernists examine how users' perceptions are modified by the contents of OI resources.

Organisational Usability. With respect to organisational use, the postmodern emphasis is less concerned with training organisational members to use OI resources effectively, and is more focused on understanding how OI resources, as critical components of the technical infrastructure, sustain organisational bureaucracy. Mark Poster presents an insightful overview of the impacts of Bell's forecasts for the Information Society. He identifies information as the sustaining materiel of bureaucracy, and he acknowledges Foucault's interpretation of online databases as the major structural component of domination in postindustrial society. But he suggests that databases also have a democratic side. In personal communication, he has associated democratic empowerment with database exchanges on the Internet to exemplify the dual potential of OI resources. In either case, the postmodern view of organisational OI resource usability can be seen to resemble the institutional view in some important ways. The end-user of the information is often difficult to identify. She may be the intermediary, the bureaucrat, or some collective identity that is amorpously referred to as 'the organisation.'

Interorganisational Usability. In postmodern discussions, the terms 'organisational' and 'interorganisational' may be used interchangeably. Clegg's analysis of modern organisations defines one of the more recent examples, the Benneton firm, "less as an organisation per se and rather more as an organised network of market relations premised on complex forms of contracting made possible by advances in microelectronics technology". Clegg does not refer exclusively to OI resources, but to IT generally speaking, when he suggests that the classic Weberian bureaucracy may be replaced by technologically enabled organisational forms such as Benneton's. Unlike Marchand and Horton's rational analysis of interorganisational use of OI resources, Clegg's analysis does not stop at the managerial methodology level. And unlike institutional analyses which call for governmental intervention to enact cultural change so that existing organisational forms can make more effective use of OI resources and traditional library bureaucracies, Clegg identifies environmental and cultural changes which are redefining the boundaries of the organisations themselves. The postmodern perspective encourages us to recognise that the boundaries which separate digital libraries, academic enclaves and commercial organisations are permeable and changeable. The roles of librarians and information intermediaries may be equally transmutable.

Temporary Archiving

The archive is in flux. Much of this has to do with the pace of technological change, and the perceived locus of control. The concept of "temporary" measures rests on an assumption that one day we will all catch up with technology. This assumption underlies much of the technology purchasing, that if we buy the "right" computer or software at the "right" time, we will finally be state-of-the-art. The reality is that Microsoft and others will continue to change operating platforms, hardware, and software every year. Manufacturers operate within a structure of premeditated obsolescence, of staggered improvement and alteration, ensuring that there will be no "end-state" program upon which we can all settle.

Because electronic media, software applications, and computer hardware will all continue to change at a rapid rate, and because policies must be developed to address that reality, the archive must change. The very notion of a permanent or fixed archive may have to give way to an ecological preservation system that is in a state of constant change.

Data grows, lives, and dies, as do delivery systems. As never before, the task of keeping data alive requires frequent adaptations to and perpetual evolution of the archival system. To keep pace with technological flux, an ongoing process of selection — of media platforms, of preservation structures, of migratory patterns — is necessary to avoid data extinction. In these various ways, there is an ecological force at work.

In fact, there are several ecological themes already in play in electronic archives. These include the encouragement of symbiotic relationships, the use of anti-extinction preservation and migratory schemes, and the deliberate adoption of cloning/breeding campaigns.

Symbiotic Archiving

Successful archiving involves assessing appropriate storage

and delivery methods for documents based on cost, usage, appropriateness, and longevity. In this case the best solution was symbiosis of electronic and paper media. By combining paper and electronic means, twin goals are achieved: an original record is maintained, and worldwide access to the material is provided.

The symbiotic, ecological relationship exists in the fact that the paper version needs the electronic version for the sake of its own preservation against constant usage, and the electronic version needs the paper version as a backup in case of technical problems or obsolescence. Symbiotic double conservation contrasts with some previous "preservation" practices such as the effective destruction of books through the removal of bindings to facilitate the microfilming process.

A careful consideration of the archival ecosystem allows for effective migration while maximising conservation in the long term. By identifying how a book or journal is most easily accessed with current technology, and best preserved, the text stands a better chance of lasting through time.

Of course, HTML, SGML, Java, JPEG, MPEG, and WAV files, etc. might go the way of the Commodore 64, and Canadian Architect and Builder and other journals archived on the Web may suffer a similar fate: technologically unreachable and/or unreadable by the Web advancements in the next five to one hundred years, they will be lost to the interested reader. They will be extinct.

Further, a Web site with a forgotten URL may, in the long term, be even harder to find than a mis-shelved book. While some search engines can be tremendously efficient at locating relevant sites by keyword now, we do not know if the search engines of fifty years hence will be able to locate the historic, first-generation sites coded late in the twentieth century and in the early years of the twenty-first century.

Preservation and Migratory Schemes

Migration is a set of organised tasks designed to achieve the periodic transfer of digital materials from one hardware/ software configuration to another, or from one generation of computer technology to a subsequent generation. The purpose of migration is to preserve the integrity of digital objects and to retain the ability for clients to retrieve, display, and otherwise use them in the face of constantly changing technology.

Crucial to that overall process is the independent certification of digital archives and a critical fail-safe mechanism. The primary function of the critical fail-safe mechanism is to enact "an aggressive rescue function to save culturally significant digital information" that may be at risk. The independent certification is a mechanism through which digital archive standards are reviewed, and whose indicators include the accessibility of stored data and the long-term protection of culturally valuable information. In 2001, Harvard University Library was awarded a major planning grant to look into repository techniques for electronic journals. Funded by the Andrew W. Mellon Foundation, the project explored the mechanism through which electronic journals are selected for preservation, commercial intellectual property negotiations with publishers, delivery format for users, costs, and the overall storage strategies to be employed.

Stanford University's LOCKSS project (LOCKSS stands for Lots of Copies Keep Stuff Safe) seek to assure the integrity of electronic publications through the maintenance of copies on multiple sites, and with periodic checks between these copies to verify informational congruency. Through cloning and distributed storage, LOCKSS hopes to minimise in advance the impact a catastrophe at any individual site may have upon (data) populations as a whole.

The Biosphere

This list of archiving and migration methodologies is by no means exhaustive. Of particular concern are the long-term prospects for the electronic resources and research undertaken in developing countries. While research libraries in the United States and other industrialised nations may have the financial resources and the available workforce to facilitate "perpetual care" activities, in other parts of the world the resources are simply not available. "Digital aid" to the universities and publishers of the developing world may prove imperative in the coming years. The ecology of the archiving process requires that the whole biosphere of electronic data must be considered in the push for preservation, not just the material of discrete territories. Even where the necessary will and resources are in place, for some electronic data the issue of long-term preservation and/or migration is somewhat more difficult. Central examples are the presentations and publications produced only in multimedia format. As one report put it, there is no "safety net" for purely digital data, "no analogous tangible version you can recapture if you lose the digital version."

While projects such as LOCKSS may provide some degree of safety, a further complication remains. If all computer platforms and software packages steadily lose their cutting-edge status via the computer industry's (apparent) maxim of premeditated obsolescence, multimedia format documents combining complex interactions of moving images, sound, and text stand the greatest risk of being lost or degraded over time. If there is a high degree of dependence between a given multimedia presentation and specific hardware or software, the process of "refreshing" — copying digital information from one medium to another — may be insufficiently compatible to maintain the exact interplay of image, sound, and text captured in the original. A two-dimensional replica may still be preserved, but the subtleties of the original may be lost, degraded in the transfer.

As has always been the case, decisions will have to be made regarding what will be preserved, either in the symbiotic sense, or in the broader ecological migration to next-generation systems. This process, as always, takes time and resources. Priorities will be set and value judgments will be made regarding what should be preserved, and how well. Despite the massive technological advances in recent decades, it is a surety that information and data will still be lost in the passage of time.

Archiving as Metaphor

The fate of data will largely depend on the strategies adopted by libraries, publishers, archivists, and individual researchers. The future of the archive depends on how information storage is conceptualised. Rather than making temporary plans in the hopes of a future permanent solution, it is advantageous to visualise all information preservation as an evolving, ever-changing ecosystem.

As technology continues to develop apace, those seeking to preserve and to update are faced with ever-expanding options of how best to do this. It is an exercise in futility to try to pick the technological winner, for "the latest" will be hopelessly outdated in ten years' time. What is necessary is a permanent strategy for handling perpetual change. This will involve periodic reassessment, the migration of material from one platform to the next, and the allocation of resources.

Technical Foundation for Digital Preservation

The vision of creating digital libraries that will be able to preserve our heritage currently rests on technological quicksand. There is as yet no viable long-term strategy to ensure that digital information will be readable in the future. Not only are digital documents vulnerable to loss via media decay and obsolescence, but they become equally inaccessible and unreadable if the software needed to interpret them—or the hardware on which that software runs—is lost or becomes obsolete.

Digital Longevity

Documents, data, records, and informational and cultural artifacts of all kinds are rapidly being converted to digital form, if they were not created digitally to begin with. This rush to digitise is being driven by powerful incentives, including the ability to make perfect copies of digital artifacts, to publish them on a wide range of media, to distribute and disseminate them over networks, to reformat and convert them into alternate forms, to locate them, search their contents, and retrieve them, and to process them with automated and semi-automated tools. Yet the longevity of digital content is problematic for a number of complex and interrelated reasons. It is now generally recognised that the physical lifetimes of digital storage media are often surprisingly short, requiring information to be "refreshed" by copying it onto new media with disturbing frequency. The technological obsolescence of these media poses a different and equally urgent threat.

Moreover, most digital documents and artifacts exist only in encoded form, requiring specific software to bring their bit streams to life and make them truly usable; as these programs become obsolete, the digital documents that depend on them become unreadable—held hostage to their own encoding. This problem is paradoxical, given the fact that digital documents can be copied perfectly, which is often naively taken to mean that they are eternal. In addition to the technical aspects of this problem, there are administrative, procedural, organisational, and policy issues surrounding the management of digital material. Digital documents are different from traditional paper documents in ways that have significant implications for the means by which they are generated, captured, transmitted, stored, maintained, accessed, and managed.

Paramount among these differences is the greatly reduced lifetime of digital information without some form of active preservation. This mandates new approaches to accessioning and saving digital documents to avoid their loss. These approaches raise nontechnical issues concerning jurisdiction, funding, responsibility for successive phases of the digital document life cycle, and the development of policies requiring adherence to standard techniques and practices to prevent the loss of digital information. However, few of these nontechnical issues can be meaningfully addressed in the absence of a sound, accepted technical solution to the digital longevity problem.

Preservation constitutes one leg of a tripod that supports informational institutions such as libraries, the other legs being access and the development and management of collections. Without preservation, access becomes impossible, and collections decay and disintegrate. Informational artifacts include documents, data, and records of all kinds, in all media, which can be refered to as "documents" for simplicity. The essence of preserving informational artifacts is the retention of their meaning. This requires the ability to recreate the original form and function of a document when it is accessed, for example, to establish its authenticity, validity, and evidential value and to allow the document's users to understand how its creator and original viewers saw it, what they were able to infer from it, what insights it may have conveyed to them, and what aesthetic value it may have had for them.

Let us focus on digital documents, which we mean informational artifacts, some or all aspects of whose intended behavior or use rely on their being encoded in digital form. The term "digital" in this context denotes any means of representing sequences of discrete symbolic values—each value having two or more unambiguously distinguishable states—so that they can, at least in principle, be accessed, manipulated, copied, stored, and transmitted entirely by mechanical means, with high reliability. The preservation of digital documents involves a number of distinctive requirements. In particular, all such documents possess a unique collection of core digital attributes that must be retained. These attributes include their ability to be copied perfectly, to be accessed without geographic constraint, to be disseminated at virtually no incremental cost, and to be machine-readable so that they can be accessed, searched, and processed by automated mechanisms that can modify them, reformat them, and perform arbitrary computations on their contents in all phases of their creation and distribution. Furthermore, new inherently digital document forms, such as dynamic, distributed, interactive hypertext and hypermedia, must retain their unique functionality, including their ability to integrate information from disparate traditional sources, such as books, periodicals, newspapers, mail, phone messages, data, imagery, and video.

In response to the difficulty of saving digital documents it is sometimes suggested that they be printed and saved in hard-copy form. This is a rear-guard action and not a true solution. Printing any but the simplest, traditional documents results in the loss of their unique functionality, and printing any document makes it no longer truly machine-readable, which in turn destroys its core digital attributes. Beyond this loss of functionality, printing digital documents sacrifices their original form, which may be of unique historical, contextual, or evidential interest.

Proposed alternatives to printing digital documents include translating digital documents into standard forms or extracting their contents without regard to their original nature. Though these approaches have traditional analogues, they are fraught with danger. The meaning of a document may be quite fragile, since meaning is in the eye of the beholder: what may be a trivial transformation to a casual reader may be a disastrous loss to a scholar, historian, or lawyer. Examples of loss of meaning abound in our daily experience of converting digital documents from their native form into that of some other software application in order to read them. At its best, such conversion often sacrifices subtleties; at its worst, it leaves out entire segments or produces meaningless garbage.

While it is often useful to create contemporary vernacular transcriptions of historical documents, society places a high value on retaining the originals so that we may verify that content has not been lost in transcription, as well as for scholarly and aesthetic purposes. For digital documents, retaining an original may not mean retaining the original medium, but it should mean retaining the functionality, look, and feel of the original document.

The preservation of digital documents is a matter of more than purely academic concern. In its short history, computer science has become inured to the fact that every new generation of software and hardware technology entails the loss of information, as documents are translated between incompatible formats. The most serious losses are caused by paradigm shifts (such as those between networked, hierarchical, and relational databases), which often require the complete redesign of documents to migrate to the new paradigm. Whenever this happens, documents that are not in continuing use may well be orphaned by the demise of their original formats, that is, they may be abandoned to save the cost of migration, while each document that does migrate may be turned into something unrecognisably different from its original, which is generally lost.

Even when migration does not involve a major paradigm shift, it can result in subtle losses of context and content. Yet aside from this ad hoc migration process, there exists no proven strategy for preserving (or translating) documents over time. The scope of this problem extends beyond the traditional library domain, affecting government records, environmental and scientific baseline data, documentation of toxic waste disposal, medical records, corporate data (such as the documentation of drug trials for pharmaceutical companies or of geologic survey data for petrochemical companies), electronic-commerce transactions, and electronic records needed to support forthcoming digital government initiatives.

The library and archives communities have identified at least some critical aspects of this problem and have recognised that preserving digital documents may require substantial new investments and commitments by institutions and government agencies. Showing admirable foresight, these communities have begun to discuss alternative economic and administrative policies for funding and managing digital preservation and have begun to develop conceptual frameworks for metadata that are not restricted to the print medium. Yet the lack of any long-term technical solution to the problem of digital preservation limits the efficacy of such explorations, since attempting to allocate responsibilities and assess costs for a nonexistent process is of questionable value.

Need for triage

The practical problem of digital preservation can be viewed at three different time scales. In the short term, many organisations are faced with an urgent need to save digital material that is in imminent danger of becoming unreadable or inaccessible, or to retrieve digital records that are already difficult to access. Yet the often heroic efforts needed to save or retrieve such material may not be generally applicable to preserving digital documents far into the future, and the techniques employed may not even be generalisable to solve similar urgent problems that may arise in the future. These short-term efforts therefore do not provide much leverage, in the sense that they are not replicable for different document types, though they may still be necessary for saving crucial records. In the medium term, organisations must quickly implement policies and technical procedures to prevent digital records from becoming vulnerable to imminent loss in the near future. For the vast bulk of records—those being generated now, those that have been generated fairly recently, or those that have been translated into formats and stored on media that are currently in use—the medium-term issue is how to prevent these records from becoming urgent cases of imminent loss within the next few years, as current media, formats, and software evolve and become obsolete.

In the long term, it is necessary to develop a truly long-lived solution to digital longevity that does not require continual heroic effort or repeated invention of new approaches every time formats, software or hardware paradigms, document types, or recordkeeping practices change. Such an approach must be extensible, in recognition of the fact that we cannot predict future changes, and it must not require labor-intensive translation or examination of individual records. It must handle current and future records of unknown type in a uniform way, while being capable of evolving as necessary.

Though most early digital documents have consisted largely of text, the generation of multimedia records has increased rapidly in recent years, to include audio recordings, graphical charts, photographic imagery, and video presentations, among others. In the digital domain, all of these media can be combined into hypermedia records, whose impact and expressivity can be expected to stimulate their increased use. Whereas the bulk of existing digital documents may be textual, multimedia and hypermedia records are likely to become ever more popular and may well become dominant in the near future. Any solution to digital preservation that is limited to text will therefore quickly become obsolete. A true long-term solution should be completely neutral to the form and content of the digital material it preserves.

Contextual issues

The preservation and management of digital records involves interrelated technical, administrative, procedural, organisational, and policy issues, but a sound technical approach must form the foundation on which everything else rests. Preserving digital records may require substantial new investments and commitments by organisations, institutions and agencies, forcing them to adopt new economic and administrative policies for funding and managing digital preservation. Yet it is impossible to allocate responsibilities or assess costs for an undefined process: until a viable technical approach to digital longevity has been identified and developed, it is premature to spend much effort attempting to design the administrative and organisational environment that will embed whatever technical approach is ultimately adopted.

Technical Dimensions

Digital media are vulnerable to loss by two independent mechanisms: the physical media on which they are stored are subject to physical decay and obsolescence, and the proper interpretation of the documents themselves is inherently dependent on software.

Physical decay and obsolescence

There is reasonably widespread awareness of the fact that digital storage media have severely limited physical lifetimes. The National Media Lab has published test results for a wide range of tapes, magnetic disks, CD-ROMs, and other media, showing that a tape, disk, or even CD that is picked at random is unlikely to have a lifetime of even five years. Vendors and media scientists may argue vehemently about such numbers, but accurate estimates are ultimately largely irrelevant, since the physical lifetime of media is rarely the constraining factor for digital preservation.

Even if archival quality media were introduced in the market, they would probably fail, since they would quickly be made obsolete—despite their physical longevity—by newer media having increased capacity, higher speed, greater convenience, and lower price. This is a natural outgrowth of the exponential improvement in storage density, speed, and cost that has characterised digital media development for the past several decades: the market makes older storage media obsolete as newer, better media become available. The short lifetimes of eight-inch floppy disks, tape cartridges and reels, hard-sectored disks, and seven-track tapes, among others, demonstrate how quickly storage formats become inaccessible.

Media obsolescence manifests itself in several ways: the medium itself disappears from the market; appropriate drives capable of reading the medium are no longer produced; and media-accessing programs (device drivers) capable of controlling the drives and deciphering the encodings used on the medium are no longer written for new computers. Upgrading to a new computer system therefore often requires abandoning an old storage medium, even if an organisation still has documents stored on that medium. The dual problems of short media lifetime and rapid obsolescence have led to the nearly universal recognition that digital information must be copied to new media (refreshed) on a very short cycle (every few years). Copying is a straightforward solution to these media problems, though it is not trivial: in particular, the copy process must avoid corrupting documents via compression, encryption, or changing data formats.

In addition, as media become more dense, each copy cycle aggregates many disks, tapes, or other storage units onto a single new unit of storage. This raises the question of how to retain any labeling information and metadata that may have been associated with the original media: since it is infeasible to squeeze the contents of the labels of 400 floppy disks to fit on the label of a single CD, label information must be digitised to ensure that it continues to accompany the records it describes. But whereas labels are directly human-readable, digitised information is not; labels and metadata must therefore be digitised in such a way that they remain more easily readable by humans than are the documents they describe. This may seem a relatively trivial aspect of the problem, but it has serious implications.

Software-dependency

Though media problems are far from trivial, they are but the tip of the iceberg. Far more problematic is the fact that digital documents are in general dependent on application software to make them accessible and meaningful. Copying media correctly at best ensures that the original bit stream of a digital document will be preserved. But a stream of bits cannot be made self-explanatory, any more than hieroglyphics were self-explanatory for the 1,300 years before the discovery of the Rosetta Stone. A bit stream can represent anything: not just text but also data, imagery, audio, video, animated graphics, and any other form or format, current or future, singly or combined in a hypermedia lattice of pointers whose formats themselves may be arbitrarily complex and idiosyncratic.

Without knowing what is intended, it is impossible to decipher such a stream. In certain restricted cases, it may be possible to decode the stream without additional knowledge: for example, if a bit stream is known to represent simple, linear text, deciphering it is amenable to cryptographic techniques. But in general, a bit stream can be made intelligible only by running the software that created it, or some closely related software that understands it. This point cannot be overstated: in a very real sense, digital documents exist only by virtue of software that understands how to access and display them; they come into existence only by virtue of running this software.

The only reliable way to access the meaning and functionality of a digital document is to run its original software—either the software that created it or some closely related software that understands it. Yet such application software becomes obsolete just as fast as do digital storage media and media-accessing software. And although we can save obsolete software as just another bit stream, running that software requires specific computer hardware, which itself becomes obsolete just as quickly. It is therefore not obvious how we can use a digital document's original software to view the document in the future on some unknown future computer. This is the crux of the technical problem of preserving digital documents. Any technical solution must also be able to cope with issues of corruption of information, privacy, authentication, validation, and preserving intellectual property rights. This last issue is especially complex for documents that are born digital and therefore have no single original instance, since traditional notions of copies are inapplicable to such documents. Finally, any technical solution must be feasible in terms of the societal and institutional responsibilities and the costs required to implement it.

Most approaches that have been proposed fall into one of four categories:

1) Reliance on hard copy,
2) Reliance on standards,
3) Reliance on computer museums, or
4) Reliance on migration.

Though some of these may play a role in an ultimate solution, none of them comes close to providing a solution by itself, nor does their combination.

Reliance on hard copy

It is sometimes suggested that digital documents be printed and saved as hard copy. This is not a true solution to the problem, since many documents cannot meaningfully be printed at all, or would lose many of their uniquely digital attributes and capabilities if they were printed. Even digital renditions of traditional documents lose their core digital attributes by being printed; that is, they sacrifice direct machine-readability, which means they can no longer be copied perfectly, transmitted digitally, searched or processed by computer programs, and so forth. Similarly, attempting to save digital documents by printing the 0s and 1s of their bit streams on paper sacrifices their machine-readability and the core digital attributes that it enables. Moreover, any such scheme destroys whatever interactive or dynamic functionality an inherently digital document may have, since the document's original software can no longer be run. For all of these reasons, saving digital documents by printing them does not offer a solution to the true problem of digital preservation.

Reliance on standards

On the face of it, reliance on standards appears to offer a solution by allowing digital documents to be represented in forms that will endure into the future and for which future software will always provide accessibility. One version of this argument offers the relational database (RDB) as a paradigmatic example of how this might work. This argument contends that since all relational database management systems (RDBMSs) are based on the same mathematical foundation, any RDB that is accessioned by an institution can be translated without loss into the specific RDB form recognised by the RDBMS used by that institution. Even if the institution later changes RDBMSs, all of its RDBs should be able to migrate to the new RDBMS without loss, since all RDBMSs support the same baseline functionality. While this argument appears convincing, it fails in several significant ways. First, precisely because the relational model legislates a standard baseline of functionality, real RDBMSs must distinguish themselves in the marketplace by introducing proprietary features that extend the relational model.

Any RDB that makes use of such proprietary features becomes at least somewhat nonstandard and will lose some of its functionality if translated into some other RDBMS. In this way standardisation sows the seeds of its own destruction by encouraging vendors to implement nonstandard features in order to secure market share. Users are motivated to use such features because they provide enhanced functionality, but using these features produces nonstandard databases that are likely to be orphaned by reliance on standards, since standards enforce strict limitations on what they can represent, and thereby preserve. In addition, far from being a paradigmatic example, the relational database is actually unique: no other kind of digital document rests on an underlying formal mathematical foundation that can serve as the basis for its standardisation.

Word-processing documents, spreadsheets, graphics and image files, hypermedia, animation, and audio and video formats are still evolving so rapidly that it is unrealistic to expect definitive standards for any of these forms to emerge in the near future. Though standards continue to be developed for many kinds of digital documents, they are almost always informal, ad hoc, and relatively short-lived. Moreover, since they lack a formal underpinning, they often compete with rival standards produced for different purposes or by different groups. The relational database example demonstrates a fundamental flaw in the standards-based approach. Just as the relational paradigm replaced earlier network and hierarchical database paradigms, it is currently under attack by the new object-oriented database (OODB) paradigm, which may well replace it or at least relegate it to the role of a low-level storage mechanism hidden beneath future object-oriented database management systems (OODBMSs). As was the case with previous database paradigm shifts, the transition from relational to object-oriented databases cannot be made simply by automatically translating RDBs into OODBs.

The paradigms are so different that such translation is typically meaningless: even when it is possible, the result is likely to possess neither the formal rigor of the original relational form nor the enhanced semantic expressiveness of the new object-oriented form. This illustrates the fact that even the best standards are often bypassed and made irrelevant by the inevitable paradigm shifts that characterise information science—and will continue to do so. Proponents of standards often argue that the way to deal with the problem of paradigm shifts is to force digital documents into current standard forms and then translate them, when current standards become obsolete, into whatever standards supplant the obsolete ones. This is analogous to translating Homer into modern English by way of every intervening language that has existed during the past 2,500 years.

The fact that scholars do not do this (but instead find the earliest original they can, which they then translate directly into the current vernacular) is indicative of the fact that something is always lost in translation. Rarely is it possible to recover the original by retranslating the translated version back into the original language. Not even character encodings last forever: ASCII (the venerable 7-bit American Standard Code for Information Interchange) is slowly giving way to Unicode (a newer 16-bit character set). Furthermore, the history of these encodings shows that successful standards do not always subsume their competitors, as exemplified by the ascendance of ASCII over EBCDIC (the 8-bit Extended Binary Coded Decimal Interchange Code long used by IBM) and the APL character set (designed for Iverson's "A Programming Language"), despite the fact that ASCII cannot represent all of their characters.

Nevertheless, standards should not be dismissed. Some standards have proven highly extensible and worthwhile within their limited scope. Since text is likely always to be a part of most documents, SGML provides a useful capability, even though it does not by itself solve the problems of nontextual representation or of representing dynamic, interactive documents. In fact, if SGML had been adopted as a common interlingua among word processing programs, it would have greatly relieved the daily conversion problems that plague most computer users; yet this has not occurred, implying that even well-designed standards do not necessarily sweep the marketplace. Nevertheless, converting digital documents into standard forms, and migrating to new standards if necessary, may be a useful interim approach while a true long-term solution is being developed.

Reliance on computer museums

To avoid the dual problems of corruption via translation and abandonment at paradigm shifts, some have suggested that computer museums be established, where old machines would run original software to access obsolete documents. While this approach exudes a certain technological bravado, it is flawed in a number of fundamental ways. It is unlikely that old machines could be kept running indefinitely at any reasonable cost, and even if they were, this would limit true access to the original forms of old digital documents to a very few sites in the world, thereby again sacrificing many of these documents' core digital attributes.

Furthermore, this approach ignores the fact that old digital documents will rarely survive on their original digital media. If an obsolete digital document and its software survive into the future, this will probably be because their bit streams have been copied onto new media that did not exist when the document's original computer was current. An old word processing file from a 1970s personal computer system will not still exist on the 8-inch floppy disk that was native to that system but will instead have migrated onto a 3.5 inch floppy, a CD-ROM, or perhaps a DVD. The obsolete document would therefore have to be read by an obsolete machine from a new medium for which that machine has no physical drive, no interface, and no device software. The museum approach would therefore require building unique new device interfaces between every new medium and every obsolete computer in the museum as new storage media evolve, as well as coding driver software for these devices, which would demand maintaining programming skills for each obsolete machine. This seems hopelessly labor-intensive and ultimately infeasible.

Computer chips themselves have limited physical lifetimes. Integrated circuits decay due to processes such as metal migration (the traces that define circuit connections on the chips migrate through the substrate over time) and dopant diffusion (the atoms that make semiconductors semiconduct diffuse away over time). Even if obsolete computers were stored carefully, maintained religiously, and never used, aging processes such as these would eventually render them inoperative; using them routinely to access obsolete digital documents would undoubtedly accelerate their demise. One role that computer museums might play in preservation is to perform heroic efforts to retrieve digital information from old storage media. If an old disk or tape is found that may indeed still have readable information on it, an obsolete machine in the museum could be used in a last-ditch attempt to tease the bits off the medium, as an alternative to electron microscopy or other equally extreme measures. A second role for computer museums might be in verifying the behavior of emulators, as discussed below. Beyond these limited roles, however, computer museums do not appear to be a serious option for the long-term preservation of digital documents.

Reliance on migration

The approach that most institutions are adopting is to expect digital documents to become unreadable or inaccessible as their original software becomes obsolete and to translate them into new forms as needed whenever this occurs. This is the traditional migration approach of computer science. While it may be better than nothing, it has little to recommend it. Migration is by no means a new approach: computer scientists, data administrators and data processing personnel have spent decades performing migration of data, documents, records, and programs to keep valuable information alive and usable. Though it has been employed widely, the nearly universal experience has been that migration is labor-intensive, time-consuming, expensive, error-prone, and fraught with the danger of losing or corrupting information.

Migration requires a unique new solution for each new format or paradigm and each type of document that is to be converted into that new form. Since every paradigm shift entails a new set of problems, there is not necessarily much to be learned from previous migration efforts, making each migration cycle just as difficult, expensive, and problematic as the last. Automatic conversion is rarely possible, and whether conversion is performed automatically, semiautomatically, or by hand, it is very likely to result in at least some loss or corruption, as documents are forced to fit into new forms. As has been proven repeatedly during the short history of computer science, formats, encodings, and software paradigms change often and in surprising ways.

Of the many dynamic aspects of information science, document paradigms, computing paradigms, and software paradigms are among the most volatile, and their evolution routinely eludes prediction. Relational and object-oriented databases, spreadsheets, Web-based hypermedia documents, e-mail attachments, and many other paradigms have appeared on the scene with relatively little warning, at least from the point of view of most computer users. Each new paradigm of this kind requires considerable conversion of programs, documents, and work styles, whether performed by users themselves or by programmers, data administrators, or data processing personnel. Even though some new paradigms subsume the ones they replace, they often still require a significant conversion effort.

Bibliography

Alfors, I. L. and Loe, J. H. "Foremothers and forefathers: One way to preserve and enhance the library research paper". *Research strategies*, 3 (Winter), pp. 4-16.

Bodi, S. "Critical thinking and bibliographical instruction: The relationship". *Journal of academic librarianship*, 14 (July), pp. 150-53, 1988.

Bodi, S. "Teaching effectiveness and bibliographic instruction: The relevance of learning styles". *College and research libraries*, 51 (March), pp. 113-119.

Bodi, S. "Scholarship or propaganda: How can librarians help undergraduates tell the difference?" *Journal of academic librarianship*, 21 (January), pp. 21-25, 1995.

Caravello, P. S. "Library instruction and and information literacy for the adult learner: A course and its lessons for reference work". *Reference librarian*, no. 69/70, pp. 259-69, 2000.

Dalrmple, C. "Perceptions of practices of learning styles in library instruction". *College and research libraries news*, 63, pp. 261-73, 2002.

Dusenbury, C. and Pease, B. G. "The future of instruction". *Journal of library administration*, pp. 97-117, 1995.

George, M. W. "Instructional services. In Academic libraries: Research perspectives", ed. by M. J. Lynch and A. Young. Chicago: American Library Association, pp. 106-42, 1990.

Gresham, K. "Experiental learning theory, library instruction, and the electronic classroom". Colorado libraries, 27 (1), pp. 19-22, 2001.

Hills, P. J. "Library instruction and the development of the individual". *Journal of librarianship*, 6 (October), pp. 255-63, 1974.

Kobelski, P. and Reichel, M., "Conceptual frameworks for bibliographic instruction". *Journal of academic librarianship*, 7 (May), pp. 73-77, 1981.

Martin, L. M. "Library instruction revisited: Bibliographic instruction comes of age". New York, Haworth press, 1995.

Oberman, C. *Library instruction: Concepts and pedagogy in the electronic environment*. RQ, 35(3), pp. 315-23, 1996.

Plum, S. H. "Library use and the development of critical thought". *New directions for teaching and learning*, 18 (June), pp. 63-78, 1984.

Shrigley, R. "Reader education". *New library world*, 82 (March), pp. 42, 43., 1981.

Young, A. P., "And gladly they teach: Bibliographic instruction in the library". *Advances in the librarianship*, 10, pp. 64-69, 1980.

Index